Screenwriting for Film and Television

William Miller

Ohio University

Allyn and Bacon
Boston • London • Toronto • Sydney • Tokyo • Singapore

Editor-in-Chief, Communication and Political Science: Paul Smith
Series Editor: Karon Bowers
Series Editorial Assistant: Leila Scott
Marketing Manager: Kris Farnsworth
Production Administrator: Deborah Brown
Editorial-Production Service: Saxon House Productions
Composition and Prepress Buyer: Linda Cox
Manufacturing Buyer: Suzanne Lareau
Cover Administrator: Jenny Hart

Library of Congress Cataloging-in-Publication Data
Miller, William Charles.
    Screenwriting for film and television / William Miller.
        p.   cm.
    Rev. ed. of: Screenwriting for narrative film and television.
c1980.
    Includes bibliographical references.
    ISBN 0-205-27299-1 (notch paper)
    1. Motion picture authorship.   2. Television authorship.
I. Miller, William Charles. Screenwriting for narrative film and
television.   II. Title.
PN1996.M62   1998
808.2'3--dc21   97-33479
                                                        CIP

Printed in the United States of Amerca

10 9 8 7 6 5 4 3   09 08 07 06 05 04 03

Contents

Preface

Film and television have dominated the entertainment industry in the twentieth century. As we move into the twenty-first, there is even more media activity. Production is up. Home video rentals and sales have surpassed domestic theater ticket sales. So have international markets, and they are growing rapidly. Networks are expanding, as are cable and direct satellite broadcasts. We're seeing the surge of CD-ROMs and interactive multimedia as traditional media integrate with computers. Virtual reality possibilities are developing. And all of these media need storytellers.

Screenwriting, therefore, offers, more than ever, excitement and challenge. The new markets offer new opportunities. The old markets are hungry for talented writers. There is always a need for someone who can tell a good tale.

Screenwriting has become very popular. Media writing courses at the university level abound. Across the United States, there are regional screenwriting groups of hopeful amateurs who share their work, encourage one another, and dream of success.

There are more resources than ever before available to the screenwriter. Videotape rentals provide access to a wide range of films and many television programs. More screenplays are being published. Computer software makes the actual word processing and printing of the script much easier.

The number of screenwriting books has also increased since this text was first published. At that time, the book was well received. I hope you'll find this totally rewritten and updated reworking equally valuable. Appropriately, I have changed the title to reflect the changes inside.

The first chapter puts writers in touch with their own creative imaginations and with the process of becoming a screenwriter. There is also advice on how to overcome writer's block.

Too many scripts misfire when they lose their central spine. A way to keep focused on a story is by working from the concept and basic story—the story overview—then expanding it to a broader story line outline, then to a more detailed scene outline, and finally to the first draft script. I call this the inverted triangle model and describe it in detail in Chapter 1. The script grows from the concept kernel, getting more detailed in the stages that follow without losing the sense of the whole that is necessary to maintain the integrity of the story.

Chapter 2 discusses how to create story ideas that have audience appeal—as what to write about is one of the most important decisions.

Creating effective characters is a big challenge and is covered thoroughly in Chapter 3. This chapter focuses on designing characters who are credible, real, unique, and individualized, and who invite audience identification and involvement. Included are checklists of character attributes and imagination exercises to help flesh out characters.

Story structure is a key element of the screenplay—many would say the most important element. Chapter 4, on structure, ranges from basic beginning-middle-end patterning, to the value of suspense and surprise in forming audience responses, to an analysis of how to develop story lines that make up film structure. Several popular screenwriting structure models are presented and discussed, including the controversial three-act plot point model. A variety of films are analyzed to show their story line structure.

Chapter 5, on diverse techniques and concerns, considers a variety of topics including the choice of title, openings, techniques of exposition and preparation, runners, maintaining forward movement, credibility and coincidence, point of view, settings, themes, and the importance of involving the audience.

Chapter 6 takes a look at the special needs of writing for television. It includes analyses of several hour and half-hour programs.

Having discussed mainstream story structure, it is appropriate to include a chapter on alternative approaches to story. While writers need to grasp the basic conventional approaches to media writing, at some point it is a good idea to consider more innovative and experimental possibilities. Chapter 7 presents alternatives.

Once a story is set and outlined, it is time to write the first draft script, and this involves constructing sequences and scenes—the action that realizes the outline. Chapter 8, on scenes and sequences, looks at what scenes do, how to structure scenes, and how to use suspense and surprise within scenes and sequences.

Chapter 9 discusses dialogue both in terms of what constitutes effective dialogue and how to avoid common dialogue mistakes. This chapter also considers uses of sound and music.

Chapter 10 covers the maxim that scripts are not written, they are rewritten. Once a first draft is completed, this short chapter on rewriting will help rework it.

Comedy techniques are useful for not just comedy but for comic relief in a serious drama. Chapter 11 presents theories of comedy, characteristics of the comic, and a variety of comedy techniques.

Since so many films are adaptations from other forms—novels, short stories, theatrical plays—Chapter 12 presents guidelines on how to adapt another form to film.

Chapter 13 is on marketing a script and contains suggestions about getting a script read, getting an agent, pitching a script, protecting a script, as well as useful references about the movie industry.

Chapter 14 presents both film and television script formats, including examples of each.

There is a glossary of common script format terms and abbreviations, and a bibliography of screenwriting books suggests further reading.

Throughout the book, I make references to many and various films and television programs. They range from classic to modern, including some silents (mostly comedies) and international productions. Though you may not be familiar with a number of the films or television programs used as examples, when they illustrate a point, I try to give enough story background so that the point is clear.

Most of the films and some of the television programs are available for video rental. Many of the scripts have been printed in book form or are available as scripts for purchase or through libraries.

This book is the result of what I've learned from years of teaching screenwriting and from working in Hollywood and smaller markets. There are so many people I could thank for this education, too many to name. I trust they'll understand and realize they have my thanks.

I would like to acknowledge the following reviewers: Janet Neipris, NYU; James D. Wilson, USC; Richard Walter, UCLA; and Allan Barber, Temple University.

Get as much from this book as you can. Read it, underline it, do suggested exercises, . . . and then . . . put it aside (close enough for reference) and write.

As a writer about to begin, it is appropriate to start with a tale.

When the great Rabbi Israel Baal Shem-Tov saw misfortune threaten the Jews, it was his custom to go into a certain part of the forest to meditate. There he would light a fire, say a special prayer, and the miracle would be accomplished and the misfortune averted.

Later, when his disciple, the celebrated Magid of Mezritch, had occasion for the same reason to intercede with heaven, he would go to the same place in the forest and say: "Master of the Universe, listen! I do not know how to light the fire, but I am still able to say the prayer." And again, the miracle would be accomplished.

Still later, Rabbi Moshe-Leib of Sasov, in order to save his people once more, would go into the forest and say: "I do not know how to light the fire. I do not know the prayer, but I know the place and this must be sufficient."

Then it fell to Rabbi Israel of Rizhyn to overcome misfortune. Sitting in his armchair, his head in his hands, he spoke to God: "I am unable to light the fire and I do not know the prayer. I cannot even find the place in the forest. All I can do is to tell the story, and this must be sufficient." And it was sufficient.

God made humans because of love of stories.*

—WCM, 1997

---

*Wiesel, E. (1966). *The gates of the forest.* Frances Frenaye, Trans. New York: Rinehart & Winston, un-numbered pages preceding text. Quoted in Kopp, S. (1972). *If you meet the Buddha on the road, kill him!* Newton: Bantam Books, pp. 20–21. (Slightly modified.)

CHAPTER 1

The Writing Process: Getting Down to Work

Why do writers write? Because it isn't there.[1]
—Thomas Berger

We dwell in a cultural mediascape. We and millions like us gorge on media hyperreality. Film, television, video, and multimedia surround us, inviting us to believe, to feel, to enjoy, to laugh, to buy. So it's no wonder that you—and many like you—dream that it could be your ideas, stories, and characters that we turn to for pleasure, that the name after the "written by" credit on the big screen might be yours. You want to become a screenwriter.

All right! Let's begin.

This chapter will help you get started, work crisply and effectively, and keep those creative currents flowing. It deals with the process of doing the writing—or the How of writing. We begin with the source of your inventiveness—the creative process.

THE CREATIVE PROCESS

Writing is an interplay of imagination and critical evaluation—the two modes of the creative process. Understanding how these interact and how to make them work can help your production. We'll work from a classic model that identifies four stages of the creative process: preparation, incubation, inspiration, and revision.

Preparation.   Preparation includes how well you know the media as well as how you approach writing a script. You're aware of what is current and have a sense of media tradition. You're familiar with genres and their development. You watch films and television programs from the writer's perspective as to how they are put together, noting what works and what doesn't work. You read screenwriting books to learn from them (while avoiding falling for quick-fix formulas). You study scripts to become familiar with their form and feel.

Research.   This is a vital part of preparation before writing a script. Not only does it help you understand your subject and give the script a feeling of authenticity, it also aids the story's credibility by the addition of important details. Research helps establish the flavor of settings, characters, and time periods.

Research also helps the writer avoid historic gaffes such as the two I recently came across—a story about a CIA agent during the Spanish-American War, when we didn't have a CIA, and another about a character who worked for twenty-five years for the Atlantic City gambling casinos, when they had been in operation for only a few years.

Research is necessary to gain a better sense of the material and verify facts. Research sources include newspapers, magazines, books, the Internet, CD-ROM databases, knowledgeable reference librarians, experts, people who are similar to your characters, and actual locations.

Incubation.   It sounds as if you're hatching something (and in a way you are). It's the time when, while not writing, you are really hard at work—unconsciously—thinking and developing ideas, stories, and characters. The incubation stage is one of the most valuable writing tools.

As screenwriter Lewis John Carlino describes it:

> Actually, the writing is really such a small part of it. I mean the mechanics of writing. What happens is that things continue to cook. . . . If a project is really formed in my head, I mean really formed and ready, it will write itself. But sometimes that takes four, six, eight months' cooking process in which occasionally maybe I'll write a note down to myself if I have an idea. . . . It's just that when it's ready, it comes.[2]

While incubating a large project can take weeks and months, incubation is equally at work in shorter periods. Describing the pressured crucible of TV situation comedy team writing, writer/producer Gary David Goldberg tells how the writing team will sit around chatting about sports or what's in the news—seemingly wasting time. But in reality, he says, what's going on is that the jokes are making their way up from the backs of their minds. It's a necessary part of the process.[3]

Since incubation works unconsciously, encourage it by taking time to put your conscious mind off to the side so the incubating work can proceed unhindered. Here are some techniques you can use to promote the process.

Dorothea Brande suggests using activities that are *rhythmic, monotonous,* and *silent.*[4] These activities keep you physically occupied and actually contribute to a light trance state that permits the unconscious work to proceed without interruption. You probably do many of these activities already and thought they were only nervous fidgeting. Tapping a pencil, rhythmic rocking in your chair, jiggling a knee, endlessly sipping water, tea, or coffee while at the keyboard all can help unconscious incubation.

One of the best techniques to court the unconscious muse is to take a walk. An easy, unhurried, strolling gait, while holding your conscious mind in casual, relaxed awareness, will help produce the light trance state that lets the unconscious do its work.

This may seem perplexing to people around you since it looks as if you're doing nothing. You putter around the house, take long walks, keep pretty much to yourself, not talking, not reading, not watching much television. What they don't realize is that you really are diligently working on your script. It's incubating.

Preparing consciously and unconsciously is an important part of what you do before writing. Many writers have idiosyncratic rituals they go through to get ready. It might be a special work place. Or the right music.[5] Pacing the floor is common. So is taking a bath, sharpening pencils, improvising on the piano, drum, or guitar before starting. A screenwriter friend must use a blue felt pen on a yellow legal pad in a room with a cathedral ceiling—he claims the tall ceiling allows more room for his thoughts.[6] All such activities help prepare you internally as well as externally. Respect them. Whatever it takes for you to court the muse, trust it and go along.

Unconscious incubation helps explain the experience reported by many writers who find that their characters become so lifelike they take over the writing, often moving the story along in unforeseen directions.

Screenwriter Edward Anhalt:

> I think what Shaw [writer/playwright George Bernard Shaw] spoke of actually happens. That is, the characters seem to be speaking themselves, they seem to be real.[7]

Buck Henry put it:

> If you can let the characters take over instead of having to force them around. If you really know who they are. If it's that kind of film and you're improvising freely enough, they can control the situation through you. It's like being a medium.[8]

It's letting unconscious processes do their work.

Inspiration.   "Eureka, I've got it!" It's that thrilling moment when unconscious insights flash into your consciousness: inspiration! Often it is dramatic. Other times it is simply a feeling that it's time to begin setting things down on paper. Either way, it's your call to action.

We often think that inspiration comes on us suddenly and compellingly. It does work this way, especially when first working out your ideas. But it also continues throughout the writing process. You are always unconsciously orchestrating your writing, resulting in a more or less continuous flow of "inspiration." The process might not feel like major inspiration, but if you can trust your unconscious, it is actively incubating and inspiring as you write.[9]

Critical Revision.   This is the final stage. The unconscious creative imagination can produce many ideas, but once on paper they have to be critiqued and reworked. The industry adage is true that "scripts are not written, they're rewritten."

Learning to balance the interaction of creative imagination and critical evaluation is a key to smooth writing.

The Creative/Critical Combo

Writing entails switching back and forth between the creative mode and the critical mode. At one moment your imagination is flowing freely and you want to get down the flood of ideas, at another moment you are evaluating and correcting what you've written. Both are necessary. It's when they begin to interfere with each other that problems occur. Let's consider each in turn.

The *creative* mode is the harvest of the imagination. Its expression is spontaneous, its source is largely unconscious. Working in the creative mode is like being swept along with a flow. Words, ideas, and images all come flooding out. Peter Elbow offers a nice image. "Producing writing, then, is not so much like filling a basin or pool once, but rather getting water to keep flowing *through* till finally it runs clear."[10]

When working in the creative mode, it's best to get the critical side out of the way and just let things gush. Don't restrict the flow by judging ideas as they come. If you continually reject what you write as not good enough, it is easy to end up writing nothing. Save the critical evaluation for the next step, after you get things down.

Realize that you're producing the raw material that you'll later temper, hone, and polish. It's not so important that the ideas come out perfectly, just that they come out. Think of the initial draft as an attempt to discover what you want to write.

Later, you'll have the opportunity to rework the material as you *rewrite*. Rewriting is an essential part of the process, and will be discussed later. Five, six, or more rewrites are common for professional screenwriters. Because no matter how much you like your first-draft script, it really becomes better as you rework it. As screenwriter Paddy Chayefsky said: "I am not a great writer, I'm a great rewriter."[11]

So as you begin writing, consider what Viki King puts in her winsome way: "Write from the heart [the creative imagination], then later rewrite from the head [the critical]."[12]

If you view a first-draft script as finding out what you want to write, it reduces the pressure to write perfection. This lets a writer work more freely to get the initial draft done. Science fiction writer Ray Bradbury had this sign by his typewriter with respect to first drafts: "Don't think."

The *critical* mode is the other side. The ideas that gushed out need to be trimmed and shaped. Now evaluate. Does what you have written work (for the audience)? Does it do what you want it to? What could make it better? How can you make it more lean and economic? More rich and scrumptious? What can you cut?

There are times the imagination dominates, such as when brainstorming an idea. And there are times the rationale reigns, such as when working out a story structure outline or making that initial assessment of whether your idea will attract a mass media audience.

Set times when you let things flow out. Set other times when you evaluate and rework. Separating the two modes will help show how the process works. If you are a new writer, beware especially of your critical side interfering with your imaginative side. Mixing the two often blocks the writing.

Most of us are very familiar with being critical; our education has seen to that. Imagination is something we know less about. Here are some exercises you might try to develop the imaginative side of the process.

IMAGINATION EXERCISES

Actors love them. Imagination exercises—theater games, they call them—help develop the creative processes. So why not use the same for writers? Consider these.

To become used to writing without critically editing as you go along, Peter Elbow suggests a freewriting exercise in which you sit for 10 or so minutes at least three times a week and simply write.[13] Do not stop for anything, especially never stop to look back or make changes. See if it doesn't become habitual.

Screenwriter Alvin Sargent[14] suggests "blind writing." Turn out the lights, close your eyes, write what your fingers want to say. Be as free as you can be. Trust that sense will come out of the exercise.

Writing to Schedule. This exercise can help you discover ideas and style as well as develop the consistent writing habit of a professional writer. Sometime in the morning, perhaps relaxing over breakfast, review the day's agenda. Then pick a specific time in the day when you definitely and unalterably can commit yourself to write. Try for at least a half hour. Consider this time a debt of honor; commit to it. At that exact time, sit with pen or keyboard. If this sounds inflexible, it's meant to be. Rigidly allow yourself no exceptions, even if it means excusing yourself from friends or other pleasures. You're trying to develop discipline within a creative framework, so be a tyrant about it. If you keep at it, day in, day out, you will soon find that you are beginning to write fluently and with control. You can use this exercise to explore story ideas or character sketches.

Developing a Story.   Here's a way to streamline the creative process and develop a rough idea into a story. Take a basic, unelaborated idea. Think about it (immerse yourself in it) for a day or two, contemplating possible directions for the action and characters without being too concrete. Alternate between focusing conscious thought on the idea and musing about it in a sort of reverie state. Try to dream about it. Then set a definite time and place two or three days hence when you will sit down and write the idea into a full narrative story. Charge your unconscious to develop this story over the next few days. Then dismiss the idea from your conscious mind. If you find yourself thinking about it, gently put it out of your mind. This is a time of concentrated incubation. You've given your unconscious the deadline. It's aware of it. Let the unconscious work toward that time.

When the day arrives, sit down and write. Work as rapidly as possible, letting the words come easily and quickly with as little conscious attention as possible. Avoid reading what you're putting down. Keep at it until you've achieved a complete story narrative—a beginning, middle, and end. Do not stop part way, complete the whole. You may be pleasantly surprised at the result.

Walking a Story.   Here's another way to try to accelerate the incubation period and develop a story or scene. Choose an uninterrupted three- or four-hour period. Begin alone and away from distractions. Get into a relaxed, pleasant, indulgent mood. Maintaining this mood, review your story idea. Visualize any scenes you've imagined. Visit your characters and observe what happens to them. Do all this in a light, easy way, allowing ideas to come to you rather than struggling for them or forcing them.

Then take the rough idea out for a walk. Begin the walk by giving your unconscious the charge to work out the story. Stroll at an easy pace while maintaining a mood of reverie or daydreaming. Avoid distractions. You are engrossed in the story on the unconscious level. Do not be concerned about what you will be writing; let it work itself out. Walk until you are mildly tired, pacing yourself so that you've reviewed the entire story in a very leisurely way. Do not return before reviewing the whole story, nor after you've exhausted the idea to the extent that you're impatient with it. When you've returned from the walk, relax. Continue your light reverie trance, avoiding distractions. Think of the story only in a desultory way, without consciously focusing on it. Relax in a dimly lit room, quieting both mind and body. Remain not quite fully awake, yet not drifting into sleep. Then, after a while, you will feel a surge of energy impelling you to write. Don't force it, permit it to come of itself. When it does come, go to the keyboard and write. The unconscious has been coaxed and focused; get down on paper what it's done.

Inviting the Imagination.   Stories, characters, images, sounds, ideas spring from a fertile imagination. Here are some ways to cultivate it.

Develop alternate ways of seeing. Most of our perception is by habit; we observe a friend just enough to recognize a familiar face. This rote observing makes it easier to move through our day, but it also means we miss much. You can sharpen your perception by practicing perceiving anew. Make the familiar unfamiliar. Become a stranger on your own streets. See for the first time what you ordinarily take for granted. Do this also with the ear (when is the last time you really listened to the sound of a friend's voice?). Take it further. Sense odors, temperature, touch. Imagine perceiving the most everyday events through the eyes of your characters. Take a walk or drive and see the world as they would.

Turn yourself into an object of your own attention. Imagine observing yourself from a camera located a little above you and off to the side. How do you look doing even simple actions such as typing, entering or leaving a room, making a purchase, walking the streets, relaxing with friends? What do you look like right now? If you knew nothing about yourself, what would you learn about yourself if you were observed by a camera above you? How do you stand? Sit? Walk? Smile? Imagine yourself in a social situation—how do you relate to the people around you? How do you feel about them?

Observe body language. Watch how people express or conceal themselves without words and how nonverbal behavior elicits responses from you and others. Consider how posture, gesture, and movement define your characters.

Speculate about the lives of strangers. What are they like? Where are they going? What for? What are they feeling? What secrets might they be harboring? What adventures are they having? What would they be like as characters in a script? Could the bow tie on the man in the gabardine suit really be a camera?

Actors use imagination exercises like these in their training all the time. Have fun with them. They encourage you to walk in the twilight land of fantasy. It's not a bad place for a writer to spend some time.

Work Habits

> *Writing is easy. All you do is stare at a blank sheet of paper until drops of blood form on your forehead.*[15]
>
> —Gene Fowler

Effective work habits create a more efficient screenwriter. Here are some suggestions.

Ideas come at odd times—inspiration frequently surprises us. Be prepared to write down ideas before they are forgotten. Carry a small notebook, pad, or comparable electronic device to make notes on. Keep paper beside your bed for late night thoughts that are likely to be forgotten in the morning. Consider carrying a small tape recorder.

Screenwriters write. For all of the emphasis on inspiration, creativity is still largely just what the old saw says—mostly perspiration. Nothing substitutes for sitting down and writing. Professional writers are disciplined into a regular habit of writing. You will want to be too. Trust that if you just go ahead and write you'll find the way to do it. Put, in garish neon colors, an imaginary sign over your desk that says: "Just do it." And then just do it.

This can be difficult. If you're having trouble getting down to writing, here are some suggestions.

Get tough. Set definite, scheduled writing periods, four or five days a week, when you commit to sit at the keyboard (or note pad) for at least a half hour but try for longer. When there, write. Stay there even if you have to sit and stare at an empty screen. This exercise familiarizes you with regular writing sessions. Realize that when you're actually working regularly, you'll want to put in much more time; it takes a while before you warm to the writing and it flows smoothly.

For professional writers, six hours is a good day's work. Usually writers work in early morning or late evening, although when meeting deadlines, entire days and all-nighters are common. If you don't know when you work best, try morning or evening.

Set up a favorable working environment, one with few distractions. And go along with whatever rituals you use to get in the mood. They help make the writer psychologically ready.

Sometimes, the most difficult moment is when you first sit down to write. As a boost, read what you wrote the previous day—sometimes even a page or two helps begin the writing. Try retyping the last page from your previous writing session. That also helps the writing start to flow.

Finally, as much as you might want to share your ideas with friends, it's better not to talk too much about your script. Talking about it can too easily replace writing it.

Writer's Block

> *Before I met Don Juan I would spend years sharpening my pencils, and then getting a headache every time I sat down to write. Don Juan taught me that's stupid. If you want to do something, do it impeccably, and that's all that matters.*[16]

The writer's B word. Maybe you've been writing happily and productively for years. Then suddenly drops the block.

It can hit in two ways. With the first, you suddenly run dry. The muse has vanished. Nothing comes. Only frustration.

The second block is procrastination. While you desperately would like to be writing, you are unable to get yourself to actually do it. There's always something else to do instead. More frustration.

Writer's block is a well-known occupational hazard. Expect it. When it comes, don't let it get you down. It isn't permanent. You can deal with it. Here are some suggestions.

Your ideas plop, your flow is drying up—you're writing but what's coming out isn't at all what you want. That's a signal to take some time and work on it.

See if some of the imagination exercises will help.

Play "what ifs"—what if they go to an amusement park instead of a restaurant, what if they don't have an affair.

Take a break. Get away from the keyboard to clear your mind. Exercise. Go for a walk. Bicycle. Swim. Go to a movie. Take a drive. A little incubation time may be all that is necessary to get the juices flowing again.

Suppose you're stuck at a particular spot in the script. What can you do? One technique is to set it aside and write a different section. Get back to the problem scene later (after you've unconsciously worked on it).

Or tackle the block directly. Take the scene and explore all its details—visual, aural, smells, and temperature. Research the specifics of the scene, no matter how insignificant. Sometimes immersing yourself in the scene can open up new options and get the script moving again.

Do imagination exercises with your characters (like those given in the chapter on characters). Talk it over with the characters. Letting them act as stand-ins for your unconscious may lead to breakthroughs.

On paper, open a dialogue with yourself about the block. Write out the problem. Explore it. Suggest solutions and see where they lead.

Tactics such as these can help overcome a particular script block.

Procrastination is a difficult problem since it often involves protecting your self-esteem. Don't fall into the perfectionist trap of believing that either you must produce great work or you are worthless. There's always a middle ground. Too many high expectations can lead to not doing anything.

Procrastination can also come from fear of how to handle the demands that you imagine come with success.

Whatever the reason, the consequence is avoidance. There's always a reason: something that needs to be done, or waiting for the "right moment." Brinksmanship—putting things off until the last minute—is another delaying tactic. By giving in to these rationalizations you will never discover what you really could do if you simply committed yourself.

Here are some ways to avoid procrastination.

Take control. Be responsible. Make active decisions about writing and stick to them. Realize that in putting things off, you are your own worst enemy. Jump right into the writing. Just do it.

Give up unrealistic fantasies of achievement and perfection; rather than trying to write the world's greatest screenplay, just do the best you can.

If the task seems overwhelming, break it up into smaller goals—so many pages, or a scene or two at a time; keeping at it will eventually get it done. Or contract with yourself to write for a short period—say thirty minutes—and just do that. Gradually you can increase the time, and you will be producing material.

Draw up a list of excuses for not writing; then realistically evaluate it. Does it make sense?

Set an agenda. Prioritize it, then follow it. (Just be sure your deadlines are realistic.)

Write material that while related to the story and characters will not appear in the script.

Deliberately try to write badly. Write the worst script imaginable.

Have a definite workspace set aside primarily for writing. Condition yourself so that when you are there, you are writing.

Most writers experience writer's block at some time; some know it quite intimately. But hang in and keep at it. It can be overcome.

Collaboration

Sometimes writers collaborate, believing that the outcome will be better than if each worked separately. Comedy writing, especially, benefits from a team effort. Television comedy series are typically written by teams of in-house writers. The ability to bounce jokes and funny ideas off one another is an important part of the process.

Collaboration has been described as a marriage without sex—some writing teams see more of each other than they do their spouses. If you decide to collaborate, be sure to pick a compatible partner.

Tools

There are all sorts of materials out there to help make writing easier for the screenwriter. A decent computer is a must, as is a quality printer that makes clear, clean copies. Most word processing programs can be tailored for script format. There are also specially designed screenwriting programs that offer advantages, such as a built-in word processing program and automatic formatting. Other programs are designed to be used in conjunction with popular word processing programs. Still others are specifically for screenplay formatting, and lack some of the enhancements of the high-end versions. All of these can speed up your writing time.

Another category of screenwriting software is story analysis systems designed to help plan the script. These programs propose answers to story problems, and supposedly lead to more effective decisions about structure, development and characters. How effective they are is an open question.

Screenwriting software programs are widely advertised in writing magazines and journals and in catalogs from stores such as The Writers Computer Store in Santa Monica, or The Write Stuff in Chatsworth, California.

Other useful tools are a good dictionary, one or more thesauruses, a book of synonyms and antonyms, a dictionary of slang, and one of those what-to-name-your-baby books to help with character names. Even if your software has a built-in thesaurus, get one or two others that are more comprehensive—one in dictionary format and another organized around concepts, such as *Roget's Thesaurus.*

SCRIPT DEVELOPMENT:
THE INVERTED TRIANGLE MODEL

It all begins on the page.

—Steven Spielberg

I conclude this chapter with a preview of what I consider the most effective strategy for constructing a script: the inverted triangle model.

Begin with the concept and develop it through each stage until it is realized in the completed script. The bottom point of the inverted triangle corresponds to the basic concept or idea—it is the succinct statement that everything else builds on. Expand it step by step, with increasingly longer and more complex development, and move up the triangle to the completed script.

The inverted triangle approach is analogous to an architect designing a building. The concept and basic story are comparable to the initial drawing of the building showing how it will look when finished—the sense of the whole. The story outline is comparable to the more detailed but not yet complete ground plan and elevations. Finally, the finished script corresponds to the complete set of detailed blueprints.

Start with an overview of the whole story and keep that concept central as you add more and more detail. The overview keeps you on track because you are always working with wholes.

The inverted triangle method also makes reworking easier. It's much easier to rewrite a few pages of an outline than to redo an entire screenplay.

Here's how to use the inverted triangle model in writing the script:

Visualize an inverted triangle (or see the diagram on page 12). Start at the bottom with the **concept**—the one- or two-sentence statement that summarizes the essence of the movie—and the slightly longer **basic story** form of a paragraph or two. This is the script's deep structure foundation.

Then expand it, moving further up the triangle, fleshing out the story to a **story narrative** of a few pages.

As you move up the triangle, get more specific and detailed.

Next, expand the narrative to a **story outline**. The outline lays out the beats—the story points—of the story lines. (In its diverse refinements it is variously referred to as a **one-liner, step outline, story line outline,** or **beat outline.** More important than the terminology is the process itself.)

The outline lays out the structure: beginning, middle, and end. Story beats logically develop one into the other: "This leads to this leads to this leads to. . . ."

Most films have more than one story line. Do separate outlines for each story line. When each of these work on their own, combine them into the overall outline of the film.

Then, still keeping the sense of the whole story, expand the outline into a long narrative **treatment, scene outline,** or **scene breakdown** that lays out the story scene by scene. Describe the action in each scene without writing the dialogue.

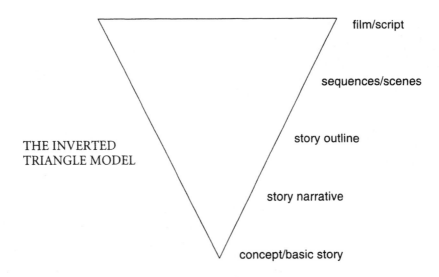

THE INVERTED
TRIANGLE MODEL

film/script

sequences/scenes

story outline

story narrative

concept/basic story

Many screenwriters outline their scenes on index cards—4" × 6" or 5" × 7"—one scene per card. This enables them to lay out the scenes—on the floor or pinned to the wall—to get a better sense of how the scenes flow. This method allows for the adding, deleting, and moving of scenes.

Now move on to the **first draft** script. This includes all scenes and sequences written out fully with action and dialogue (to be followed by subsequent rewrites until the **final draft**).

While every screenwriter outlines in one way or another, not all go through every step in the inverted triangle process. Whether you choose to follow the entire process or skip the middle stages, they are there for your service. Taking the steps one at a time insures the integrity of the story before you begin writing the full screenplay.

Sometimes students want to just sit down and begin writing the script without outlining. If this is the only way you can work, then you have no choice. But I consider it a major mistake. Such a script is likely to lack the tight structure demanded of most media stories. Besides, it is easier to make major structural changes in a shorter preliminary version than in a 120-page script.

Following (at least most of) the steps in the inverted triangle screenwriting model is the best approach I know to efficient and effective script writing.

The Filmscript. The final filmscript times out at about a minute of screen time per page, and typically will be between 105 to 125 pages. Don't let the script fall too far outside this range (although comedies will run a bit less, maybe 95 to 115 pages).

A one-hour series teleplay in film format will run around fifty-five to sixty-five pages. Live (on tape) television uses a different format and times to less than a minute a page. A situation comedy script to be shot before a live audience will run between thirty-five and fifty-five pages.

Scripts are always written in the present tense; use it for concepts and outlines as well. (It is best to avoid the authorial "we" as in "we see . . ." and "we are . . ." as this is outmoded usage.)

Script style is lean and economic, not literary. Description should be in the active voice, punchy without being gimmicky or pretentious. As concisely as possible, paint vivid word pictures. Make your script as exciting a read as possible.

Later, we'll discuss in detail how to use the inverted triangle model. For now, simply note the way in which it helps you write a script systematically, getting each successive stage right before moving on to the next until you have a finished screenplay.

SUMMARY

We've examined the How of writing—how to stimulate the creative process, how to develop effective working habits, how to combat writer's block, and how to approach writing the script.

Creative writing involves a balance between the unconscious creative imagination and critical evaluation. Inspiration can be nurtured by keeping busy with rhythmic, monotonous, and silent activities while letting the unconscious do its work.

Being a writer involves knowing your medium—watching what is currently being produced and analyzing its structure. Research lends authenticity to the work and helps avoid factual errors.

Effective work habits include ritual activities to set the mood, tools to make writing easier, and a commitment to sitting down and getting it done.

Writer's block is an occupational hazard, but it can be overcome.

Although most screenwriters work alone, some, including many comedy teams, collaborate.

Exercises to stimulate the imagination can be useful in getting started, working in a disciplined way, and overcoming blocks.

The inverted triangle model proceeds step by step from the concept/basic story through outlines, scene descriptions, and the finished script. Check each stage to see that it works. This approach retains a sense of the whole story through increasingly detailed developments.

ENDNOTES

1. Berger, T., quoted in R. Byrne (Ed.). (1988). *1,911 Best Things Anybody Ever Said.* New York: Ballantine, p. 45.

2. Carlino, L. J., quoted in W. Froug. (1972). *The Screenwriter Looks at the Screenwriter.* New York: Dell, p. 21.

3. Interviewed in the program *Inside Family Ties,* produced, directed, and reported by Michael Hirsh, WTTW Chicago, PBS.

4. Brande, D. (1934). *Becoming a Writer*. New York: Harcourt, Brace and Co. Fortunately, this useful book has been republished by J. P. Tarcher, Los Angeles, 1981.

5. Writer/director Quentin Tarantino has said that when he has an idea for a film, he goes through his record collection and starts playing songs until he finds one that has the spirit of the movie.

6. Miller, W. (Summer 1984). An interview with Terrence McDonnell. *Journal of Film and Video, 36,* 3, 51–57.

7. Froug, p. 276.

8. Froug, pp. 194–195.

9. Some earlier aesthetic research had painters draw to a poem and poets write to a picture, each free associating continually for the half hour of the exercise. The researcher could trace the idea that became the final work as it first appeared, dropped back into consciousness, reappeared in somewhat different form (reflecting unconscious work on it), with the process continuing until the half hour was done and the final work appeared. Patrick, C. (1935). *Creative Thought in Poets: Archives of Psychology, 178,* (R. S. Woodworth, Ed.), and (July 1937). Creative thought in artists. *Journal of Psychology, 4.*

10. Elbow, P. (1973). *Writing Without Teachers*. New York: Oxford University Press, p. 28.

11. P. Chayefsky, according to DiMaggio, M. in *Writing for Hollywood* (videotape), Writers Connection, Cupertino, CA, 1990.

12. King, V. (1988). *How to Write a Movie in 21 Days*. New York: Harper and Row. While King's structure model is much too formulaic, her suggestions on how to get the writing done have worked for many students. If you're having trouble getting started, her book may help.

13. Elbow, p. 3.

14. Described in Field, S. (1989). *Selling a Screenplay: The Screenwriters Guide to Hollywood*. New York: Dell, p. 203.

15. Fowler, G., quoted in Byrne, p. 46.

16. Attributed to Carlos Castenada. Author's note: Though I am sure this quote belongs to Mr. Castenada, I have been unable to locate the source of this quotation in his works.

CHAPTER *2*

Deciding Your Story

In my early days of writing, I was afraid that working it all out in advance would destroy the creative impulse. Now I don't even start seriously writing until it's all worked out on paper first.[1]

—Dan O'Bannon (Screenwriter)

First comes the idea—what to write about. In this chapter we'll look at choosing and developing an effective and marketable story idea, considering trends and genres, and tapping sources for ideas.

CHOOSING YOUR STORY IDEA

Choosing what to write is an important decision. Don't waste time writing something that won't attract a large, mass audience—domestic and international. Mainstream media are so expensive to produce that a script needs to demonstrate audience potential in order to attract financing. Considering that so many scripts are too mediocre to be made—some 90 percent of submissions to studios are a clear pass—why risk your effort on a weak idea? This doesn't mean catering to the lowest common denominator. It does mean that you must honestly evaluate whether your idea will attract a sufficiently large audience to justify the huge cost of producing it.

Rigorously evaluate the script idea. Is it marketable? Will audiences commit time and money to view it? Does it fit in with current trends? Is it unique enough to avoid being boringly derivative, but not so bewilderingly aberrant as to alienate viewers?

GENRES

One way to relate your script idea to trends and traditions is to situate it within a classic genre.

Genres identify similar film (or television) types. This may be because of plot similarities, typical characters, themes, settings, or even the "look" of the film. When we think of westerns, we expect to see cowboys, gunslingers, schoolmarms, dance-hall women, homesteaders and farmers, cattle barons, and saloon keepers. We look for horses, six-guns, western dress, and small towns with wooden sidewalks and tall storefronts. In the classic western we expect plots in which a heroic gunfighter comes to the aid of the honest settlers who are about to be wiped out by the powerful villains. And what is a western without the final shootout on the dusty streets?

Similar elements characterize other genres: action/adventure, romance, comedy, situation comedy, science fiction, gangster, film noir, doctor/hospital shows, and horror, to name just a few of the genres that have been identified by film scholars, the media industries, and movie audiences.

This doesn't mean that a genre film or television program has to follow a rigid genre formula. Part of the fun of writing in a genre is the freedom to play around with the conventions in new ways—as can be seen in the gangster genre films of Quentin Tarantino. Still, you'll want to be aware of the structures and conventions of the genre you write in so that you can modify it by design.

Genres are also important for marketing considerations because at different times some genres will be more popular than others—action/adventure is a perennial favorite, while for some time now musicals have been a decidedly hard sell. Let's look at some familiar genres.

Action/adventure stories range from a realistic, personal story such as *The Fugitive*, to a mix of humor and adventure in such films as the *Lethal Weapon*, *Die Hard*, the *Beverly Hills Cop* series, and Jackie Chan movies (although martial arts films may be considered their own genre), to the special effects extravaganzas of *Under Siege*, *Sudden Death*, and *Speed*. Because they depend more on action than dialogue, action/adventure films do well internationally.

There is always an audience for **romantic** stories. We like to see a couple made for each other finally get together; *When Harry Met Sally*, *Sleepless in Seattle*, and *Pretty Woman* are three films that have this quality. A film like *Ghost* shows us how malleable genre films can be. *Ghost* successfully combines a moving romantic story with an action story. One of the most enjoyable variations on romance, the **screwball** comedy, is itself considered a genre. Popular in the 1930s and 1940s, screwball comedies were unique in their emphasis on witty dialogue and the battle of the sexes. In these films, strong women usually gave better than they got from the men they were involved with. Part of their appeal came from poking fun at the wealthy at a time when America was going through a depression.

Comedies are always marketable, sometimes even becoming blockbusters (as did *Ghostbusters* and *Home Alone*). For television, situation comedies are the most common comic narrative form, although a prime-time animated series such as *The Simpsons* demonstrates that other forms are possible.

Horror film scripts have been a difficult sell lately, the exception being low-budget horror releases direct to home video. Interesting variations in the horror-movie theme are the comic or erotic elements of such vampire films as *Love at First Bite* or *Dracula: Dead and Loving It.* Placing the vampire story in contemporary America is one way of modifying the form; this has given us both the striking *Near Dark*, which transposes the story to the modern American southwest, and the less effective *Vampire in Brooklyn.*

As much as we might be drawn to large-scale **science fiction** and **sword-and-sorcery**, these are not recommended genres for beginning writers since their high production costs make them investment risks. However, there are many possibilities for lower-budget science fiction and fantasy material. *Star Trek, Deep Space 9, The Pretender, Profiler, Dark Skies,* and *The X-Files* have all done well on television.

Fantasy is a broad classification that can include a mix of genres. Films like *Alien* and *Jurassic Park,* for instance, effectively combine the monster threat of horror films with science fiction.

In spite of the success of Merchant Ivory films and the Jane Austen adaptations that appeared in the 1990s, new screenwriters are advised to stay away from **period pieces**—anything before about 1970—since they involve period costumes and settings that run up the budget.

Westerns, dead for many years, have had a comeback with films like *Unforgiven, Geronimo,* and *Dances with Wolves*; it's hard to tell if this will last.

This is not a good time for **musicals**.

A decade or so ago it was thought that **television situation comedies** were dead. Then along came *The Cosby Show* and sitcoms skyrocketed; they are still popular. Then it was claimed that one-hour shows (generally **action/adventure**) were finished—they were expensive and difficult to syndicate. Nevertheless, they came back. For many years **doctor/hospital** shows and **westerns** were off the tube. They, too, came back.

Additional genres include gangster, combat/war, sports, docudrama, real life, film noir, the quest, biography, big screen epic, disaster films and the television "disease of the week"—an unflattering label for a once popular TV movie-of-the-week pattern.

To write within a genre, it is necessary to study the form. Who are the heroes (gender, type, characteristics) and how are they portrayed? What are typical settings? What are the elements that help define the genre (a western has cowboy outfits, horses, six-guns and western settings)? What functions do other characters serve? What ritualistic elements (such as the final shootout) are usually present?

To write for episodic television, know the series thoroughly. Know the characters, their typical actions and characteristic dialogue. Make note of the sorts of situations that repeatedly appear in the show. Analyze the show's structural development. Try not to depart too much from the pattern of the series. Although series often go through major changes, it's the producers and staff writers who make the changes, not freelance writers.

When submitting scripts to a series, it's been suggested that you send in scripts for a series other than the one you are targeting. The weaknesses of your script are bound to be glaringly obvious to a producer or story editor familiar with the show in question. Submitting scripts for another series may be a better way to showcase your talent.

STORY THEMES

Certain story themes, while lacking the traditions and conventions of genres, recur in film after film. Here are some themes that speak to basic human interests.

The likable underdog is a consistently popular theme. We like to see a deserving character come through in the last reel. We've seen this work in such films as *Rocky*, *First Blood*, *The Karate Kid*, *Forrest Gump*, *Clear and Present Danger*, and *The Fugitive*, as well as in those classic Frank Capra films about ordinary idealists fighting the corrupt, greedy, and powerful (*It's a Wonderful Life*, *Mr. Smith Goes to Washington*).

We enjoy getting an "inside look" at some operation or adventure to see how it was pulled off—how do you steal the crown jewels? rescue terrorist's hostages? destroy a killer shark (*Jaws*)? help a Soviet submarine to defect (*Hunt for Red October*)? as a kid alone protect yourself from marauding burglars (*Home Alone*)? get a disintegrating spacecraft safely back to earth (*Apollo 13*)?

Because the film audience is young, teenage films—rites of passage or coming of age—are popular (*Fast Times at Ridgemont High*, *Risky Business*, *The Breakfast Club*, *Amarcord*, *Gregory's Girl*, *Clueless*, and on a younger level *Stand by Me*, *Forbidden Games*, *Small Change*).

Friendship stories include "buddy" movies in which we like the interaction of the two protagonists (*Midnight Cowboy*, *Butch Cassidy and the Sundance Kid*, *Lethal Weapon*, *Thelma and Louise*).

A popular formula is the "fish out of water." A likable (and often oddball) character is thrust into a strange territory and must confront a threatening new reality (*Big*, *E.T.*, *Rain Man*, *Back to the Future*, *Star Trek IV: The Voyage Home*, *Die Hard*, *Die Hard 2*, *Private Benjamin*, and *Beverly Hills Cop*).[2]

STORY SOURCES

Where do ideas for stories come from? Check out newspapers, magazines, the Internet, your immediate environment, and places you travel. Historical events gave us *All the President's Men*, *The Day of the Jackal*, *JFK*, *Malcolm X*, *Missing*, *Nixon,* and *Schindler's List*. Read the alternative press.

The classics are another source for stories. *Rosemary's Baby* is a variation of the Faust legend. *The Warriors* was inspired by the story of a small band of Greek warriors who had to fight their way home through the Persian army (from the Sol Yurick novel drawing on Xenophon's *Anabasis*). *West Side Story* retold an updated *Romeo and Juliet*. *Apocalypse Now* drew on Joseph Conrad's *Heart of Darkness*. *Ran* was an adaptation of *King Lear*. Other sources include Bible stories, fairy tales, and folk stories such as Robin Hood.

People you know can become story characters, especially if you imagine them in intriguing situations. These characters have the advantage of being based on life rather than clones of what you see in the media.

Things that happen to you or others can suggest stories. Things you care deeply about are an especially good choice.

DEFINING THE STORY: THE "WHAT IF . . ."

In the early stages of forming your story, explore as many possibilities as possible. Brainstorm. Unconsciously incubate the idea. Play with alternatives. Give yourself many options as you consider the directions it could go.

Make use of the magical *"what if . . ."* as you investigate possibilities.

What if they crashed in a desert instead of a jungle?

What if she doesn't go on the trip?

What if he loved his father too much rather than hated him?

What if it were her story and not his?

What if he runs into his double?

What if's can lead to some interesting ideas. Some ways to use them are to:

Reverse things. What if she were rich and he poor instead of vice versa? What if the villain was cool and sophisticated, rather than the hero? What if he is the hero instead of she? What if it's a love story rather than an adventure story? What if instead of responding modestly to publicity, your character turns out to be a braggart who revels in it? What if your B story (secondary story line) were to become your A story (primary story line)?

Expand it. What if the story took place in a large city rather than in a small midwestern town? What if it involved the World Cup championship rather than a local soccer club?

Reduce it. How about a sailboat rather than an ocean liner? What if the story involved local street gangs instead of organized crime?

Think of *alternatives.* Could the characters be older? younger? What other situations could you put characters in? What else could happen to them? What other characters might be involved?

HIGH CONCEPT

Your story idea will be even more compelling if you can express it as high concept. High concept is hot.

High concept is an industry term for a story concept that can be expressed clearly in a sentence or two (like a television log line description) and that will, on its own, attract an audience. It just sounds like something you'd want to see. The movie industry wants high-concept scripts since they're considered an easier sell. High concept is almost a necessity with TV movies (it makes good TV-listings log lines). Some excellent, complex, and successful films don't lend themselves to encapsulated, high-concept log lines. But if yours does, it will have a much better chance of being made. Here are some examples of high concept.

Back to the Future: A teenager finds himself propelled 20 years into the past and must not only get back, but must unite his parents despite his young mother-to-be's having fallen in love with him.

E.T.: A cute, lovable outer space alien gets stranded on earth and needs the help of some children to get home.

La Cage aux Folles or its American adaptation, *The Birdcage:* An outlandish, gay entertainer must get approval for the marriage of his son to the daughter of an official on a morality crusade.

Twins: Twins discover each other at the age of thirty-five; one is the short Danny DeVito, the other is the large and powerful Arnold Schwarzenegger.

Jurassic Park: Scientists at an island theme park populated with reconstituted dinosaurs fight for their lives when the creatures escape and attack.

Apollo 13: When an oxygen tank explodes, astronauts race against the clock to bring their deteriorating spacecraft safely back to earth.

High concepts are always in big demand; they are an easier sell. How does your concept sound? Can you express it in one or two sentences?

BROAD-STROKING THE STORY

When working out a story idea, keep it broad-stroked. Frame the story in the most general terms, add details later. As specific ideas for scenes occur to you, make notes and set them aside for later. By thinking in too much detail at this early stage, you risk getting locked into story action that may get in the way of forming a complete story. First see the forest, then later describe the individual trees. Setting specific scenes and actions too early often makes it hard to let go of them when they no longer work in the story. Screenwriter William Goldman describes his file of best scenes, all marvelous, that he had to drop from his scripts when they no longer fit.

Make sure your story has enough substance to fill the required length. Don't underestimate the story beats (story points). I've seen too many feature film ideas that would really fill only a half-hour.

THE ESSENTIAL STORY

Is there a paradigmatic media-story model that fits most of what appears on the screen and yet is broad-stroked enough to avoid the pitfalls of writing to formula? I think there is and that in generalized form it includes the following elements.

To work with an audience, a story needs *emotion* (and/or *humor*) to involve us emotionally and make us care. We want to see *characters* we can get involved with, *heroes* we can identify with, who have something *vital at stake* in achieving a *clear, strong goal* that they must achieve or else. *Conflict* with a strong *antagonistic force*—usually a *villain* that opposes the hero—gets us involved.

We want to be hooked on *suspense* throughout the story as we wonder how each new crisis will be resolved. We want to be *surprised* at unexpected twists of the plot. Generally we want a clear *resolution,* and typically a happy ending. Usually there will be at least one strong *secondary story line* (B story).

If your story is a comedy, we want it to be *funny.*

It helps if there are strong acting roles since a script that attracts a star has a much better chance of being made.

SUMMARY

This chapter considered that crucial question—what to write about? It discussed the value of audience appeal, and the particular attractiveness of high concept. Factors to consider in forming a story idea include industry trends, popular themes, and genres. Ideas come from many sources, including current events, literature, and personal experience. The chapter concluded with a concise account of what comprises the essential media story.

ENDNOTES

1. O'Bannon, D., quoted in W. Froug. (1991). *The New Screenwriter Looks at the New Screenwriter.* Los Angeles: Silman-James Press, p. 311.

2. In a sense, identifying common story themes is not unlike the notion that there are only so many basic plots. Various analysts have tried to reduce all plots to a fundamental few, but they don't agree on what these are. I've seen different lists that claim the number of basic plots is 7, 10, 15, 20, and 36. I don't find any of them very convincing.

CHAPTER 3

Characters

THE ACTOR: *He's my character, I created him.*
CECILIA: *Didn't the man who wrote the movie do that?*
—Woody Allen, *The Purple Rose of Cairo*

What is the most basic description of a film story? I would answer that question as Alan Armer does: a film story is most simply about a character with a problem.[1]

We experience a dramatic story through its characters. We see ourselves in their struggles, triumphs, and failures. We care about and identify with them, like or dislike them, worry about them, root for them, take sides in their clashes, and share their problems and adventures.

Memorable characters stay with us: Chaplin's Little Tramp, Rhett Butler and Scarlett O'Hara, James Bond, Charles Foster Kane, Sherlock Holmes and Dr. Watson, Dracula, Dorothy and her companions on the yellow brick road, Darth Vader, R2D2 and C3PO, E.T., Indiana Jones, Hannibal Lecter, and Captain Kirk.

Creating interesting, involving characters is one of your most important challenges. In this chapter we'll consider ways to do that. First, some preliminaries.

A film usually has three to five major characters. Six or seven are possible, but then it begins to get unwieldy. With film/television scripts, don't include a page describing the characters (as is commonly done in theatrical playscripts). A script reader's sense of the characters comes from what they do and say, from how they talk about themselves, and from how others react to them and talk about them.

When a character first appears in the script, include a very brief description. Keep this to a sentence or two that conveys the highlights of the character. Supply gender, age, appearance, and perhaps a choice phrase to convey the character's personality. (Linda Seger gives two examples of clever character descriptions: "A sweet-faced guy who's probably done his job too long," and "A big woman with small illusions—180 Guatemalan pounds squeezed into a pink lace teddy.")[2]

Try to include two or three strong, meaty acting roles in the script. Interesting characters make for better scripts, and can attract popular, bankable stars. It isn't usually a good idea to write a character designed for a particular actor; if the actor is unavailable or uninterested, the script could languish unmade. On the other hand, some screenwriters find that having an actor in mind—living or dead—helps to concretely visualize a character. Try this if your characters seem abstract and undifferentiated.

EFFECTIVE CHARACTERS

You'll want your characters to be interesting, involving, original, and memorable. See how many of the following qualities of effective characters apply to those in your script.

Effective Characters Seem Real

For many viewers, television characters seem more real than the people who live down the street. Television actors frequently find that their fans confuse them with the characters they play. In some four years of *Marcus Welby, MD*, the show received over 250,000 letters addressed to the character, many requesting medical advice. While this doesn't speak well of fan comprehension, it does indicate that these characters worked in one way—they came across as being real.

Effective characters convey the feeling that they are complex human beings with a personal history—a past that has made them who they are—and a life outside the story. They seem involved in the process of living their lives and of working out their destinies rather than being mere puppets of the writer. We see them as complex human beings within the world of the film.

Try to model your characters on real people. This doesn't have to be a direct transposition. It is possible to change appearance, circumstance, age, and gender and still retain those qualities that make the person, and now the character, real for you. Try combining the qualities of several people into a single character. Or use one person for a number of characters. Drawing from life will help you avoid one-dimensional characters.

Stereotypical characters—oversimplified, cardboard types—are easily recognized by the audience: the starving artist, effete poet, alcoholic reporter, stuffy professor, bigoted and overweight southern sheriff, solemn and pontificating clergy-man, or whore with a heart of gold. Whatever authenticity these clichés once possessed has been lost through overexposure and distortion.

This doesn't mean that you can't use a type. The character type may have certain prominent characteristics, but still avoid caricatures. What can you add to the stuffy-professor type to make it less trite?

We build expectations based on stereotypes, so surprise us. Thwart our expectations without resorting to equally simplistic reversals (such as turning the soft-spoken, mild-mannered librarian into a martial arts expert).

The Nazi Colonel in *Schindler's List*, for instance, contains all the cruelty of similar types in low-budget World War II movies, but with some added dimensions that makes the character believable. Unlike the stereotypical Nazi, he at first dispassionately plays with moral choices by toying with Schindler's suggestion of exercising power by *not* killing. In addition, the Colonel is attracted to his Jewish housekeeper despite his racist beliefs.

Giving characters a personal history and unique personality traits, helps make them real for the audience.

Effective Characters Are Credible

In spite of the best efforts of writers, directors, and actors, sometimes we see characters that we simply can't believe, and so we get turned off to the story.

Believable characters make effective characters. Because the credibility of a story depends largely on the believable actions of the characters, their behavior must be consistent with who they are, what they know, and what we know about them.

Credibility means that characters respond with the depth and insight appropriate to them. They must believably handle the situations in which the story places them. In the case of excessive melodrama, for instance, the characters express strong emotion, but to us it feels counterfeit because the character's responses are out of sync—either with the story or with their own personality. We recognize their actions, but don't share them. We are shown rather than invited along.

Credible characters also have realistic weaknesses. Sometimes writers care so much for their heroes that they want them to be good, wise, beautiful, and virtuous. The result can be unrealistic. Don't make characters too perfect. Be willing to step back and see their human frailties. They'll be better characters for it.

Nor will the audience identify with heroes who take themselves too seriously. To compensate, some films add humor—often self-deprecating humor—to their characters (as in the *Indiana Jones, Die Hard,* and *Lethal Weapon* films).

"In real drama, all characters must be in the right—that is how God sees them, i.e., how they are."[3] Unless you're doing action/adventure melodrama, try not to make your characters simplistically "good" or "bad." Complex individuals who are more than just bad guys make the best villains. This doesn't mean that they have to be presented sympathetically, but simply that the reasons for their actions must be understood.

Effective Characters Are Unique and Individualized

Most effective characters are unique, complete with their own actions, speech, movement, rhythm, dress, values, and style. Think of Chaplin's shuffle and flipping cane. Or the unkempt, ill-mannered Ronin Samurai of *Yojimbo* and *Sanjuro*. In *Harold and Maude*, Harold is at first somber and weird; he stages suicides and goes to funerals. Maude is vibrant and full of life (and also goes to funerals). The couple in *Natural Born Killers* are amoral, violent, and at odds with the world. Annie Hall has such a characteristic mode of dress that it created the Annie Hall look.

Little details help make a character unique. In *Chinatown*, Jake kicks out the red lens of a tail light in order to better follow a car. In *The Way We Were*, Katie's hair is frizzy. Later it is straightened. At the film's end, it is again frizzy.

Sometimes it can be an attitude, such as Reggie Hammond's nervy commandeering of a country-and-western bar in *48 Hours*. Or it might be the carefree, humorous, ironic mannerisms of Indiana Jones, Butch Cassidy and the Sundance Kid, or Lt. McClane of the *Die Hard* films. The witches of *Rosemary's Baby* are hardly the usual, sinister sort; they are unique witches. Minnie is earnest and fussy. There's a silly one who wears thick glasses. The Japanese witch is more like a tourist, running around taking pictures.

Dominant traits are the ones that inevitably stand out in a capsule description of the character. Jake (*Chinatown*), McMurphy (*One Flew Over the Cuckoo's Nest*), and Harry (*Dirty Harry*) are direct, challenging, and aggressive. James Bond is suave and coolly effective. Hawkeye Pierce (*M*A*S*H*), Lt. McClane (the *Die Hard* series), Indiana Jones, and Butch Cassidy are witty and ironic.

Chances are that the audience will only be able to register three or four major characteristics for each character. Screen time doesn't permit many more. Define these when writing the notes to yourself about your characters.

One technique is to **tag** the character with some distinguishing label, mannerism, gesture, appearance, behavior, or speech. Tags are the sorts of things an impersonator exaggerates. While a tag helps make a character distinctive, be careful not to overdo it to the point of caricature. Some examples of tags are the character who sucks on a child's pacifier in *Boyz 'n' the Hood*, the "I reckon so" spoken by the outlaw Josie Wales, the friend in *When Harry Met Sally* who keeps repeating "I know, I know, I know I should" when told she should break off her affair with a married man. There's Leo's "Okay, okay, okay . . ." (*Lethal Weapon 2* and *Lethal Weapon 3*), the Chief Samurai's habit of stroking his shaved head (*The Seven Samurai*), Rocky's halting "ya know" (*Rocky*), Mr. Spock's ears (*Star Trek*), Oliver Hardy's tie flutter, Chaplin's walk and cane swing, and Harpo Marx's business of "giving his leg."

Effective Characters Have a Strength

Characters must project a presence strong enough to involve us and carry the drama. The source of a hero's strength can be physical, emotional, intellectual, or spiritual. Even "weak" characters must portray weakness effectively. Hamlet is the classic example. But consider also Guido in *8½*. Both men vacillate, yet each conveys a strong presence. (Be wary, however, of characters who feel sorry for themselves. Their feeling often preempts our ability to empathize with them.) We like a hero who continues to struggle when the odds are overwhelming (*Places in the Heart*), even if those odds eventually overwhelm them (*Butch Cassidy and the Sundance Kid*, *Viva Zapata!*, *Braveheart*).

Effective Characters May Be Ambiguous

There's often a certain ambiguity about effective characters. Just as with real people, there's a sense of mystery, of an unknown area. This touch of ambiguity leaves room for the audience to project our own feelings and motivations onto the character.

In *8½* we are never clearly told why Guido is having trouble completing his film, yet we share his turmoil. Nor are we ever quite sure what Bobby is running from in *Five Easy Pieces*, even as we participate vicariously in his quest. In *The Passenger* we are given only hints as to why Locke switches identities with the dead Robertson. In *The Day of the Jackal*, there's an enticing mystery about the hired assassin. Even when the plot is exposed and his backers are removed, he continues with the assassination out of some sense of professional challenge—we never fully understand why. And at the film's end, no one knows who he was, or even his nationality.

In *Lawrence of Arabia*, the complexities of Lawrence's strange drive and sense of destiny are as much a part of the written character as they were of the actual man. In *Silence of the Lambs*, we never know what makes Hannibal Lecter the monster he is. Nor are we ever certain why Schindler acts at so much risk to himself in *Schindler's List*. Although we want to understand a character's motivation, there is always room for something unknown and ambiguous. Let the audience fill in the blanks.

Effective Characters May Have Intrinsic Conflicts

Film characters are often given conflicting values and objectives in order to make them more interesting. Arthur is torn between his desire to remain wealthy and his love for Linda (*Arthur*). Bobby in *Five Easy Pieces* tries to span two worlds—his escape world as an oil driller and the world of his family with its refinement, quiet retreat, and classical music.

The father in *Through a Glass Darkly* is torn between sympathy for his daughter's mental illness, and his almost morbid curiosity about the degenerative progression of the disease. Throughout *Boyz 'n' the Hood*, Tre is caught between commitment to his friends and his father's admonitions to avoid violence and waste.

Effective Characters Invite Audience Identification

In large measure, audiences experience the story by identifying with the characters, vicariously taking on the objective, the conflicts, and the struggle toward a final resolution.[4]

Empathy is one of the most powerful ways to get involved with characters. We put ourselves in a character's place; we share their adventures, desires, and troubles. From the time of tales told around the flickering glow of primeval campfires, we've enjoyed identifying with the hero's journey.

As a screenwriter, you can nurture the empathy by the way you present the hero. Specific techniques can be used to invite audience involvement.[5] Find ways to present the character as sympathetic, likable, quirky, funny, attractive, brave, caring, skillful, in jeopardy, charismatic, having a tragic flaw, or in a moment of self-disclosure.

Sympathy.   We care about characters we feel sorry for. Audiences sympathize with characters suffering unwarranted physical, mental, emotional, or social distress. In the early minutes of *Back to the Future*, Marty is shown being castigated by a high school administrator. A finger is waved in his face. He is called a slacker like his father before him. We sympathize with Marty, and thus begin identifying with him.

When we first meet Rocky (*Rocky*), we quickly see that he's a loser. Yet when he is supposed to break a guy's thumb but only lectures him instead, he gains our sympathy.

When police chief Brodie in *Jaws* is slapped and blamed by a distraught widow for her son's being eaten by the shark, we know he doesn't deserve it because he had tried to close the beaches but was opposed by the town's economic interests.

Sympathy also works for characters with whom we can't readily identify. Hannibal Lecter is a despicable character, yet he suffers sadistic little torments from a sleazy psychiatrist, and this creates some sympathy in us. We feel uncomfortable with Rupert in *The King of Comedy*—he's such a schmuck—but we can't help feeling sorry for him.

Another way to create sympathy is to present a character whom no one believes, although the audience knows better (*Sisters, Rear Window, Beverly Hills Cop*). Still another technique is to show a character struggling to overcome a handicap or battling difficult, perhaps overwhelming, odds.

Likability.   It almost goes without saying that you want to create a likable hero. Let us enjoy them as people we might like to know (if we were in situations like those of the story). A character who rescues a cat from a tree in the first act is someone we're going to like. George Bailey in *It's a Wonderful Life* is the prototypical nice guy, habitually sacrificing his own ambitions for the good of the community.

Quirky.   We like quirky, off-beat characters who follow their own drummer, such as one who plays a tuba and chases fire engines (*Mr. Deeds Goes to Town*), those who inhabit the homeless world of *My Own Private Idaho,* or a free spirit such as Maude in *Harold and Maude.*

Funny.   We like characters who are funny, and who don't take themselves seriously. Arthur is such a character. When we first meet him, he is laughing boisterously and making jokes at his own expense. We nevertheless detect his loneliness and need for affection. The same is true for most Woody Allen characters.

Attractive.   Make your heroes attractive—not in the sense of being glamorous, but in having qualities that attract us to them. They should be special, interesting people who are grappling with life in interesting ways.

Bravery.   We like a hero who's brave, who takes risks. The young boy in *E.T.* who takes a flashlight out to investigate the alien, then invites it into his room gains our admiration. So does the boy who resists the robbers in *Home Alone.* This needn't be physical bravery. We also admire people who stand up for their beliefs, and who are free enough to express their feelings openly.

Caring.   *E.T.* illustrates something else we appreciate in characters—that they show a concern for others. The same is true of the hero in *Schindler's List.*

Skillfulness.   We admire characters who are good at what they do, whether the skills be physical, social, or intellectual. When the Sundance Kid is asked, "How good are you?" he demonstrates by shooting the man's gun belt from his hips and across the floor. James Bond movies often open with examples of 007's prowess. Early in *The Hunt for Red October,* Ryan figures out that Ramius is trying to defect with the Red October; no one else has this insight. In the beginning of *Three Days of the Condor,* we admire Robert Redford's explanation of how someone could be shot without any bullet being found (it was made of ice and melted). We also enjoy the fact that he learned this from Dick Tracy comic strips.

In Jeopardy.   Putting characters in jeopardy is another effective technique. Place them in situations that threaten them—physically or emotionally—and the audience will identify with the character's predicament. Opening jeopardies are well used in the beginning of the Indiana Jones films. This technique works with even minor misfortunes. At the beginning of *Die Hard 2,* McClane gets a parking ticket and his car is towed away. He tries to talk his way out of it, but to no avail. It's a situation the audience easily identifies with.

Charisma.   We get involved with characters who show charisma—a forceful, winning, quality of leadership. Charisma can also be used to get us involved with less likable characters; we may dislike them, but we admire the power they convey. This quality is often seen in films about historical, larger-than-life figures (*Patton, Citizen Kane, Lawrence of Arabia, Braveheart, Viva Zapata!*).

Tragic Flaw.   Another way to handle unappealing characters is to show us their tragic flaw. We like to see them trapped by their nature—their ambition, greed, or ruthlessness driving them relentlessly to self-destruction. Two of my favorite examples are films from the late 1950s that both have excellent scripts.

Lonesome Rhodes in *A Face in the Crowd* is a charmingly charismatic character who goes from being a small-town radio personality to a television talent so powerful that he can sell out to politicians and promote potential presidential candidates. While we are attracted by his charm, his desire for power is his undoing, and we eventually see what he is really like.

I don't think there is a single likable character in *Sweet Smell of Success*. Their craving for power and fame make them distasteful but fascinating characters.

Identification in such films is often negative—antipathy rather than empathy. We seem to identify more with the moral lesson they negatively represent, a lesson that invites involvement by reinforcing our own values.

Even likable characters often reveal flaws. We like characters who show that they can be vulnerable, even foolish. These are human foibles that we all share.

Moment of Self-Disclosure.   A useful technique that often appears later in a script is the moment of self-disclosure, a moment of vulnerability when the character's innermost feelings are expressed. Don't place this moment too early. It should come when we know the character well enough to accept such a disclosure.

In *Silence of the Lambs*, Clarice relates the experience of hearing the lambs crying before they are slaughtered and of unsuccessfully trying to save one. This is a private and painful memory for the character, and we strongly respond to it.

Sometimes an entire film is built around self-disclosure, as with the students in *The Breakfast Club* who reveal their hopes and fears to each other over the course of one day.

CHARACTERS FORM THE STORY

We'll continue our discussion of creating effective characters by examining the ways in which characters drive the story.

Character Goals Form Story Lines

We've sketched out a broad-stroked overview of a media story as one in which the protagonist's motivation impels them toward a goal. The hero's struggle to reach the goal in spite of the obstacles is what forms the story line. The audience wants to see if the hero can prevail against strong opposing forces.

In planning a story line, make sure the protagonist has a clear objective. Here's a suggestion how to do this. Express the character's goal using an active verb form: "To ___(do something)___," to *catch* the criminal, to *win* a love. This defines the story line dynamically. It describes your character's action in striving toward the goal, something the character can play out over the story line.

What is true for the protagonist is equally true for all the major characters in a screenplay. Each wants to do something; each has a goal.

To better understand your characters and their actions, be sure to identify their goals. These won't necessarily be acted out in the story—you only have time to tell so much—but they will give you a better sense of how and why the characters behave as they do.

What about our initial simple definition of a story as a character with a problem? This amounts to the same thing. The character's problem—overcoming obstacles in order to achieve a goal—creates the dramatic conflict of the story.

There Is Something at Stake

The story objective must be one that is immensely important to the hero. The stakes must be high. The hero must succeed—or else. In order to hook the audience, the alternative to success must be (physically or emotionally) catastrophic. In *Places in the Heart,* the young widow's two friends say that they can't get her cotton picked in time. So she lays it out for them: if they fail, one will be back begging his meals, another will be put in a state home, and she will lose her farm as well as her surrogate family. For her—and them—it is virtually a matter of life and death.

On the other hand, a loss of dignity that wouldn't faze some people may be devastating to others. In the Danish film *Babette's Feast*, it is not really a life-or-death matter for Babette to prepare a scrumptious meal, but the act takes on enormous symbolic significance for her. In *Ikiru,* Watanabe's desire to get a small park built before his imminent death gives his life meaning.

Heroes Are Proactive

Film/TV heroes are proactive rather than reactive. They define and move the story along by their actions, either initiating or actively responding to the actions of others. A common error in ineffective scripts is to have a detached, observing hero who simply watches what others do. Although a few films may be able to sustain an inactive hero, this approach doesn't usually work and should be avoided.

The hero's actions move the story along. They initiate and define the story (to catch the criminal, win love, rescue prisoners, uncover a secret), and drive the story to its end. Keep your hero proactive.

Characters Grow and Change During the Story

Characterization is an ongoing process; characters grow over the course of a film. They change as they are shaped by events and by their interactions with other characters. The changes may be in terms of values, attitudes, emotions, or insight. This growth/change process is often referred to as the **Character Arc** or **Transformational Arc.**

Typically, it is the main character who changes. In *Arthur*, the death of his friend and valet helps give Arthur the courage to stand up to his family and risk the loss of his fortune. By the end of *Jurassic Park*, paleontologist Alan Grant has changed his attitude toward the children, becoming more responsive to them and even entertaining the idea of having some of his own.

Not all heroes change. The heroes of such action/adventure films as the James Bond, Indiana Jones, and *Die Hard* series go through no major transformations. Other characters, however, do change. In *Die Hard 2*, it is the Airport Security Captain who changes (from being McClane's antagonist to supporting him). In *Beverly Hills Cop*, Axel Foley doesn't change, but the Beverly Hills police do. In *Pulp Fiction*, Jules gives up his life of crime. (Although he is an important character, this film doesn't have one clear protagonist in the classic sense.)

It's difficult for a television series character to undergo major changes, given the short span of an episode. Nor is it a good idea to quickly change a character whom viewers expect to behave in certain ways. Instead, a television episode may reveal something new about the character—new to us and perhaps new to the character as well. Characters in a long-running series often go through significant changes once the series becomes established (*M*A*S*H* being a prime example).

Characters Interact in Relationships

Characters continually interact with other characters. One way to develop interesting relationships is to provide contrasts among your characters. Form your characters so that conflict or at least tension between them is inherent.

One reason to contrast characters is to make it easy for the audience to distinguish them. A film featuring all California blondes could easily cause confusion. An obvious way to deal with this is for the production to cast actors who are identifiably different. You can help by writing characters with clearly distinct qualities.

Contrast also adds spice to a story. Contrasting characters can be made to conflict in interesting ways (and even generate their own story lines thereby). "Buddy films" frequently feature contrasting heroes. In *48 Hours*, in addition to the Caucasian/African American contrast, Jack Gates is coarse, uncouth, slovenly, drinks on duty, and drives a junky Cadillac convertible; Reggie Hammond is cool, suave, a sharp dresser, and cons others with his cocky attitude. In *Jaws*, the police chief is a normal guy, ignorant of boats, and scared of being on the water. The scientist is educated, casual, and from a wealthy background. The Captain is crude, working class, and obsessed with the shark chase. Their different temperaments contribute to interesting relationships as well as plot development.

Annie Hall plays contrasts for laughs: Alvy's New York Jewish chutzpah, Annie's midwest, white-bread Americana. *Ghost* gains immeasurably from the marvelous storefront medium who adds humorous relief to the tender emotions we feel for the lovers.

In *Star Wars*, Luke Skywalker is boyish, idealistic, dedicated, and ready to believe in goodness and right. Han Solo is cynical, sarcastic, wise-cracking, mercenary, and a maverick. Princess Leia is gutsy, challenging, commanding, independent. Wookie is a mix of good pet and dangerous predator. Obi-wan Kenobi is knowing, in the tradition of the wise men of legends and folktales. R2D2 has something of the pet about him. 3CPO plays the fussy, petulant, sometimes dithering "gentleman's gentleman." Han is something of an older brother to Luke. He and the Princess compete and bicker in a way that inevitably leads to romance.

The **television family** is a staple of that medium. In some cases it's a literal family (*The Cosby Show*, *All in the Family*, and *Fresh Prince of Bel Air*). Other times it's a work "family" or social "family" (*Cheers*, *Wings*, and *Seinfeld*). The *Star Trek* "family" has stayed with us from the original series through at least six feature films. Much of the attraction of series like these is the reassuring familiarity we feel with a continuing family of characters.

Paul Lucey offers this description of the character personalities of the *Cheers* family.

> Sam's earthy sexuality conflicts with Diane's intellectual romanticism. . . . Norm is a lonely and rather sad fellow who hides from his wife night after night, preferring the company of Cliff the mail carrier. Cliff is a Reader's Digest intellectual, a bachelor who is afraid of women. Coach has a simple, literal mind. Carla is tough, scrappy and narrow minded.[6]

An ideal recipe for the interaction that made *Cheers* such a favorite.

Characters Are Convincingly Motivated

Just like you and I, characters are motivated to act the way they do. There is a reasonable "why" behind a character's objectives and behavior. Motivation works a number of ways.

Psychological Dynamics.   Motivation comes from the inner psychological dynamics that underlie and impel the actions of a character. These include the need for survival, for security, for interaction with others (affection, intimacy, recognition), and for personal fulfillment (success, self-confidence, self-respect, commitment to duty, a moral code, and personal honor). Motivational dynamics justify the actions of your characters. By exploring your characters' deep-seated motivations, you will better understand them and their behavior.

A character's struggle with conflicting motivations can be a central issue: love versus financial security (*Arthur*), success versus self-respect (*Sweet Smell of Success*), duty versus ethics (*Platoon*, *The Fugitive*).

As we'll discuss later, an **internal story line** is often constructed around a character's conflicting inner motivations.

Story Line Motivation.   If a story line is the movement of a character toward a goal, motivation is the justification that drives a character toward that goal. It is the character's intention within the story: to catch the criminal, to win someone's love, to discover meaning, to indulge a passion.

Michael Hauge makes an interesting distinction between what he calls a character's **outer motivation** and **inner motivation.**[7] The outer motivation is what the character hopes to outwardly achieve. It drives the story (to catch the criminal, etc.). The inner motivation is *why* the character wants to achieve the outer motivation (for example, a desire for self-worth). Inner motivation, he points out, is often revealed through dialogue. This is a useful way to look at motivation because it allows you to further delineate the main characters.

Scene Motivation.   In each scene, your characters want something: to escape from prison, repair a malfunctioning engine, or convince another of a course of action. These motives produce the action within the scene. Conflicting motives between characters will produce scene tension and excitement. In virtually every scene, each character should want something. Know what that something is as you write the scene.

Wants and Needs.   You might find it useful to make a distinction between a character's **wants** and a character's **needs.** A character may want one thing, but need something else—something they aren't yet aware of. Often the audience is aware of this need and enjoys seeing the character discover it. Try to determine for your main character—perhaps even for all your principal characters—what they *want,* and then—if it is different—what they *need.*

A character's motivation need not be explicitly spelled out for the audience. Some ambiguity allows us to project our own emotions onto the character.

To uncover a character's motivation when it isn't clear, explore possible reasons for the character's actions. For example, suppose a female character overreacts to the sexual advances of a male character; she's angrier than the circumstances warrant. What motivates her extreme reaction? To find out, ask: why? Perhaps she wants more respect than she feels he has shown her. Press further. Why is respect so important to her? Competing in a man's world, perhaps she has experienced discrimination; perhaps she should be doing better than she is, given her education and talent. Now the character's dynamic is taking shape. Probe further. What else could motivate this response? Well . . . maybe her mother was talented but never realized her potential because she married early, had children, deferred to her husband, and so on. Use this inner character dialogue to probe character motivation and better understand the character.

Character Story Roles

Since a story is told through its characters, we can identify functions that these characters play. All a story really needs is a hero and some antagonistic force. Most stories, however, are much more complex. The most common characters are:

Hero or Protagonist

Villain or Antagonist

Love Interest (if there's a romance)

Helper or "Buddy" (to the hero)

Catalyst

Comic Relief

The **hero** and **villain** are at odds. The hero strives toward a goal, which the villain tries to block (usually because the villain has a contrasting goal).

The **love interest** is, of course, the dominant element in a romantic story. But in what is primarily a task story, a common way to add complexity is by developing a secondary romance.

The **helper** can act as a confidant, someone the hero can reveal himself to. We learn more about the hero through this interaction.

The **catalyst** is someone who by their behavior impels the hero into action. The catalyst's actions often initiate the inciting incident that leads to the hero getting involved in the story. (In *Witness*, Samuel, the young boy, witnesses a murder, then later identifies the killer, leading to the hero's involvement).

A **comic relief** character lightens things up (R2D2 and C3PO in *Star Wars*, the medium in *Ghost*).

In addition to these, Linda Seger has identified a number of other character roles we sometimes see in films:[8]

A **contrasting character** helps define the main character by their contrast to the main character. In *Witness*, Daniel is the Amish suitor who, while less exciting than the hero John Book, is a more appropriate romantic interest for Rachel. He thus forms a contrast to John; he is something John cannot be. It is not a matter of better or worse, just that they are different.

A **balance character** makes sure the film's theme is not misread. In *Boyz 'n' the Hood,* the brutal African American cop who harasses the hero and shows a lack of sympathy for those in the neighborhood provides a balance by showing that African Americans can also represent prejudice and abuse of power.

Voice of . . . characters present various points of view that contribute to the film's theme; Eli in *Witness* presents the Amish perspective on nonviolence.

Writer's point-of-view characters are occasionally used to present perspectives the writer wants expressed. In the first two films of the *Star Wars* series, Obi-wan Kenobi and Yoda perform this function.

An **audience point-of-view character** is found in some scripts. This character points us in the right direction with respect to another character or situation. In *Arthur*, Hobson, the valet, serves this function by letting us see Arthur through his caring (yet reproving) eyes.

Lesser characters can supply **mass** and **weight,** which highlight the importance and power of a main character; these characters include bodyguards, secretaries, chauffeurs, gang members.

Seger points out that in many stories characters fulfill more than one function. She also suggests that one useful purpose of identifying character functions is that they can indicate unnecessary characters.

As useful as it is to assess characters in terms of their story functions, don't let this device become formulaic. Some of the most effective film characters are there simply because they are interesting, add ambiance, or contribute to a secondary story line. Don't start off by defining the balance character, the point of view character, and so on. Determine the story and then, as you review it, see if what is lacking can be corrected by adding characters who perform some of the functions we've described.

Consider Actors

Give some consideration to the fact that your characters are played by actors. Try to have two or three meaty roles that will attract quality actors. Creating a juicy part that will appeal to a major star is often a requirement for getting a script produced in the movie industry.

Consider giving each major character in your script a big moment. Actors appreciate these.

Trust actors to know their job. Don't overdo parenthetical comments on how actors should play the lines—these should be used sparingly (as we'll note in the section on screenplay format).

Much in a film is conveyed by character reactions: looks, gestures, and facial expressions. Visualize how these can enrich your scenes; leave room for them.

As was mentioned, sometimes you write a character with a particular actor—living or not—in mind; it's called "blue sky casting." This is useful if it helps you visualize the character and imagine your dialogue actually being spoken by a person. But it's best not to make it too obvious.

Villains, Antagonists, and Other Oppositions

Villains deserve special mention. Often they have their own special charms and attractions. (Remember Darth Vader, Goldfinger, and the marvelous witches of *Snow White* and *The Wizard of Oz.*) Give your villains attention just as you do your heroes. Heroes look better if they have strong opposing villains.

Make your villains complex human beings who are struggling with their own demons. Let the audience see what has made them what they are. Playwright/screenwriter Harold Pinter can say, "Every single character, even a bastard like Goldberg in *The Birthday Party*, I care for."[9]

Be sure your villains don't overshadow your heroes. Often a screenwriter wants the hero to be nearly perfect. After all, they are the hero. And you are very close to them. The result can be a hero who is bland and boring. Villains are not so inhibited; they have the freedom to transgress. Watch out for making them more interesting than your heroes.

The antagonistic force opposing the hero doesn't have to be a person. Heroes often struggle against ideas and social ideologies. Or against internal forces. Inner conflicts and struggles enrich a script. An inner/personal story line that augments the main task story line can add texture and complexity to your script. First set your main story line (which will often be a task story line), then consider if an inner/personal story line or two won't add additional enrichment. (We'll discuss this further in the next chapter.)

When formulating your story concept, it's helpful to define the antagonistic forces by using the phrase **"in spite of."** Can the hero achieve the goal **in spite of** the obstacles? Such a concept for *Jurassic Park* would be: "Can the visitors escape the island in spite of the dinosaurs, the storm, and the villain who is destroying safety devices?" As we'll discuss later, using "in spite of" helps clarify the problems the protagonist faces in the script.

Minor Characters

Minor or secondary characters give ambiance and richness to the story. Screwball comedies (and in particular the films of Preston Sturges) are especially noted for their colorful minor characters. Because they are often on the screen for only a short time, you'll want to sketch your minor characters quickly, highlighting only a unique quality or two.

Consider the officer in *Dances with Wolves* who sends Lt. Dunbar to the frontier. How vividly he is presented, although he appears only for one brief sequence. He calls Dunbar "Sir Knight," folds up his orders into a tiny square, calls a wagon driver a peasant, urinates in his pants—then puts a pistol to his head and shoots himself.

Another memorable minor character is the Chief in *One Flew Over the Cuckoo's Nest*. At first withdrawn and silent, he is gradually drawn out by McMurphy. In the end, he mercifully smothers the lobotomized McMurphy and symbolically rips the heavy sink from the floor—the one McMurphy bet he could lift but couldn't—throws it through the window, and escapes into the night.

If your minor characters aren't essential to moving the story along, review what other functions they might serve (Seger's listing on pages 34–35 is useful for this). If they don't appear useful, you may need to drop them. If they are important, look for ways they can enrich the film beyond their functions. Consider contrasting them with the main characters—in appearance, temperament, style, and so on. Can they add humor as well as fulfilling their other functions? Work with your minor characters.

Comic Characters

Characters are often exaggerated for comic effect. The range extends from the farcical characters of the Marx Brothers, *Saturday Night Live,* and *Monty Python* to screwball comedies and the films of Woody Allen. Many comic characters are built around a popular comedian/actor: Chaplin, W.C. Fields, Laurel and Hardy, Buster Keaton, Harold Lloyd, Peter Sellers, Seinfeld, Robin Williams.

Serious dramas often use humorous characters for comic relief (the robots in the *Star Wars* films and the medium in *Ghost*), thus breaking up the heaviness of a drama.

Many films guard against excessive melodrama by giving their adventure heroes humorous qualities. Even very straight characters can be put in humorous situations; the humor often serves to make the serious scenes all the more intense.

INTRODUCING AND DEVELOPING CHARACTERS

Some characters develop slowly; getting to know them is a progressive revelation. Usually, however, it is best to characterize your main characters quickly, giving us an immediate feeling for them. This means meeting them early in the story set-up (usually in the first few minutes). Often we meet them with a bang.

Early in *Dirty Harry*, he clashes with his police department superiors, then uses an empty gun to bluff a bank robber, thus establishing himself as an aggressive outsider—and giving us the line "Make my day." The Sundance Kid's virtuoso performance with a gun at the beginning of *Butch Cassidy and the Sundance Kid* grabs the audience's attention. The Indiana Jones films, too, are noted for exciting, adventurous openings.

Beverly Hills Cop introduces Axel in a wild cop car–bashing chase through the streets of Detroit. The opening establishes him as a cool undercover cop able to bluff hijackers with his con, an aspect of his character that amuses us throughout the film.

Quick characterization is not only a staple of action/adventure films. The arguments between the two characters in *When Harry Met Sally* establish their contrasting styles, as well as hinting that opposites will attract. The montage during the opening titles of *Tootsie* quickly lets us know that Michael is a talented but difficult actor.

The opening ten minutes of *Arthur* establish him as a cute, funny guy with problems. We sympathize with him, partly because of his ability to laugh at himself.

Entrances and exits are key moments for characters, especially in situation comedies. Use dramatic or comic entrances or exits to emphasize a powerful line or visual, or to get a desirable laugh.

Keep in mind that any time a character is on the screen, they are being characterized. Let them grow and change (their **character transformational arc**) as appropriate. Let them be consistent with who they are in the circumstances. Be sure we are getting the right impressions of them as they move through the story.

Names

Baby Jane, Dr. Strangelove, Angel, Rocky, Mork, Hawkeye Pierce, Alex Foley, Darth Vader, Indiana Jones, Butch Cassidy, Radar O'Reilly, Alvy Singer, R2D2, Rambo, and Hannibal Lecter are intriguing names. What do you name your characters, and why?

Names carry associations; they can suggest character types and convey cultural connotations. Different connotations are suggested by such names as Orville, Scott, Reba, Rosie, Harvey, Percival, Rodney, and Gertrude. Agatha sounds like an aunt, Priscilla would be quite prim, and Havensacker suggests a bureaucrat.

Very simple names like Bill, Tom, Sue, Jane, Mary, Smith, and Brown are probably best avoided as too commonplace.

Sometimes a name goes against type. Humphrey, Sylvester, and Arnold might not ordinarily be considered macho virile names, but they have very different associations when connected with Bogart, Stallone, and Schwarzenegger.

A telephone book is a fine source for names, as are what-to-name-your-baby books. Try out names for their sound. The soft vowels in Lisa, Laura, and Larry have a different feel than the hard consonants in Dick, Buck, and Vicky.

Names and nicknames can be used to expand character interactions. When a friend of Jim Rockford (*The Rockford Files*) who usually refers to him as "Rockfish" calls him "Rockford" at a key moment in one episode, both Rockford and viewers are surprised. Archie Bunker calls his son-in-law "Meathead." In *One Flew Over the Cuckoo's Nest*, everyone calls McMurphy "Mac." Nurse Ratched, however, first calls him "Mr. McMurphy," then "Randle" (his first name), underscoring their antagonism. (At one point he calls her "Mildred" in reprisal.)

On *The Mary Tyler Moore Show*, everyone calls Lou Grant "Lou" except Mary, who calls him "Mr. Grant" (he calls her "Mary"). The protagonist, Gittes, in *Chinatown* is called "Git-tes" (two syllables) by everyone except the plutocratic villain, Noah Cross, who pronounces it as one syllable, "Gitts."

COMPOSING CHARACTERS

This section will examine techniques to create unique, believable characters. Use whatever works for you.

Knowing and Researching

Characters based on people you know are more likely to seem real. Diane English, creator of the television series *Murphy Brown*, created the Eldon character because for years she had construction workers working on her house. The parade of secretaries for Murphy came from English's own string of secretaries.

Research is another way to better understand a character—to uncover the small details that add originality and credibility to a character. New writers often choose characters they've seen on television or at the movies. CIA agents, lawyers, law enforcement officials, drug dealers, prostitutes, and corporate executives are some of the choices that often don't ring true. While nothing can match direct knowledge, be sure to research unfamiliar characters. Observe them, interview them, and read everything available on the subject.

Character Biographies

Is it helpful to prepare biographies of the major characters? Some screenwriters find short biographies invaluable in giving a sense of the character's personal history and motivation. For others this is too intellectual an exercise; they fear losing an instinctive sense of the character in biographic details. Once again, see what works best for you.

One approach is to begin with the character's family background, and sketch out the highlights of their life up to the time of the story. Give special attention to formative events, personal traits, feelings, romance, friendship, parents, and significant others. Consider the cultures and subcultures that have influenced the character. For a shorter version, describe the five most important experiences in the character's life. These sketches can be written as straight narrative or as a monologue spoken by the character.

Or write an impressionistic sketch of the character, highlighting the traits that appeal to you. Here's such a short, impressionistic, biographical sketch done by a friend about a person she knew.

> She comes in all starry-eyed and laughing. Black hair and blue eyes. The face of a choirboy who can't tell a lie. At twenty-five she looks like a fourteen-year-old paperboy. The little munchkin is as explosive as a keg of dynamite. A strike of the wrong word can set her off. "Expose and intimidate, expose and intimidate, a hand in the dark is a hand in the dark, that's what I've always said." A prophet with her hand in the dark. Lyrical lover, she can only read political poetry to her band of followers. That sense of politics. A balance of power. An insulation of emotions. Under the guise of a Gemini, she swings from artificial assuredness to manufactured doubt. She needs all that she can get. She feels sorry and won't forget. A tumbleweed connection, an incessant child. It takes a child to be a woman. A preacher of the faith, the protector of the female species, an incurable realist. She deals with the spaces without. A true utilitarian. A radical at best.

Known for her sudden outbursts of radical therapy. A contradictor. T-shirts and painted jeans. A pulse of one hundred fifty. The pride of being Jewish. A sixties hippie child. She broke her ankle during a riot at Kent State jumping off a car. A Walter Cronkite special. A sexual spokeswoman. Anything for an argument. Anything for a scene. She breaks the ice with self parody. "Make 'em laugh and you know you've got 'em." Consistently nostalgic. Painfully self-conscious. An intellectual Pinky Lee. Life of the party. An outgoing recluse. Separation of words and actions. She cares too much. With thumb in mouth, she theorizes Marx and Lenin, folds her pajamas under her pillow, never travels without her bedroom slippers. She doesn't like to sleep alone. Showers constantly, chews gum for hours, hates smokers and wants to be magic.[10]

Still another approach is to sketch a character lifeline. Outline the high and low points of the character's psychological and social development from birth to the (story's) present. Then project it beyond the story into the future. J. D. Salinger described his character Franny as a girl destined to "one day marry a man with a hacking cough. So there was *that* in her face, too."[11] What will the character be doing five years after the end of the story? How will the character die? At what age? What will the eulogy be? What will appear on the tombstone? These future projections can help to better grasp the character.

Here are a series of questions that may offer insight to your character.

What is the character's biggest problem?

What is their favorite fantasy?

What do they want from life?

What do they most like about themselves? What least like?

How would the character briefly describe themselves?

What is the character most afraid of?

What does the character avoid?

What makes them angry?

What typical psychological games do they play with others?

What kind of child was the character?

What does the character do when no one is watching?

If you took some candid photographs that revealed the essence of the character, what would the pictures look like? What would they reveal?

What kind of places does the character frequent?

Whom do they socialize with?

How does the character appear to the public? to co-workers? to friends? to lovers?

If someone very close to you asked what the character was like, how would you answer?

What does the character spend their time doing? What do they invest their energy doing and talking about?

What films and TV do they watch? What did the character watch as a child? What books did they read? What video games did they play?

What do others know about the character that they don't know?

What do they do that they aren't aware of (such as criticizing others)?

What does the character hide from others?

If you were to describe the character as a metaphor, what would it be?

What will be the character's epitaph?

In what subtle, physical ways does the character express personality?

What do the major characters want from each other?

What does your main character want?

What do they need?

What does this character contribute to the script?

Why will the audience like (or dislike) the character?

Whether as hero or villain, why will the character stay in our memory?

Character Checklist

A checklist of characteristics can be a useful tool, but don't let it get in the way of the natural feel you have for the characters. Avoid the pitfall of mechanically constructing characters by list making.

PHYSICAL/BIOLOGICAL CHARACTERISTICS

Age (How do the characters show age? How do they feel about aging?)

Sex/Gender (How do the characters affirm or deny their maleness or femaleness?)

Height and weight

Color of hair, eyes, skin

Physical defects (disabilities, abnormalities, diseases)

Physical body: carriage/posture (casual, relaxed, stiff)

Physical body: build/body type (athletic or not, ectomorphic, isomorphic, mesomorphic)

Movement: rhythm and way of walking (cat-like, fast, jerky, slow, smooth)

Facial expressions, characteristic look

Mannerisms ("stage business," characteristic gestures, ways of non-verbal expression)

Voice/Speech: texture and quality (high or low pitch, clipped, guttural, smooth and flowing) What's the most striking thing about the character's voice?

Verbal expressions (favorite expressions, idioms, use of language, use of slang)

Heredity (the character's inherited physical characteristics)

Clothing/Dress (style, uniqueness)

Appearance (attractive, clean, mod, neat, unkempt)

How does the character physically express tension?

Sexuality (How do the characters express their sexuality? What sexual hangups do they have?)

PSYCHOLOGICAL CHARACTERISTICS

IQ/Intelligence (intellectual? common sense? street smarts?)

Abilities (skills, talents, languages)

Introvert, extrovert, ambivert?

Disposition/Temperament (easygoing, optimistic, pessimistic, rebellious)

Other qualities (awareness, imagination, judgment, poise, sensitivity, sophistication, taste)

Complexes/Maladjustments (compulsions, hangups, inhibitions, obsessions, phobias, prejudices, superstitions)

Frustrations and major disappointments

Nicknames (and what do they mean?)

Feelings (most common emotions? most comfortable/uncomfortable emotions?)

Attitudes toward life (militant, nervous, relaxed, resigned)

What does the character most like about themself? What do they least like?

What aspects of their personality does the character deny and not accept? (anger, sexuality, tenderness)

How does the character feel about the other characters?

Is the character a winner or loser?

Do they want to be part of the group?

Do they want to control others, achieve power?

How much do they give and receive affection?

Hidden aspects of the character's personality (What do these reveal? What parts of themself does the character know but keep hidden from others? What is unknown to them but known to others? For example, a character may seem cool and in control but actually exist on tranquilizers, or may act the upright citizen while taking part in secret orgies)

INTERPERSONAL CHARACTERISTICS

Family background

Friends and lovers

Co-workers, employers, and employees

Others with whom the character interacts

CULTURAL CHARACTERISTICS

Birthplace

Ethnic background

Education

Occupation (satisfaction and dissatisfaction on the job)

Socio-economic status

Environment (How does the environment affect the character? Room, apartment house, neighborhood, town or city, car?)

Historical period (if not the present) and its ethos

Interests, hobbies (such as fast cars, wines, hunting, tennis, growing orchids)

Special abilities, skills (martial arts, weapons skills)

Religious beliefs

Political attitudes

Values (moral response to life)

Lifestyle (street life, jet set, suburbia)

Distinctive traits (What one or two traits are most distinctive of the character?)

Major events in the character's life (psychological, financial, physical, cultural)

Goals/Ambitions (immediate and long-range. Put in terms of "I want to . . ." Consider unspoken desires as well as those expressed in the film)

What does the character want?

What does the character need? (And when does the character realize it?)

Dominant impact of the character (use adjectives such as aggressive, ambitious, amoral, anxious, arrogant, artificial, authoritarian, awkward, bitchy, brave, cantankerous, careful, careless, caring, casual, cheerful, clever, competitive, compulsive, confident, conservative, cowardly, cruel, cunning, depressed, dirty, domineering, egotistic, energetic, exhibitionistic, extravagant, fearful, finicky, fickle, flirtatious, friendly, fun, generous, gentle, graceful, hostile, humorous, immoral, insolent, jealous, kind, miserly, modest, moral, naive, nervous, obsessive, optimistic, perfectionist, pessimistic, phony, playful, possessive, radical, rigid, rude, ruthless, secretive, seductive, selfish, shrewd, slow, snobbish, sophisticated, strong, stupid, subdued, submissive, tedious, treacherous, vain, violent, vulgar, weak, withdrawn, worldly).

IMAGINATION EXERCISES

Fascinating characters are a script's major asset. Here are some ways to stimulate your imagination and help bring them to life.

Take your character through a typical day. How do they feel when they get up? What do they feel when they look in the mirror? Do they sing in the shower? What do they eat for breakfast? How do they get to work? Do they like their work? What do their subordinates think of them? Their superiors? Who do they interact with during the day? What do they think about? Worry about? Daydream about? What do they do in the evening? When do they go to bed? And note how different it would be if the character were a soldier of fortune in some jungle. Or in outer space.

Think of some common yet revealing actions and describe the way the character performs them. What, if anything, does the character like to cook? How do they eat pasta? What kind of laugh do they have? When is the last time they cried? How do they kiss?

Sit quietly in a darkened room and listen to your character. Ask questions, and hear the replies. Let them do the talking—likes and dislikes, feelings. Don't force the replies; just let it happen. Get into that creative attitude of relaxed, passive awareness and listen to what your character tells you of themselves.

Imagine a screen on which the character appears. See them concretely. What do they look like? What do they have to say? Or try having a dialogue with the character on paper. Write out questions and answers.

What about the character most strikes you physically? Psychologically?

Exaggerate the character's dominant traits. Pick two or three crucial characteristics, then imagine their opposites. How does the character express contradictions? Let their strong self interact with their weak self, their loving self talk with their hating self, their tender self with their macho self. How does each try to assert control?

Become the character in your imagination. Sit like them, move like them. Get into their rhythm. When walking outside, imagine that you are following your character. Observe them. What do they do?

What do the character's surroundings (room, car, books, furnishings) and their clothes say about them?

Take a crisis situation from the story and imagine how the character physically feels the crisis. Do they express this non-verbally? Do they hide it?

If your character has an internal conflict, let the two sides talk with each other.

Put two characters together and have them say things that they can't or won't express during the film.

Imagine the character metaphorically. If they were a car, what kind of car would they be? Why? Or an animal, a novel, a painting, a flower, a tree, a piece of furniture, an article of clothing, a type of food, a drink, a color, a song, a style of architecture, an odor, a metal, the weather, or a period in history.

How does the character deal with anger, tenderness, fear, hatred, rage, intimacy, aggression?

Have your character complete the following sentences: "I have to . . . ," "I choose to . . . ," "I keep people from getting close by . . . ," "I refuse to face . . . ," "I would let people know me if . . . ," and "I am trying to give an impression that . . ."

Screenwriter Frank Pierson doesn't find writing character histories helpful; what is important is the way they feel about what has happened to them, and the sense memories that make them who they are. Pierson suggests asking characters: "What was your most embarrassing moment?"; "Did you ever feel like a fool?"; "What are the worst things that ever happened to you?"; Did you ever throw up in a public place?" Or imagine two characters having lunch. One sends food back to the kitchen, which embarrasses the other. How do they deal with it? Do they argue? How would they change a tire on the Santa Monica Freeway in the rain? How would they get change for a $100 bill in Detroit after midnight?[12]

Imagination techniques uncover the details that bring a character to life. They help you to better know the character, and encourage the character to develop a life of their own. That is creativity at its best.

SUMMARY

This chapter considered a major subject for screenwriters: creating effective characters who invite audience interest, involvement, and identification. It considered the various aspects of effective characters: They seem real. They are credible. They are unique and individualized. They have the strength to carry a story. They may be ambiguous, and thereby encourage audience projection. They often have intrinsic conflicts. They invite identification through empathy; identification can be solicited by making characters sympathetic, likable, quirky, funny, attractive, brave, caring, skillful, in jeopardy, charismatic, have a tragic flaw, or give us a moment of self-disclosure.

Character goals form the story line. They have something vital at stake in the story. They are proactive in defining and moving the story. They grow and change, interact with each other, and are convincingly motivated.

Characters function in story roles such as hero, villain, love interest, helper, catalyst, and comic relief.

The screenwriter must be considerate of actors, and give special attention to villains, minor characters, comic characters, and character names.

When composing characters, it may be helpful to write character biographies, refer to a checklist of character attributes, and try the imagination exercises.

A CHECKLIST FOR WRITING CHARACTERS

Is the protagonist proactive?

Does the protagonist define and move the story?

Are the characters' inner and outer motivations clear?

What do the characters want?

What do they need?

Are story lines based on character goals/objectives?

Are goals clearly expressed as active verbs ("to _____")?

Does the hero have something significant at stake?

Is the hero strong enough to sustain the struggle?

Do one or more characters grow and change?

Can you trace their transformational arcs?

Do the characters seem real?

Have you avoided stereotypes?

Are your characters credible?

Do the characters have realistic weaknesses?

Do they have intrinsic conflicts?

Do they have a certain ambiguity?

Are they unique and individualized?

Do they invite audience identification?

Do you use techniques to encourage our involvement by making your protagonist: sympathetic, likable, quirky and offbeat, funny, attractive, brave, caring, skilled, in jeopardy, charismatic?

Have you contrasted the characters?

Have you appropriately used functional characters, such as the confidant, the catalyst, and the comic relief character? Do your characters contrast or balance each other? Do they express themes?

Have you written some meaty roles?

Is there a strong, complex villain?

Are there interesting minor characters?

Can you quickly characterize the principal characters?

What do the names say about the characters?

Have you researched the characters and their world so they seem real and credible?

Do you like your characters?

ENDNOTES

1. Armer, A. (1988). *Writing the Screenplay.* Belmont, CA: Wadsworth.

2. Seger, L. (1990). *Creating Unforgettable Characters.* New York: Henry Holt, pp. 27–29. The descriptions are by two of her clients: the first by Roy Rosenblatt, the second by Sandi Steinberg.

3. Hebbel, F., quoted in A. Kaplan. (Spring 1966). The aesthetics of the popular arts. *Journal of Aesthetics and Art Criticism, 24,* 361.

4. While in most films we identify with characters, there are exceptions in which other elements such as unusual story twists dominate. It's been claimed that in some Hitchcock films, the audience is voyeuristically positioned to observe rather than participate. This is particularly true in films in which the main character is not that attractive (as in *Psycho,* in which the first major character is killed off in the middle of the film).

5. There is a good discussion of identification devices in Hauge, M. (1988). *Writing Screenplays That Sell.* New York: McGraw-Hill, p. 41ff. Some of my discussion draws on his listing.

6. Lucey, P. (1989). *Sit-Com Story Analysis. "Cheers" Episode.* Los Angeles: University of Southern California, p. 2.

7. Hauge, M. p. 41ff.

8. Seger, L. (1987). *Making a Good Script Great.* New York: Dodd, Mead.

9. Pinter, H., quoted in Bensky, L. M. (Fall 1966). Harold Pinter: An interview. *Paris Review, 10,* 12–37.

10. Mitera, D. (1975). "For Danni." (unpublished).

11. Salinger, J. D. (1955). *Franny and Zooey.* New York: Little, Brown and Co., p. 126.

12. Pierson, F., interviewed by Holmes, D. C. (September 1986). *Hollywood Scriptwriter, 385* (76), 4.

CHAPTER *4*

Story Structure

Let's begin with the story. Human beings are storytelling animals. We domesticate our world by narrative, by myths. . . . We are hungry for a story that will dramatize some meaning we can hold to. The need for a myth that begins "Once upon a time," and ends with "The hero finally triumphed after many trials and returned home," still sleeps in our substance.[1]

—Sam Keen

In this chapter we consider structure—how you form the story so that it works for the audience. Structure organizes the story, and thereby structures our experience of that story. That's a point worth repeating. Story structure doesn't simply pattern the narrative—as important as that is—it also structures our experience throughout the story.

Screenwriter William Goldman: "Screenplays are structure. Screenplays are structure, that's all they are. They are structure."[2]

A caution as we begin our study of structure. Screenwriting texts sometimes offer simplified structure formulas—sort of easy write-by-the-numbers (or pages) patterns. These may work for some stories, but only for some. Taken to extremes, they can result in predictable, assembly-line clones. As we explore media structure, here are four important maxims to keep in mind.

There are no magic structure formulas.

There are no rigid, unbreakable rules.

No preset pattern replaces inventiveness.

What I and others write are suggestions, not gospel.

THE STUFF OF STRUCTURE

Classic Dramatic Structure

Classic structure moved audiences in ancient Greece, and it is still an effective model of the dramatic story. Classic dramatic structure contains a beginning-middle-end pattern usually represented by a rising (then slightly falling) curve that graphs the increasingly intense and suspenseful **development.** It begins with a **conflict** (or commitment to a **goal**), progresses to the **climax** in which the conflict is resolved, and finishes with a **denouement** (or "letting-down time") in which loose ends are tied up.

The curve rises overall as events *accelerate,* building in intensity as we approach the climax. The graph line isn't so much smooth as sawtoothed (in order to represent the *rising and falling action* as the story moves through a series of high and low moments). A crisis occurs and is solved, only to be replaced by another crisis, then another, and so on until the climax.

With only slight modification, this pattern fits modern media stories. In film, climaxes come nearer the end, and television plots generally adapt to commercial breaks.

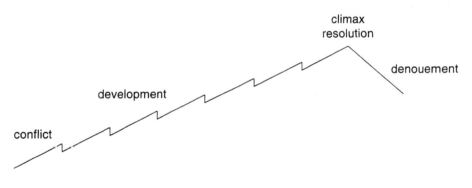

Beginning, Middle, and End

Classic dramatic structure has three basic divisions: **Beginning, Middle,** and **End** (also referred to as **Act I, Act II,** and **Act III**). Each has its functions. The Beginning engages our interest, sets up the story, and introduces the conflict or commitment to a goal that begins the story proper. The Middle holds our interest and develops the story. The End climaxes and resolves the story, leaving us with a feeling of completion.

Typically, very generally, the Beginning (Act I) takes up the first quarter of the film or television program, the Middle (Act II) takes up one-half, and the End (Act III) takes up one-quarter. So we can roughly divide the Acts of a two-hour movie into 30-60-30 minutes. A one-hour TV drama divides into 12-24-12 minutes of story playing time (taking into account commercial breaks). A one-half-hour TV comedy runs roughly 6-12-6 minutes of playing time.

The sections that follow are defined by their function in the story. The Beginning is the **Set-up**; the Middle is the **Development,** or **Complication,** or **Confrontation;** the End is the **Resolution.** Let's consider each of these in detail.

Beginning (Act I): The Set-Up.   The Beginning sets up the story. It gives us the time, place, mood, style, atmosphere, and tone. If a comedy, it quickly sets the comic tone. The major characters are introduced: their motivations, wants, and needs. The initial story situation is introduced. Some sense of what the story is about is given, as is background information about the characters. (We get this **backstory** through **exposition,** which we will discuss later.)

The actual **story begins** close to the end of the Beginning (Act I). This may seem odd. Doesn't the story begin when the film begins? Of course in one sense it does, but we will consider that the story proper begins after it has been first set up—which is why the Beginning is called the Set-up. Only after we have met the characters and understood the situation—in a film this takes twenty to thirty minutes—can the story proper begin.

Think of the story as beginning when the protagonist commits to a goal (to solve the problem). Other beginnings are possible, but this one is the most common. It is usually a powerful and unmistakable event that shoots the film in a new direction. This new direction is the story.

Sometimes the story beginning closes Act I, corresponding to what is referred to as the **Act I Plot Point** or **First Act Break.** Or it may occur somewhat earlier, in which case some other turn of events will define the act break.

The set-up may include an **inciting incident** that triggers events that quickly set the plot in motion.

In *Star Wars,* the inciting incident occurs when Princess Leia, about to be captured, sends a message to Obi-wan Kenobi via one of the drones. This sets in motion events that lead to the start of the story proper when Luke Skywalker commits to getting the Death Star plans to the rebels.

The inciting incident in *The Fugitive* occurs when Dr. Kimble's wife is killed (and he is convicted of the crime). The story begins when Kimble escapes on his way to prison and sets out to find the killer.

The Middle (Act II): Development.   The Middle intensifies the story through complications and confrontations. Crises succeed each other in a cascade of reversals for the hero. No sooner is one obstacle overcome than another appears. Crises occur regularly during the Middle, and keep us involved in the vicissitudes of the protagonist. (The sawtooth rising and falling action of the classic dramatic graph represents this development.) Depending on the type of story, these major story beats (or story points) come every 10 or 15 minutes, occurring more frequently near the end of Act II. In a television episode, the beats occur at even shorter intervals.

The end of the Middle is sometimes marked by an intense, decisive beat referred to as the **Act II Plot Point** or **Second Act Break**. This beat spins the story in a new direction and sends it rushing toward its climax. It may be a low point; a time when the outlook is bleak for the hero. Or it may be a moment when the hero recommits to the goal with renewed energy.[3]

A strong Second Act Break usually presents the protagonist with a powerful challenge. Because Act III is just beginning, the protagonist still has time to struggle with the challenge and its implications.

In *Witness* the second act break occurs when the villains learn where John is hiding and come to get him. In *Star Wars* the break occurs when Luke joins the rebels in their attack on the Death Star.

The Middle is usually the hardest section to write. It must sustain the story and our interest. This can be done by an effective series of crises that keep us in suspense as they move us toward the climax.

The End (Act III): Resolution.   The End features the emotional high point of the film—the **climax**. With the climax, we know whether or not the protagonist has succeeded. The suspense is resolved, and the story proper is over.

The End is the final shootout between the marshal and the villains (*High Noon*), the blowing up of the Death Star (*Star Wars*), Dorothy revealing that she is really Michael (*Tootsie*), Harry meeting Sally for keeps (*When Harry Met Sally*), the Jewish workers being freed due to Schindler's efforts (*Schindler's List*), and E.T. going home. The climax may involve some surprise twists. In *Casablanca* the police chief covers for Rick—"the beginning of a beautiful friendship." In *Harold and Maude*, Maude takes her suicide pill and "moves on."

The climax usually comes within 5 minutes of the film's conclusion. It is followed by only the briefest denouement—to tie up loose ends, or perhaps to bring us down a bit from our tense involvement.

Since the climax is the dramatic highpoint of the story, it often involves the last, most powerful challenge.[4] In both *Witness* and *High Noon*, the villain holds a gun on the hero's loved one and insists the hero surrender. In the romantic comedy *Sleepless in Seattle*, the two lovers rush toward their long-awaited meeting, but just miss each other. The story climaxes when one of them returns for a forgotten knapsack and they unite. In *Star Wars*, Luke's shot destroys the battle station just seconds before it would have destroyed the rebel base.

Before discussing story structure, let us consider some of the relevant elements—suspense, surprise, objectives, conflict, high stakes—and then briefly revisit the essential media story.

Suspense and Surprise

Perhaps the key requirement of a screenplay is that it grab and hold the audience's attention.[5] The two elements most important in that regard are **suspense** and **surprise.** Suspense maintains the audience's attention. Surprises keep the story from getting too predictable. Mastering the use of suspense and surprise will produce audience-involving story structures.

Suspense.   Suspense sets dramatic enigmas; it raises puzzling questions that hook us and keep us involved. What is going to happen next? Will the hero best the villain (in spite of the difficulties)? Will they escape from the burning building? Will they find true love? Can they get to the rendezvous in time?[6]

Suspense involves **anticipation** and **expectation.** We anticipate the next exciting plot development, the next dilemma for the protagonist, the clever way they will deal with it (or the consequences for them if they don't).[7]

Suspense often follows a **cue-delay-payoff** pattern. The audience is cued that something is going to happen—perhaps a bomb is ticking under the table. Then there is a delay to develop anticipation—those in the room get up to leave, but then sit down again for another item of business. Finally, there is the payoff—the bomb explodes.

Suspense operates at many levels. At the overall **story level,** the film story is based on suspense. It asks: will the protagonist achieve the objective in spite of the strong opposing forces? Because of the strength of the obstacles, we **doubt** that the protagonist will easily triumph, and we want to see what happens. The suspense continues until the climax when we learn whether or not the hero did succeed, and our suspense is over.

Suspense also works in the **scene crises** the protagonist encounters along the way. Will Fergus shoot the fleeing Jody (*The Crying Game*), will the boy escape the overturned car, will the group outrun the pursuing tyrannosaur (*Jurassic Park*)? Each crisis scene creates its own suspense, which serves to hold our interest as we move toward the climax.

Suspense often involves **managing story information** between the characters and the audience: who knows, who doesn't know, who needs to find out. What we don't know, we want to find out. What we know but a character doesn't makes us want to see what their reaction will be when they find out. By manipulating the pattern of character and audience knowledge, you can build suspense.[8]

You create suspense whenever you present an enigma that must be resolved or a question that must be answered. When planning the story, think of how events could encourage audience suspense and involvement.

Surprise.   Hand in hand with suspense comes **surprise,** the sudden shock of the unexpected. Audiences enjoy being kept off balance by frequent surprises in both plot twists and scene action (such as the sudden revelation of gender in *The Crying Game* when Dil—whom Fergus [and most of the audience] assumed was a woman—is revealed to be a man).

Suspense and surprise interact effectively to produce an involving story. Surprise can add spice to the payoff of a suspense build; the payoff might come as we anticipated, but in a way we didn't expect. Or surprise can trigger plot development, sending the story spinning in an unexpected direction.

Consider these suspense and surprise examples.

Bugs Bunny slips Yosemite Sam a stick of dynamite. The fuse burns down as Sam sweats. Then it goes out. "Whew," he sighs. *Then* it explodes. A cue-delay-payoff pattern.

Suspense and surprise mingle beautifully in a scene from *The Conversation*. Harry breaks into a hotel room fearing foul play for a couple that used to meet there. He finds it empty and immaculate. He prowls around. What will he find? (Suspense!) He checks out the bathroom. The bathtub faucet is dripping. He flings back the bathtub curtain—we hold our breath. Nothing. The toilet is also dripping inside its tank. He flushes it. And it fills with blood. (Surprise!)

For suspense in comedy, consider the famous mirror bit from the Marx Brothers' *Duck Soup*. Groucho stands before what is supposed to be a full-length mirror. Only it isn't; it's Harpo pretending to be Groucho's image. A suspicious Groucho puts Harpo through some hilarious testing. (Suspense: how will the imposter finally mess up?) Surprising bits keep the scene from becoming repetitive: at one point Groucho twirls around and strikes a pose—Harpo just strikes the pose without the twirl.

An interesting interplay of suspense and surprise occurs in *Alien*. The crew of the spaceship starts out to capture the alien creature that has come on board. Searching warily, they pick up a life-form reading. Cautiously they hunt it down, ready with net and protective weapons. (Suspense.) They trace it to a locker and get ready to open it. (Increased suspense.) They fling open the locker door . . . only to be met by a hiss from their pet cat. (Surprise!) When the cat runs away, we are thrust into the new suspense of having to get it back.

Consider the suspense/surprise element in the first act of *Three Days of the Condor*. The main character comes into a conservative-looking New York brownstone, which appears to be some sort of library or literary society. It appears very scholarly, but the receptionist keeps a gun in her desk drawer. (That's strange!) A man in a car parked nearby is watching the building and checking off names. (What's going on here?) Heading out to buy lunch for everyone, the protagonist ducks out the back door (to avoid the rain). A postman comes in to make a delivery, but instead starts shooting. Everyone in the office is killed. The hero returns carrying lunch, only to find his colleagues dead. What does he do? Where can he run to? He knows no more about what happened than we do.

The film *Witness* is another good example of the development of suspense/surprise highlights.[9]

Suspense and surprise are principles that underlie and operate throughout story structure. They are basic techniques that form audience responses. They hook and involve the audience in the film/television story.

Objectives

We've defined a story as a character with a problem (or goal). Let's discuss some other ways to define a story. While they amount to the same thing, one of these definitions might be a bit more relevant to your particular story. A story can be defined in terms of the following:

An **objective** or **goal** to be attained

A **conflict** to be resolved

A **problem** to be solved

A **lack** to be filled

A **threat** to be managed

A **decision** or **choice** to be made

A **challenge** to be met

A **mystery** to be solved

An **obstacle** to be overcome

Conflict

Conflict is essential to drama. The conflict between protagonist and antagonist drives the story. The uncertainty of its resolution creates suspense. Implied in every conflict is the question: how will this be resolved?

Traditionally, conflicts have been designated by a set of oppositions:

Person vs. person (hero vs. villain)

Person vs. self (internal conflict)

Person vs. natural forces

Person vs. society

Person vs. god or cosmic forces

It is usually more dynamic, however, to transform the conflict into an objective that the protagonist must attain. This makes it active rather than passive—"to _____" [do something].

While the conflict in *Jaws* is persons versus shark, it takes on a dynamic, animated quality when defined as the chief's overwhelming desire to destroy the shark.

Story goals make for conflict because there are always obstacles to achieving them. (Can the protagonists seek and destroy the shark in spite of . . . ?)

Conflict not only drives the story, it adds texture to the story as well. Conflict can make every scene in your script more effective. (Examples of the breadth of conflicts in a film are given in this endnote.)[10]

High Stakes

Whatever the conflict or objective, make it important to the character. Something big must be at stake. Wells Root refers to the "dreadful alternative" and the "or-else factor."[11] The audience becomes involved by imagining the dreadful consequences that will occur if the hero is not successful.

This fate could be physical (the criminal might kill the detective), it could be emotional (losing the chance for true love), or it could be psychologically devastating (losing self-respect).

In *Silence of the Lambs,* if Clarice was already an FBI agent the story would change little, but making her a trainee who desperately wants to *become* an agent (because of her father's death in the line of duty) raises the stakes as she tries to catch the killer.

For the characters in *Jurassic Park* and similar stories, it is literally a matter of life or death.

The Media Story[12]

Here again, in broad-stroked, capsulized form, is the basic film or television story.[13] As you review it, note the way its elements create responses in the audience (structuring not only the story but also the audience's experience of that story).

A **character** (hero/protagonist) has an **objective/goal** (such as solving a problem, resolving a conflict, or making a decision). This goal must be **extremely important** to that character (it may be a life-and-death situation), and cause us to **care** about, be **involved** with, the character's task. There is a **strong opposing force** (antagonist or villain) that makes us **doubt** that the hero can achieve the goal.

As the story develops, the character encounters numerous **obstacles**. A series of **crises** makes things worse; three or four of these are major crises. Each crisis creates moments of **suspense** and develops with some **surprising twists**. As the plot **builds**, it **accelerates**. The outlook is bleak as we near the climax. With the **climax**, the story is **resolved** and our suspense as to the outcome is finished.

STRUCTURING THE STORY

The film experience resembles a fun house attraction, a wild ride, the
itinerary of which has been calculated in advance but is unknown to the spectator.
By spurts and stops, twists and roller coaster plunges, we are taken through a dark
passage, alert and anxious, yet confident we shall return satisfied and unharmed.[14]

—Dudley Andrew

With this understanding of what constitutes a media story, we now turn to the in-verted triangle approach to writing that story—starting with the concept, and mov-ing through various stages to the completed script.

The Concept

Begin with the broadest overview of your story—the essential story idea, compact and concentrated. This is the **concept.** Let's consider two forms of the concept, both of which can be valuable to forming the story: the short, TV-listings log-line form, and the slightly fuller version that includes the resolution.

A log line captures the gist of the story, the problem that faces the protagonist, but doesn't include the resolution (TV listings don't give the ending away). The fuller concept takes this further by adding the resolution.

A good place to begin the story is to identify the protagonist. Who is the "char-acter with a problem"?

Whose Story Is It?   Know who your protagonist is. In Truffaut's *Day for Night*, each of the three central characters—actors in a film-within-a-film—are interviewed about that film. Each sees the film as his or her own story. Alexandre thinks "it's the story of a man in his early fifties who has a son. . . ." Alphonse, the son, believes "it's the story of a young man who marries an English girl. . . ." And Julie, the English-woman, claims that "*Meet Pamela* is the story of a young Englishwoman who falls in love with. . . ."[15]

While this may say much about actors' egos, it also pinpoints the decision a writer must make about whose story it is. Who experiences the conflict, has the goal, goes through the complications, and reaches the climax?[16]

Be open to the possibility that the story might belong to someone other than your first choice. Writers may think they have a protagonist, but when they look at who really is proactive they realize that the hero is another character altogether. Check to determine who really has the problem, conflict, or objective, or who proactively goes through the crises and realizes the climax and resolution. This is your protagonist, whose story it is.

Forming the Concept.   With your hero in hand, formulate the concept. It can take different shapes. The simplest way to put it is a short statement or a **"What if . . ."** log line that presents the problem provocatively. Including the phrase **"in spite of"** in your concept is a good idea because it emphasizes the antagonistic forces that block the hero. Here are some short-form movie concepts.

> Will John Book catch the criminals in spite of finding himself wounded in an (alien) Amish community—and with the Philadelphia police after him as well? (*Witness*)

> What if a drunken but lovable millionaire playboy must choose between marrying his father's choice and retaining his inheritance or giving up the money for true love? (*Arthur*)

> What if the genetically reconstructed dinosaurs in an island theme park break loose and threaten the visitors? (This doesn't mention the protagonists, but with a premise this exciting, it isn't necessary.) Or: Scientists at an island theme park populated with reconstituted dinosaurs have to fight for their lives when the creatures escape and attack. Or: Will the scientists be able to stay safe and then escape from the island **in spite of** there being a wild storm, the electricity going out, and the dinosaurs being so formidable? (*Jurassic Park*)

A fuller concept that includes the resolution will give a better sense of the whole story.

> Drunken, lovable, millionaire playboy Arthur must choose between obeying his father's injunction to marry a woman Arthur doesn't love and thereby retain his inheritance or following his heart with a poor but electrifying woman from Queens. After much vacillation, he chooses love, only to discover that he gets the wealth as well. (*Arthur*)

> A young boy accidentally left behind when his family goes on vacation has to confront two bumbling burglars intent on robbing his house. By the end, the boy has driven the burglars crazy. (*Home Alone*)

How you frame the concept depends on what you want to do with it. A short, high-concept hook may be useful in evaluating the appeal of your idea, and helpful in selling it. A fuller statement helps clarify the story. Even more useful in this regard is the Basic Story.

The Basic Story

Having defined the concept, you'll want to expand it to what I call the **basic story**. This lays out, in microcosm, the essential elements of the story. It forms the foundation from which to build the completed script.

A basic story is still fairly short—perhaps a page or so—and broad-stroked—at this stage too many details would get in your way and keep you from seeing the whole story. The basic story lays out the beginning, middle, and end, and highlights some of the major beats (crises).

Allow a separate paragraph for each act in order to indicate act breaks. If there are secondary story lines, simply add another paragraph summarizing them.

Consider this an outline of your story in narrative form. The basic story will include the following:

The locale and time period of the story

Whose story it is—your protagonist

Some sense of the motivation that drives your character

The antagonist and other crucial central characters

The conflict (or objective) that initiates the story

A brief description of the dominant plot developments (perhaps two to five major beats)

The climax and resolution

Your major act breaks (if you wish)

Here's a sample basic story for the contemporary action/adventure thriller *The Fugitive.*

> Chicago physician Dr. Richard Kimble finds himself wrongly convicted of killing his wife. When the prison bus crashes, he escapes and vows to find the actual killer—a mysterious one-armed man—even though he must also avoid recapture by a relentless U.S. Marshal (Samuel Gerard).

This paragraph sets the scene for us, gives the time and place, introduces Kimble, his problem, his motivation, and his goal. While avoiding recapture by the persistent Gerard is a secondary goal, it is the cause of numerous crises. The end of the first paragraph marks the end of Act I (the Beginning).

> In spite of almost being caught a number of times, Kimble manages to search hospital records on prosthetic arms, and after some false leads discovers the killer's identity. Gerard stays close on Kimble's trail, even while uncovering evidence that points toward other suspects. Kimble learns that his wife's murder is somehow connected to a cover-up concealing the fact that a major new drug causes liver damage. At first he suspects a pathologist, but later learns that the man died under suspicious circumstances. Finally, Kimble discovers that his friend, Dr. Charles Nichols, has falsified tissue samples—and may have hired the killer. But before he can confront Nichols, Kimble is almost shot by the one-armed-man, and in the process is blamed for the death of a policeman. Now he has the entire Chicago police force ready to take him down.

The second paragraph includes some of the highlights of the Middle (Act II). It sometimes closes on a strong act break, but where the act break comes in this story is not clear. (It doesn't have to be. There doesn't have to be a strong second act break. All we need is to build toward the climax.)

> With Gerard and the police closing in on him, Kimble confronts Nichols in the middle of a speech to a medical convention. There is a chase and a showdown. Kimble bests Nichols, saving Gerard's life in the process. The real villains are captured and Kimble is on his way to freedom.

This third paragraph marks the End (Act III) of the story. Kimble's problem is solved. The villains are caught. Gerard knows Kimble is innocent, and will see that he is set free. Kimble has achieved his goal.

It is important to be able to write the basic story—a capsule summary and guide to what the film will be. (For two additional examples—one of an historical story, the other of a comedy—see endnote.)[17]

If your basic story is working—if it clearly expresses the essential story you are writing, beginning, middle, end, with no obvious story problems and with promise of much audience suspense and surprise involvement—you are ready to move on to the story outline. However, if you are at all unsure about the story, you might choose to take an intermediate step and expand the basic story into a five- to fifteen-page **story narrative.** In effect this means that you are writing it as a short story. It's another way to firm up the story and make sure that it holds together in a longer and more detailed form.

Story Lines

We've been talking mostly in terms of the film's story. Although the term **story line** means much the same thing, it makes speaking of more than one story in the film easier. We can then refer to primary and secondary story lines. (Another industry practice—especially in television—is to speak of the **A story, B story,** and so forth in order to describe various story lines. I use both terms, but favor story lines.)

Because a story line is, in effect, a story, each story line has the same elements as a story: beginning, middle, end, character with an objective or problem, dramatic build, complications, climax, and resolution.

A **story line outline** outlines the story line in terms of its **beats,** an industry expression for the plot points or elements that compose the story line. Depending on its complexity, a major story line will have roughly fifteen to thirty beats. Lesser story lines will have fewer. On television, some sitcom secondary story lines have had as few as two or three beats, although this is unusual. A story line beat usually corresponds to one scene. Put another way, one scene equals one story beat. Sometimes, however, one beat may span several scenes, or one scene may contain two or more beats.

When outlining a story line, it helps to insure that each beat is a step in the protagonist's movement toward (or away from) the objective. If the hero's objective is to catch a thief and recover the missing painting, then their winning a game of tennis isn't a beat unless it advances that story line. For example, if winning the tennis game gets the protagonist into the social circles of a suspect.

This is something to check as you write the story line beat outline. Anything that doesn't help the protagonist move toward or away from the objective will slow things down and risk losing our involvement. You generally want to be clear that each beat moves the story line along. While there are exceptions, the general principle stands.[18]

As screenwriter William Goldman says:

> So ultimately when I say that screenplay is structure, it's simply making the spine, and you must protect that spine. . . . Can't say it often enough . . . you must decide what the spine is and protect it, keep it clear, keep it clean.[19]

Story Beats/Scene Action

There's an important distinction between **story beat** and **scene action.** A story beat is a unit of the story. It moves the plot along. Scene action is what happens to realize the beat, and is obviously more detailed. You don't want to confuse the two in your outline.

A sequence from *Arthur* clearly illustrates the difference. This is the crucial event that starts the story and marks the end of Act I (the first-act break) The **story beat** is: Arthur meets Linda and falls in love, changing his life forever.

There are many ways this beat can be realized in **scene action.** They could bump into each other and spill packages. They could fight for the same cab. She could rescue him from a mugger. Instead, in the film the beat is realized by scene action in which Arthur sees her steal a tie, covers for her, and gets her to agree to go out with him.

You'll want to outline your story with generalized story beats rather than getting distracted with too much detailed action. Once the story is set, then you'll work out the scene actions that realize its beats.

Multiple Story Lines

Many, perhaps most, films and television programs have a number of story lines. What we've called "the story" is the **dominant story line** (or **primary, major,** or **main story line**). There may be others, such as a romance story line, but trying to include too many story lines can be confusing. A film with more than a half-dozen story lines becomes unwieldy. Most films have one or two story lines (a few have three or four).

The main story line, especially in television, is often called the **A story,** with additional story lines referred to as the **B story, C story,** and so on. Story lines belonging to characters other than the protagonist are typically referred to as **subplots.**

The dominant story line runs from its beginning near the end of Act I through the climax in Act III. Other story lines can begin and end anywhere.

Needless to say, a character may have more than one story line, such as a task and a romance. But just because a character wants something and tries to get it doesn't mean they have a story line. Every major character in your story wants something. A story line needs substance and development over time; it needs all the elements we've defined for a story. (The antagonist's opposition to the protagonist does not itself form a separate story line; it is considered part of the same story line.)

Story Line Types

It's useful to identify three types of story lines: **task, relationship,** and **internal.** Any or all can appear in a script.

Task Story Lines.   These typically form the main story. The protagonist's objective is to sink the ship, catch the criminal, save the dying patient, or successfully complete the secret mission.

Relationship (Interpersonal) Story Lines.   These are about emotional interactions between characters: winning a lover, making a friend, reconciling with a family member. Many films have a main-task story plus a romance story line.

Internal (Inner, Personal) Story Lines.   These deal with a character's internal growth and change. Such story lines are concerned with values, attitudes, and beliefs. A character may need to achieve personal insight, open up to intimacy and vulnerability, give up an illusory ideal, or simply accept who they are. An internal story line might involve overcoming false pride, developing confidence, or resolving a conflict between personal desire and sense of duty.

An internal story line often involves making a decision, as in *American Graffiti* when Curt needs to decide whether or not he should leave his small California town to go away to college. In *The Graduate,* we see Benjamin move from being confused and uncertain about his direction to knowing what he wants and getting it (this also includes a romance story line). In *Fried Green Tomatoes,* Evelyn needs to gain self-confidence and be more assertive, especially with her husband.

An internal story line is not to be confused with the growth and change transformational-arc process that a character might trace.[20]

After determining the dominant story line, consider whether or not the film would benefit from additional story lines. An internal story line can add complexity to the main character as well as texture to the film. If your script seems short, adding another story line or two can fill it out.

When you compose the **basic story,** include secondary story lines as separate paragraphs and trace them out just as you do the main story line.

The Story Outline

Once you've devised a basic story that you're happy with, you're ready to move on up the inverted-triangle writing model to the next major step: the **story outline.**

A story outline or **story line beat outline** is stronger if it focuses on how each beat works in the story and how one beat leads to the next. One way to do this is to link your beats with expressions like "but," "and," and "leads to."

A spirited way to show how the beats work on the audience is to exaggerate their effect by adding comments such as (Suspense!), (Surprise!), (Wow!!), or (!!!). Put in what an engrossed viewer might think: "Oh, no!" "How will he survive?!" "Look out!" "Hooray." After all, this outline is only for you, so feel free to identify the emotional reactions that you want to invoke in the audience.

With more than one story line, outline the beats of each story line separately, thus ensuring that they work independently as story lines. Check that each has beginning-middle-end development, builds tension and excitement, and offers suspense and surprise.

Once each story line works effectively on its own, interweave the various story line beats together in the order they'll appear in the script. Note when and how you change from one story line to another. Moving between story lines helps form the narrative rhythm of the story.

Here's an example of how a half-dozen beats from the middle section (Act II) of *Star Wars* might look in a story line beat outline. I've added embellishments to highlight the fun.

I've also included plus (+) or minus (−) signs to indicate whether the beat is positive or negative with respect to the hero's succeeding in his task of getting the plans to the rebels so they can destroy the Empire's battle station. This follows observations by F. A. Rockwell[21] that a film story development often follows a plus/minus pattern; no sooner is one crisis solved (+) than another one arises (−). This is especially applicable to Act II.

We begin as Luke and Obi-wan Kenobi are trying to get a pilot to fly them to the planet Alderon.

—Luke and Obi-wan recruit Han Solo and his ship. After a close call,   +
they escape into outer space. (They're away!)

—But they find Alderon destroyed and a tractor beam draws their   −
ship captive into the huge battle station. (Oh no!)

—But they escape and rescue the princess. (Hooray!)   +

—Only to be trapped by storm troopers. (More problems)   −

—But they manage to escape into a garbage chute. (Whew!)   +

—Only to be almost crushed when the walls compact. (!!!)   −

An effective story line beat outline will indicate whether or not the story works. If something isn't working, now is the time to make the necessary changes. (For more complete examples of beat outlines, see the film analyses given at the end of the chapter.)

Scene Breakdown

All this outlining seems a lot of work, but virtually all screenwriters outline before writing the script. The few writers who prefer to knock out a full script and then go back and rework it often end up doing an after-the-fact outline, and risk throwing away much of what they've done. An added danger is the writers' becoming so enamored of what has already been written that they may be unwilling to let go of it. I'd rather work with a student who has just an idea than one with a finished script since the latter usually requires much undoing and struggle over things the writer can't easily let go.

As screenwriter Dan O'Bannon put it:

> In my early days of writing, I was afraid that working it all out in advance would destroy the creative impulse. Now I don't even start seriously writing until it's all worked out on paper first.[22]

I definitely recommend outlining.

Now that the story line beat outline works, you're ready to proceed to the next level of the inverted triangle—the **scene breakdown.** This is a scene-by-scene outline of the film, written as a narrative (without dialogue, although including an occasional phrase for flavor isn't a bad idea).

Now is the time to imaginatively create **scene action** that best realizes each story beat. This is a marvelously creative time. The story has been successfully outlined, now you can compose the engaging scene actions that tell the story.

Some screenwriters work out the scene breakdown on paper. Others transpose their outline to 3" × 5" or 4" × 6" cards, allowing one beat (or scene) per card. This way they can move the cards around to better determine where the beats/scenes should fall. Use the scene outline to determine the flow of the story, its pace and rhythm. Be sure that there is a build in intensity and pace as you rush to the climax. Imagine how it will look unfolding on the screen.

For an example of a scene-breakdown outline, let's jump back to the time of television bionics: Act One of a *Six Million Dollar Man* episode written by Terry McDonnell and Jim Carlson. It is representative of many such outlines they prepared as freelance television writers (and turned in to producers who wanted to check scene development before okaying a "go to script").

This particular act follows a teaser in which the secret, top-speed experimental plane XJ-7 disappears in the Edstrom Quadrant . . . attacked by a World War II Messerschmitt! Steve has to come to the rescue. (Following television practice, the scenes/beats are numbered—you needn't do this.)

1. McMillen, the only pilot to ever successfully come out of the quadrant, is questioned by Steve and Oscar in the mental ward. He has nervous exhaustion and traumatic amnesia. Oscar plans that Steve will take McMillen back in, jog his memory, and backtrack to find the XJ-7.

2. Gen. Kraven, in charge of the XJ-7's flight, won't let Oscar take McMillen out of the mental ward . . . wants to keep him there and interrogate. Oscar wants to find that plane now! Jurisdictional dispute! Kraven appears to win.

3. Alone with Steve, Oscar tells Steve he wants that plane! He won't ask questions about how Steve manages to find it.

4. Bionically, Steve breaks McMillen out of the mental ward.

5. On the phone, Kraven reports (we don't know to whom) that Steve and McMillen split . . . probably headed for the Quadrant.

6. Driving a jeep in the desert, Steve and McMillen see the long missing and presumed dead Dr. Martin Edstrom! He warns them to go back then dematerializes before their eyes!

Once you've completed a workable scene breakdown, corrected all problems, moved things around to the places they work best, patched up weak or slow spots, and done the many other things that must be done when working through the outlines, you are ready to begin writing the first draft script.

(Some screenwriters perform still another step—a long narrative **treatment** that can run thirty to sixty pages for a feature film. In fact, Terry and Jim would often take the brief scene outline given above and flesh it out to two, three, or four times that length in order to better realize what happens in the story/script. Other writers go directly from the short scene breakdown to the script. Do what you find most effective.)

On to the Script(s)

Start with "FADE IN:". You are on your way to writing the first draft. You'll pick up suggestions in the chapters on scenes/sequences, dialogue, and format. Before long you'll have a first draft.

Other drafts will follow. Rewriting is part of the process. (Viki King says you write your first draft to see what your movie is about, to discover what you want to write.)[23] Most screenwriters go through four, five, six or more drafts. (Don't panic, not all of these are complete rewrites; some are only polishes.)

Rewriting can seem daunting, and it is hard work. But once you get into it you'll discover that rewriting is remarkably creative. Something that didn't quite work can suddenly click. Scenes that were only okay can be reworked until they sparkle.

Look forward to rewriting. It's a truism: **scripts aren't written, they're rewritten.** (We'll discuss rewriting in more detail later.)

At the end of this chapter I've included abbreviated structure analyses of various films. Observe how they are structured, how the different story lines develop. Then do some similar analyses of your own. Such analyses can help develop a feel for film structure. The first few analyses are abbreviated since they present multiple story lines in tabular form. The others are more like condensed story line beat outlines.

The next few pages present some additional ways of considering story structure. There may be something in the various models that you will find useful for your script.

STRUCTURE MODELS

A model is a map, a template, a schema. At its best, it can present a design that will be useful for your story. At its worst, it imposes a formula that restricts your creative freedom and becomes predictable and hackneyed.

Multiple Story Lines Model

Here's a very simplified schema (and not meant to be accurate) showing how four different story lines might range over a film. ("Mins" refers to minutes into the film.) The lines represent segments of the film given over to each story line. Note that there are overlaps since the same scene can be a beat in different story lines.

(1)	--------------------------		----	----		----		----	-------
(2)		----				---	---	----	
(3)		----	----	----			-----	---	---
(4)				----		----		-----	
Mins	0	15	30	45	60	75	90	105	120

(1) Main task story line
(2) Internal story line
(3) Relationship romance story line
(4) Subplot belonging to another character

Three-Act-Structure/Plot-Point Models

Syd Field offers one of the most popular (and controversial) three-act-structure models.[24] It stresses writing to act breaks and three other middle section plot points. While applicable to a number of films, it doesn't apply to a great many others. Numbers in the model refer to both pages and minutes (since a film times to about one minute per page).

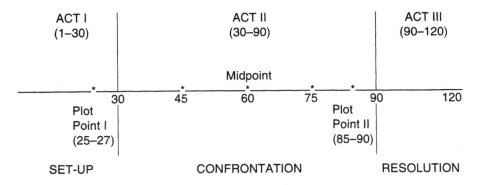

Major plot points I and II are incidents or events that spin the story in another direction and move it forward. Field says the midpoint (60) bridges the two halves of Act II, while the two "pinch" points at 45 and 75 tie things together and keep the story on track. He suggests that the screenwriter identify these points in the outline and write to them.

Linda Seger elaborates the three-act model.[25] She suggests starting with an image that gives a visual sense of the mood and style of the film (such as the waving grain and Amish environment in *Witness*). Next, present the location, characters, situation, and so on. What Seger calls the **catalyst** then initiates the action. Samuel witnessing the murder in *Witness* is such an inciting incident. Then you must **raise the central question**, which will remain unanswered until the climax. Seger stresses that the **turning points (act breaks)** raise this question again, raise the stakes, and present a different stress for the action. These points often require a decision or commitment by the hero. The second turning point (Act II break) accelerates the story.

She designates specific types of story points. An **action point** drives the story forward by causing a reaction, by demanding a response. This is usually followed by another action point. (Turning points are clearly action points.) A **barrier** action point is an obstruction that forces the character to go in a new direction, take a new course of action, make a decision. A **complication** is an action point that doesn't produce an immediate payoff but anticipates the inevitable payoff. (In *Tootsie*, Dorothy/Michael's realizing John will try to kiss her/him is a complication that will have to be dealt with later.) Complications produce suspense. A **reversal** is the strongest kind of action point since it turns the story around 180 degrees, as in a horror film the monster springs just when the characters start to feel safe. It's a reversal in *Jaws* when they realize that the first shark they've caught is not the killer monster that they are after. *Body Heat* is structured around a reversal. A dominant man who appears to rape a beautiful, young woman turns out to be her victim.

Michael Hauge draws on his character model of inner and outer motivation (where the latter refers to what I've called a task story line) and defines each act in terms of the hero's outer motivation. He claims this motivation can be divided into three stages with separate but related goals that correspond to the three acts. He gives the example of *War Games* in which Act I shows the young computer hacker trying to break into the system to play a game, Act II has him trying to escape from the FBI and to alert NORAD of what's going on, while in Act III he wants to stop the computer from starting World War III. The screenwriter begins writing by first determining the hero's overall outer motivation, then dividing it into its three segments (it will change twice), which are the motivations for each act. The writer can then work on the act-break scenes that signal the changes in motivation.[26]

Viki King's "clothesline model" is a formulaic version of the three-act-structure model.[27] She specifically spells out what should happen on various pages. For example, on page seventy-five she calls for a "Letting Go" scene in which it looks as though the hero will not achieve the goal and so has to give up—let go—in order to go on; to let go of what he thought he wanted, in order to get what he needed all along. (This model fits very few films.)

The Three-Act-Structure Controversy

For some time now the three-act-structure model has been controversial. Few question the validity of a general Beginning-Middle-End, three-act approach; it is the prescribed plot-point formulas that make it questionable. Should you adopt a three-act model?

Obviously Act I needs a strong break if it is to begin the story. (Even this isn't always so clear. The interesting modern vampire film *Near Dark* has an uncertain first-act break. So does Steven Spielberg's exciting early film, *Duel*.)

The Act II act break is much more dubious. Some films have such a break, many others do not. As a film nears its end, it's more important to develop a rush of crises to the climax than to have a second-act break.

Screenwriter Frank Pierson doesn't like the concept of "acts" at all since these imply each act coming to an end.[28] A film flows; a curtain doesn't come down at the end of an act as in the theater. While supporting beginning-middle-end structure, he opposes the notion of acts. Paul Mazursky finds three-act structure too formulaic although he admits it's possible. He simply gets the story rolling and sees where it goes; he doesn't think in three acts.[29] Larry Gelbart says he never thought of a movie in three acts.[30] *Tootsie*, which he co-wrote, doesn't use three-act structure.

In *The New Screenwriter Looks at the New Screenwriter*, Bill Froug explored the three-act-structure issue in interviews with a dozen screenwriters.[31] He asks each if they follow the three-act model. About half say they do, half say they don't. In a recent book, Froug says of Syd Field's book:

> It is *not* valuable to recommend that new screenwriters write by the numbers . . . like all formulas, this tends to wear itself out with repeated use. . . . The great American movies usually deny formula writing.[32]

After pointing out many William Goldman films that don't follow the three-act structure, he says, "The reality is that there are no clearly defined 'Acts' in screenplays. An 'Act' is wherever you choose to say it is."[33] Of the tight three-act model he concludes, "The results are a lot of formula-written movies that look and feel alike."[34]

Many academic writing teachers find three-act-structure models too formulaic. Dancyger and Rush specifically address this issue in their book *Alternative Scriptwriting.*[35]

My own opinion is mixed. It is one thing to suggest that every ten or fifteen minutes a major beat is needed to maintain audience interest, but quite another to maintain that these have to occur on pages forty-five, sixty, and seventy-five. Nor is it appropriate to mandate the functions that these various points must serve. I find this too formulaic.

One of my biggest concerns with many three-act models is that they slight the climax. Stressing the questionable second-act break, makes it seem more significant than the climax toward which the entire story has been building.

A second act break can be powerful. The death of Hobson leads Arthur to defy his family and choose his true love. But a second-act break is hardly a necessity for all films. My suggestion is to stay with the beginning-middle-end story line development and use a more specific model only if it seems to fit your story.

Other Structure Approaches

We have mentioned Rockwell's helpful underscoring of the plus/minus, positive/negative, progression of the crises that develop the story. Each crisis is a minus trap that the hero springs with a plus effort, only to meet a new obstacle that must be overcome. These build to the major **Crisis**—the hero's worst challenge—just before the climax, as the following schematic shows:

Protagonist
and Purpose   Crisis Climax

$$- \; + \; - \; + \; - \; + \; - \; + \; - \; + \; - \; + \; - \; + \; - \; + \; - \; + \; - \; +$$

Rockwell advocates a multiple story line model: develop a story line for each prominent character, then interweave the story lines. While the hero has a problem or goal, an antagonistic force is equally committed to a conflicting goal. Rockwell suggests the writer thoroughly develop the arguments on both sides of the contest—the plot and **counterplot.** Let the counterplot be as strong as the main story line.[36]

Vale describes how the hero's **motive** produces an **intention** to achieve a **goal.**[37] **Conflict** comes from the intention clashing with the difficulties involved in achieving the goal. Vale describes three types of middle complications. **Obstacles** are circumstantial, such as a mountain that must be climbed. **Complications** are accidental, as when the plague delays the friar's getting Romeo's message to Juliet. **Counterintentions** are the result of the counterplot—the attempts of the antagonist to block the protagonist's intentions.

He offers a striking image to describe how a film works on an audience. He asks us to imagine the main goal of the story as a powerful magnet that pulls the hero (and us) toward the climax. This carries the obvious implication that the closer we get to the goal/climax, the more powerful the tug of the magnet; so events accelerate as we approach the climax. For much of the story, however, the magnet is still far away.

To keep the story's **forward movement** going, we need a number of smaller magnets along the way, each one representing an auxiliary objective that arises with respect to each crisis. Vale suggests these should often overlap because forward movement stops if one auxiliary goal is achieved without there being another one to involve us. (This is a useful notion although I think he overstates it. Break moments can be built into a script without the audience losing emotional involvement.)

Vale insightfully points out that it is the audience's anticipation—suspense— of auxiliary goals that causes forward movement, not rapid pacing of dialogue or action. There's a valuable lesson here. Especially during the middle section, forward movement is maintained by suspensefully involving the audience in a series of (often overlapping) crisis goals.

Beker doesn't so much present a model as a way of working.[38] She asks her students to break the length of the film into twenty-four segments (of five pages/ minutes each) and then fill in a plot point for every five pages. (She admits this is arbitrary—it could be six or more.)

Lucey might not call his approach a model either, but it contains some interesting elements.[39] He suggests having a **simple story but complex characters.** He has a three-act approach. In Act I, the hero takes on the problem, and the twist at the end of the act spins the story in a new direction. In Act II, the hero seems defeated by the problem, with another twist at the end of the act. In Act III, the hero solves the problem. Lucey makes the writing task seem less daunting by pointing out that once you get the story set, a number of scenes fall into place:

The opening orientation scene, often without dialogue, which psychically puts the audience in the film

A scene that presents the statement of the dramatic problem and that tells the audience what the story is about

The meet-the-hero scene

The meet-the-problem scene

The meet-the-villain scene

The "Button" that starts the story—ten minutes or so into the film

The twist reversal at the end of Act I

The twist at the end of Act II

The girding-for-battle scene in Act III

The fighting-through-to-the-villain scene in Act III

The climax

The denouement

Whether or not one accepts his model, a number of these scenes are likely to occur in any script.

Brenner suggests a **false goal/real goal** model.[40] The hero has been pursuing a false goal, unaware of the true goal until he gains insight at the climax. For example, a character may want to marry a supposedly ideal person, then realize that the two are not right for each other and chooses someone else. In *Gregory's Girl*, Gregory—a rather immature Scottish high-school student—learns to give up his infatuation with Dorothy to begin a relationship with Susan.

Dancyger and Rush rework the three-act model into what they call a **restorative three-act structure**.[41] Here, each act rises to an intense highpoint: the act crisis or climax which forms the act-break plot point. After each act break there is a point of relaxation before the new act begins to build. Each act builds to a greater intensity than the previous act.

The Act I ending break is a point of no return. Once the hero has moved through it, they can never turn back. (In *The Graduate*, once Benjamin has sex with Mrs. Robinson he can never go back to his previous innocence.) The Act I plot point seems to answer the hero's problem, but it is a false solution.

In much of Act II, the audience is ahead of the protagonist. We know the hero's course of action will not be successful, but the hero does not. At the end of Act II, the hero finally faces the implications of the false solution at the end of Act I. The hero realizes that what he tried before doesn't work. The hero has finally caught up with the audience.

In Act III, having recognized the earlier failure, the character is able to reenergize. The internal conflict is usually solved first. The rest of Act III is devoted to resolving the external conflict. Typically, the character triumphs.

It's commendable that Dancyger and Rush attempt to remodel three-act structure. However, I do not find that their model fits a great number of films. It might work with *The Graduate* and a few other films, but it really seems too limited.

Recently there has been a slight renewal of interest in **myth and folktale models**. Some of this can be traced to the work of Vladimir Propp who decades ago analyzed folktales looking for a common structure; however, I don't find his analysis useful for media stories.[42]

Christopher Vogler champions the archetypal hero's mythical journey, or **hero's quest**, based on the writings of Joseph Campbell.[43] Volger lays out a twelve step model:

Act I: (1) introduce hero, (2) the call to adventure, (3) refusing the call, (4) older mentor or helper motivates the hero, and (5) the threshold—a leap of faith (or a push).

Act II: (6) making allies, enemies, going through tests, (7) the inmost cave—overcoming an obstacle, (8) the supreme ordeal—hero confronts his greatest fear, (9) the seizing of the sword—overcoming the villain or dragon, taking the treasure, or finding romance, and (10) the road back—often a chase scene with the villain pursuing the hero.

Act III: (11) the resurrection—the hero must be purified, and pass the final test, and (12) returning with the elixir, bringing something back to share.

While interesting because of their roots in folktale and myth, I find these models much too restrictive to be of that much use in media writing unless you happen to be doing a classic mythic tale. (George Lucas is said to have adapted a myth model for *Star Wars*.)

We've had a long journey looking at story structure. There's a lot here to consider. Digest it. Then go back to the basic story and story line structure. Following are some sample film analyses that should help you to recognize story line structures. When you've finished examining them, prepare your outline and go on from there.

SAMPLE FILM ANALYSES

The African Queen

The African Queen is a classic. It has two story lines: an adventurous task and a romance. It closely follows three-act structure with clear act breaks. The development here is not so much cause and effect (with one event leading to another) as it is a succession of obstacles/crises to be overcome. Some beats reflect both story lines. (Here I number beats, but don't time them.)

Beat	Task Story Line: To get down river and sink ship	Romance Story Line: To romance
	ACT I	
1	SET-UP: Intro characters, situation, WW I.	
2	SET-UP: Germans burn village, brother dies, Charlie and Rosie leave in Queen.	
3	Rosie persuades Charlie to go after Louisa in spite of difficulties.	
	ACT II—25 minutes in	
4		They modestly bathe.
5		It's raining, they share tent.
6	Rapids. R says go on.	
7	C drunk, says won't go on.	
8		R dumps C's gin bottles.
9	R sulks until C agrees to go on, and they do.	
10	German fort.	

11 Heavy rapids.	
12	Kiss, then make love.
13 Falls, broken propeller.	Repair it together.
14 Mosquitos.	
15 Stuck in marshes, pull out.	
16 Leeches.	
17 Stuck. Resigned to death. She prays. We see lake nearby.	
18 Rain, float onto lake.	
ACT III—85–88 minutes in	
19 See ship, prepare torpedoes.	
20	Quarrel over other staying; both go.
21 Queen sinks in storm.	
22 About to be hanged.	
23	Captain marries them.
24 Louisa hits Queen's torpedoes, blows up. CLIMAX.	
25	As Mr. & Mrs., they swim to shore.

Approx. number of beats: 16 | 9

Witness

Witness has a task and romance story line, and closely follows the three-act model. You can see the progression from the timing. Samuel is the young boy, Paul is the villain, Daniel is Rachel's suitor. Note how beats occur more rapidly near the climax. (In the following example, I have numbered and timed the beats. Mins refers to the number of minutes into the film.)

Beat	Mins	John Book Task Story Line: To capture villains and avoid being killed	John and Rachel Romance Story Line: To romance
		ACT I	
1	00	(Rachel's husband dead.) She and son go to Philadelphia.	

2	15	Samuel witnesses killing.	
	18		John & Rachel meet.
3	29	Policeman id'd as killer.	
4	32	John shot, realizes cops in on it.	
		ACT II	
5	43		Rachel nurses John.
6	44	Paul tries to locate John.	
7	51		R gives J husband's clothes.
8	56	J tells partner what up against.	
9	62		Daniel visits Rachel.
10	66		J & R dance, almost kiss.
11	69		R clashes with father over J.
12	70	Partner questioned by Paul.	
13	74		Barn raising. J & R getting involved, many looks exchanged.
14	80		J watches R bathing, almost sexual encounter.
15	84	J learns partner killed.	
16	85	J threatens Paul on phone.	
17	87	J hits punk, Sgt. learns, & we assume notifies villain.	
18	91		J & R embrace, wild kiss.
		ACT III	
19	93	Villains arrive to get J.	
20	99	J buries villain in grain.	
21	103	J gets shotgun, kills villain.	
22	104	P holds gun to R, J drops gun. Shows J's feelings for R.	

23	106	Amish arrive, J gets P to surrender. CLIMAX.	
24	109		J leaves, Daniel arrives.

Approx. number of beats: 14	11

Tootsie

Tootsie is interesting for identifying five stories all belonging to Michael/Dorothy:

1. To act, make money and put on his friend Jeff's play (in which he and Sandy would star). (This is the main story line. To be a successful actor—even if in drag as Dorothy—is not the main story line since this is achieved early on, around p. 75.)

2. To win Julie, the strong romance story line.

3. To avoid Julie's father, who is wooing Michael/Dorothy.

4. To remain friends with Sandy. Michael's sleeping with Sandy is the result of a subterfuge. Trying on one of her dresses (imagining how it would look on Michael/Dorothy), Sandy catches him stripped to his underwear. Embarrassed to be thought a transvestite, he claims he stripped out of passion for her.

5. To avoid John, a lecherous older actor. He's trying to hustle Dorothy. (I may be stretching with this one, it may not be a full story line but just part of the complications.)

This is a film that doesn't so readily fit the three-act model. While the first-act break is clear enough, there seems to be simply a progression of accelerating events building to the climax rather than a clearly demarcated second-act break.

Mins	Story Lines: To act, make $, put on play	To win Julie	To avoid Julie's father	To stay friends with Sandy	To avoid John
	ACT I				
6	Wants to do play.				
12				Helps Sandy with part.	
18	Agent says unemploy-able.	Meets Julie.			

Time					
20	Wins role (in drag).				
	ACT II				
	Reaffirms $ for play.			Sleeps w/ Sandy.	
30		Meets Julie on set.			Warned about John's kisses.
36	Successful improv.	J off with director.			M/D kissed by John.
	Hassle with Jeff.				
40				Misses date.	
			Meets father.		
	Some success.	Director two-times J.			John attracted.
				Stands up S.	
45		Falling for J.		S criticizes Dorothy.	
55	Success!				
		At party, M rejected			
60		by J.		Puts off Sandy.	
70		Farm: more in love.	Father falling for D.		
			Father sends candy.		
	Stuck in				
75	option.				
		J breaks with director.	Father to see D.		
80		Tries kiss, thought			
85		lesbian.	Father		
90			proposes.		Serenades, thinks D with Jeff.

(Where's act break?)			Breaks up with Michael, still to do play.	
95 Wants out of show.	Not see Dorothy anymore.			
100 CLIMAX. Reveals as Michael.	J punches M.		Sees M.	Sees M.
M in Jeff's play.				
105		Father & M reconciled.		
110	M & J together.			
Total Beats 11	12	6	7	7

Die Hard 2

Die Hard 2 has a single story line: Police Lt. John McClane has to foil the villain's plot to rescue the captured cocaine kingpin. In the process, McClane must save the airliners circling overhead, in one of which his wife is a passenger.

The characters are McClane, the hero Colonel Stewart, the villain and ex-special forces officer, the Wife, airport police Captain, airport control tower Supervisor, special forces Major, obnoxious TV Reporter in plane, TV reporter in airport, and an airport janitor.

I also indicate **preparation** and **exposition**, two techniques we'll discuss later. A **runner** is a recurring bit that adds spice to a script; a **running gag** is a humorous version of a runner.

Mins

ACT I

00   Meet hero as he gets parking ticket at airport (introduces runner, which will Frame story). TIME: contemporary, Christmas season. PLACE: Washington, DC airport.

EXPOSITION (on TV): captured cocaine lord, who was a military general, flying in.

Meet villain as he does martial arts exercises.

PREPARATION: hero's beeper—call wife on airphone.

PREPARATION: woman in plane shows wife her stun gun.

06   Villains take over church near airport for headquarters.

EXPOSITION: weather terrible, getting worse.

PREPARATION: hero lights cigarette with his lighter.

12   Hero fights two villains in baggage transport area, kills one, other escapes.

PREPARATION: villain drops hand-held two-way radio.

16   Wife confronts obnoxious reporter whom she punched in first *Die Hard.*

20   Hero chews out airport security captain for not doing his job.

22   Meet general, captive on plane flying in, dangerous guy.

22   Hero sneaks dead villain's prints, learns from cop on coast that villain was special forces soldier and listed as dead for two years. (SURPRISE and SUSPENSE) (INTERCUTTING between hero, general, villains, and wife gives fast pace.)

30   Hero warns captain and airport manager that they're facing pros. Runways go dark. (SURPRISE) Control systems go down. Villain calls, demanding a 747 so he can escape with general, or else! (SUSPENSE) Hero clashes with captain; ejected from control tower.

ACT II

40   Airport tries to set up alternate control system, fails, and security SWAT team is destroyed. Hero wipes out some villains.

51   In retaliation, villains cause plane to crash. Hero tries to warn it off with torches but fails.

60   Wife and reporter. Reporter's assistant has a radio.

62   Army counterterrorist major and platoon arrive and take control. Hero doubtful they can handle it, but again is shut out of involvement.

66   Airport rigs alternate transmitter. Reporter picks it up.

69   General overpowers guards but loses cabin pressure, must land immediately.

72   Hero overhears on hand-held radio (that villain lost earlier). (PREPARATION PAYOFF)

75   Hero captures general on landed plane. But villains get general back. Hero barely escapes.

81   Hero clashes with captain and major.

83   Hero discovers villains in church, but wife's call on his beeper alerts guard. (PREPARATION PAYOFF) Fight. Hero kills guard.

86   Major and special forces platoon arrive, fight villains who escape on snowmobiles.

     PREPARATION/SUSPENSE: Villains switch ammo magazines.

90   Hero chases in snowmobile, crashes. Perplexed he didn't kill villain with gun he got from villains.

94   SURPRISE: Major and platoon revealed as villains as they kill a new replacement. (We know but good guys don't yet know.)

97   PREPARATION PAYOFF: Hero convinces captain that troops are also villains as he shoots captain with villains' gun loaded with blanks. *Now* good guys know. Captain mobilizes his men.

     ACT III

98   Plane reporter broadcasts situation; panics airport crowd. Wife stun guns reporter in middle of his transmission. (PREPARATION PAYOFF)

102 Hero gets TV-news helicopter to drop him on wing of villains' escaping 747; hero jams an aileron. Wife's plane must land, runway lights or no—it is out of fuel.

104 On 747 wing, hero fights major, who dies when sucked into jet engine. Hero fights Colonel Stewart and is knocked off wing, but not before he unscrews fuel tank cap. Fuel streams out from wing tanks.

110 CLIMAX: Hero uses lighter (PREPARATION PAYOFF) to ignite fuel, blowing up villains' plane and leaving lighted stream that wife's plane and other airliners can follow in order to land safely.

115 Hero and wife unite. Reporter lies helpless in snow.

116 Captain tears up hero's parking ticket. (FRAME)

     END

Jurassic Park

Jurassic Park has one primary story line (to escape from the dinosaurs) and two story lines so minor they are almost runners: will Dr. Grant change and want to have children? will Dr. Malcolm romance Dr. Sadler away from Dr. Grant?

This story doesn't neatly follow the typical three-act structure. The first-act setup lasts an hour. One might call the attempt to turn on the power (91 minutes into the film) the second-act break. But while this does follow the quieter ten-minute break, it doesn't have the impact usually ascribed to a major plot point. Rather than following the three-act model, *Jurassic Park* simply develops from one suspenseful event to another, up to the climax.

Drs. Grant and Sadler are the main protagonists although the two children have their own moments of adventure. Dr. Malcolm is a flippant chaostician. John Hammond is the creator of the park. Dennis is a villainous technician, although the real antagonists are the carnivorous dinosaurs.

Beat Mins

1	00	Loading an unidentifiable creature into a compound, a worker is dragged into its cage and killed. (SUSPENSE)
2	03	Lawyer visits amber mine, concerned over worker's death.
		PREPARATION: Find amber with mosquito inside.
3	05	Hammond visits digging site of Drs. Grant and Sadler and promises them future funding if they come and endorse his park. Meet heroes.
		PREPARATION: Grant tells how velociraptors attack you from side while you are tracking the one in front.
		Second Story Line: Sadler wants children, Grant doesn't.
4	14	Dennis makes deal to sell embryos. Meet villain.
		PREPARATION: But will have only eighteen minute window to catch boat off island.
5	15	In helicopter to island, meet lawyer (again) and Dr. Malcolm.
		Third Story Line: Malcolm flirts with Sadler.
6	20	At island, first view of the dinosaurs.
7	23	EXPOSITION: Learn how dinosaurs were raised from DNA found in amber-encased mosquitoes. (PAYOFF)
		PREPARATION: Malcolm warns that even by growing only female dinosaurs they won't control breeding—"Life finds a way."
8	31	PREPARATION: Velociraptors are fed a cow, Aussie overseer says they are very smart creatures.
9	34	Both Malcolm and Sadler warn of bad consequences.
10	38	Hammond's grandchildren arrive (boy and girl), begin guided tour.
		Second Story Line: Grant annoyed by children.
		Third Story Line: Malcolm flirtatiously rides with Sadler.
11	40	Storm coming. (SUSPENSE DANGER)
		Tour doesn't see any dinosaurs.
		PREPARATION: These are dinosaurs who spit poison at their prey.

12	42	(INTERCUT MUCH OF FOLLOWING ACTIONS)

Tyrannosaur Rex not seen in his paddock.

Third Story Line: Malcolm flirting with Sadler, touching her arm to make a point.

13	48	Dennis—the evil computer expert—begins to shut down systems.
14	49	Tour people find an ailing Triceratops. Sadler stays with it, others continue.
15	52	Tour cut short because of coming storm.

Third Story Line: Grant lets Malcolm know that he and Sadler are involved. (RESOLVES THIRD STORY LINE)

16	55	Dennis steals embryos, escapes in jeep in storm, rushed because must meet boat. (PAYOFF)
17	59	Control room loses control of systems.
18	60	T-Rex attacks tour cars, Malcolm knocked out, Lawyer killed.
19	71	Dennis stuck in mud, attacked by poison-spitting dinosaur. (PAYOFF)

Dennis loses embryos. (POSSIBLY SETTING UP NEXT FILM)

20	78	Sadler and park doctor find Malcolm, are chased by T-Rex and barely escape.
21	81	Grant and children climb tree to be safe, adopt a pet—plant-eating dinosaur. Grant stays awake and keeps watch. (QUIET INTERLUDE)

Second Story Line: Grant getting close to children.

22	84	Hammond and Sadler talk in dining room about his past and his dreams. (QUIET INTERLUDE CONTINUING)
23	90	Grant and children find hatched eggs. Dinosaurs are reproducing! (POSSIBLY SETTING UP NEXT FILM PREPARATION AND EXPOSITION: Learn girl is a computer hacker.)
24	91	(POSSIBLE ACT BREAK)

In control room, shut down all systems and restart in attempt to regain control. It works, but now must turn on circuit breakers in a distant bunker. Technician goes.

25	94	Grant and children watch herd of dinosaurs moving like birds, T-Rex catches one.
26	95	Power not yet on, Sadler and Aussie go to check breakers. Being hunted by velociraptors. Sadler gets power on. (SUSPENSE)
27	101	Grant and children climbing wire barriers just as power comes on. Boy shocked, not breathing. (SUSPENSE)

28	102	Sadler attacked by velociraptor, learns technician dead, barely escapes.
29	103	Aussie killed by velociraptor that sneaks around to side when he is hunting one in front of him. (PAYOFF)
30	105	Grant revives boy with CPR. Enters dining room with children. Children stay, Grant goes looking for others.
31	107	Children hunted by velociraptors. Close escapes. (SUSPENSE)
32	112	Everyone in control room, but velociraptor at door, which Grant and Sadler must hold shut. (SUSPENSE)
		Girl uses computer and restores power to door so Grant can close it. (PAYOFF)
33	114	Velociraptors break in. Another chase. Then people are trapped in the foyer. Suddenly (SURPRISE) T-Rex breaks in and attacks velociraptors, allowing the people to escape. (CLIMAX)
34	117	On board helicopter, returning to safety.
		(SECOND STORY LINE RESOLVED) Grant happy, holding sleeping children, suggesting he will now want some of his own.
	120	END

Sleepless in Seattle

Sleepless in Seattle is a feel-good romantic comedy in which two deserving people find each other. It contains a single (relationship) story line with separate portions for each character.

This film does not manifest three-act structure. There is no clear first-act break—Annie's hearing the radio show comes too early, Jonah's reading her letter and working on Sam comes too late. Nor is there a clear second-act break (Jonah's talking about going to New York doesn't have the power such an act break usually requires).

Sam is the single parent. Annie is the woman who falls for him. Jonah is his son.

00	After the death of his beloved wife, Sam moves to Seattle.
05	Annie and Walter—with his many allergies—get engaged. But then, Annie hears a radio call-in talk show in which Jonah appeals for a new wife for Sam, and Sam describes his relationship and loss. Annie is moved to tears.
31	Sam gets tons of mail from sympathetic listeners, many offering romance.

44   Having fantasies about Sam, Annie hears a rebroadcast of his radio comments. She writes him a letter.

53   Jonah reads the letter and decides Annie is the one, but he can't convince his father. Jonah would like to take her up on her offer to meet at the Empire State Building on Valentine's Day (something she got from the film, *An Affair to Remember*).

54   Sam goes on a dinner date; the woman has a grating laugh.

61   Listening to the radio call-in talk show, Annie hears Jonah complaining about Sam's date. She flies to Seattle, purportedly to do a story on talk shows, but really to check out Sam.

65   At the airport to see his date off on a trip, Sam notices Annie and is drawn to her, but they don't meet.

68   Annie watches Sam and Jonah playing, and is further attracted.

70   Annie determines to meet Sam, but when she sees him embrace a friend outside his house, she thinks they are involved and quickly leaves. But not before Sam notices her and is once again attracted.

74   Annie gets a letter from Sleepless in Seattle, but finds it simplistically written—it was actually written by Jonah.

75   Sam tells friends of his strange attraction to a woman he's seen.

83   Urged by a friend, Jonah decides to fly to the Empire State Building rendezvous in New York.

85   Annie determines to give up her fantasy and commit to Walter.

93   On the verge of going on a weekend trip with his date, Sam argues with Jonah, stressing that he will not go to New York. When the sitter arrives, Jonah can't be found.

98   Jonah goes to New York. Sam flies after him.

104   Annie breaks up with Walter. She happens to see the heart design lit up on the Empire State Building and goes there. Meanwhile, Sam finds a disappointed Jonah. Annie arrives and they almost miss each other, but Sam and Jonah return for Jonah's forgotten knapsack. All meet, and go off together, hand in hand.

105   Close on the lighted Empire State Building with its Valentine heart.

The Fugitive

Adapted from an older television series, *The Fugitive* features Dr. Richard Kimble trying to prove his innocence after being convicted of killing his wife. To do this Kimble has to trace down the mysterious one-armed man (Sykes) while avoiding a relentless U.S. Deputy Marshal, Samuel Gerard. Near the end he discovers that the villain behind the killing was his friend and colleague Dr. Charles Nichols. The crimes (there was an earlier killing of a pathologist that we hear about) were committed to avoid exposing the information that a new drug about to be approved by the FDA (and worth millions to the pharmaceutical company producing it) causes liver damage.

The story has an unusual adversary/villain structure. Through most of the film, Kimble's major adversary—the major threat to achieving the objective is Gerard, but he's more a complication. Sykes is the immediate villain, and we do see him—but not clearly—in the beginning commiting the murder. Except for some hazy flashbacks, Sykes doesn't figure in the story in a major way until nearly an hour and a half into the film. Near the end we learn through a twist that the prime villain is Kimble's friend Nichols.

An interesting feature of the film is that it uses a great deal of intercutting, primarily between Kimble and his pursuer Gerard. This makes for fast pacing and good suspense. It also means many beats overlap.

The film follows a rough three-act structure, although the act breaks are not that clear. Does the first-act break come when Kimble escapes from the prison bus (20 minutes in), or when he commits to finding the one-armed killer (44 minutes in)?

00   A woman (Kimble's wife) is killed by an unrecognizable assailant.

09   Kimble claims that the killer, whom he struggled with, was a one-armed man. Nevertheless, Kimble is convicted and sent to prison for the crime.

13   When the prison bus crashes, Kimble escapes, injured.

20   Gerard starts his rigorous search for Kimble.

25   Kimble goes to hospital (where he was once a doctor) to treat his wound, is almost detected by a guard.

     (INTERCUTTING GERARD AND KIMBLE)

30   Kimble is almost caught by Gerard, but escapes by leaping into the waters of a large dam.

39   Gerard continues searching, convinced Kimble may have survived, while Kimble recalls his fight with the one-armed man and commits to finding the man.

46   Gerard shows how cold-blooded he is when he shoots another escaped convict who is holding one of his men hostage.

50   When Kimble calls his attorney, Gerard learns he has returned to Chicago.

54   After getting some money from his friend Nichols, Kimble checks in prosthetics department of the hospital for a lead as the Chicago police join the marshals in searching for him.

59   Gerard can't get Nichols to help him find Kimble. Gerard is beginning to learn what kind of man Kimble is; he begins to suspect that Kimble may be innocent.

61   Kimble is startled when police break into the house where he has rented a room, but it turns out they are there to arrest the landlady's son.

65   Kimble sneaks into hospital computer files and finds the records of five prosthesis users.

67   The landlady's son identifies Kimble to police.

68   In the hospital, Kimble correctly diagnoses a boy, and gets him to an operating room, thus saving his life, but this arouses suspicion. Kimble barely escapes exposure.

73   Gerard realizes Kimble has checked prostheses records and does the same.

75   Both Kimble and Gerard go to the county jail to check out a prosthetic user (a false lead). Kimble narrowly escapes capture by melding into a parade outside.

84   Gerard is being pressured at a press conference that raises the issue of Kimble's possible innocence.

85   Following up a lead, Kimble breaks into Sykes's residence and discovers a picture of Sykes with the pathologist. Kimble puts things together and realizes Sykes is the killer. He leads Gerard to Sykes.

90   Interviewing Sykes, Gerard realizes he is lying.

95   Suspecting the pathologist and Sykes, Kimble telephones Nichols and tells him that the murder was about a bad drug deal. Sykes gets a call and goes after Kimble.

100   Kimble checks out the liver samples from the drug testing and realizes they were faked. But when he learns the pathologist was killed in a mysterious car accident, he realizes who must be involved.

104   Gerard realizes Nichols lied to him and goes after him.

106   Kimble is almost shot by Sykes who kills a policeman before Kimble overpowers him. Now the Chicago police think Kimble is a cop-killer. They go all out to "take him down."

110   At a medical convention banquet, Kimble confronts Nichols in the midst of delivering a speech, and accuses him of being behind the faked samples.

115   Kimble and Nichols argue. Gerard arrives. Police have orders to shoot Kimble on sight.

120   In the final fight, Kimble gets Nichols just as Nichols is about to kill Gerard. Gerard knows Kimble is innocent.

125   Gerard drives off with Kimble, who will soon be released. Nichols and
        Sykes are in custody.

SUMMARY

This chapter explored screenplay structure. It began with the contents of structure:
the classic dramatic model with its Beginning, Middle, and End structure, suspense
and surprise, conflict, and media story. Then it considered stages of the actual writing process, progressing from concept to basic story to story line outline to scene
breakdown.

Also considered were a number of structure models that—while often too formulaic—may contain suggestions useful to the screenwriter. The three-act-struc-
ture-model controversy was reviewed. Finally, there were a number of sample film
analyses to illustrate story outlines.

A CHECKLIST FOR STORY STRUCTURE

Is the suspense throughout the story strong enough to make the audience want
    to know what happens next?

Are there enough unexpected surprises to avoid making the story predictable?

Have you managed basic information: who knows what, when?

Is there a clear beginning, middle, end?

Is the major story line clear and clean?

Does each story beat lead to the next and clearly tell the story?

Do we understand early on what the story is and where it's going?

Does the opening grab us?

Does the beginning set up the story?

Is there an inciting incident, if necessary?

Does the story begin with a problem, conflict, or objective?

Do we meet major characters in Act I?

Is there clear dramatic conflict?

Is the protagonist's objective clear?

Is there sufficient doubt the protagonist can achieve the goal?

Is there a dreadful alternative, an "or else" factor that comes into play if the
    protagonist isn't successful?

Are there major turning points at the ends of Acts I and II if appropriate to your story?

Do the protagonist's actions move the plot along?

Does the story clearly belong to the protagonist?

Does Act II hold our attention through repeated crises?

Does Act II develop the story line without getting sidetracked?

Are all additional story lines clear and clean?

Is life difficult enough for the protagonist?

Does the story develop logically, with one thing leading to another?

Does the story move well—without dead spots?

Is there conflict and tension throughout?

Does your middle section have −/+ crisis development?

Does your story maintain forward movement by always keeping us involved?

Is there a powerful emotional climax?

Does the story accelerate as it moves toward the climax?

Do you need a Crisis just before the climax?

Is there a clear resolution?

Do you have a clear, concise concept?

Have you written a short but complete basic story?

Does the basic story convey what you want to write?

Have you considered other story lines: task, relationship, internal?

Have you written a strong and complete story line beat outline?

Have you laid out your sequences?

Have you done a scene outline (if needed)?

Have you done a treatment (if needed)?

Are your outlines complete enough to enable you to write the script from them?

Do we care about the story?

ENDNOTES

1. Keen, S. (December 1977). Don Juan's power trip. *Psychology Today, 11,* 42.

2. Goldman, W., interview in T. Sanders and F. L. Mock. (1981). *Screenwriters: Word Into Image* (film series). Santa Monica, CA: American Film Foundation. An expanded tran-

script of the interview was published as *Word Into Image: Writers on Screenwriting.* (1981). Santa Monica, CA: American Film Foundation. Goldman restates his view on screenplays—capitalized, set apart, and repeated—in his book *Adventures in the Screen Trade.* (NY: Warner Books, 1983.) (The other statement he so emphasizes is, "Nobody Knows Anything," a revealing comment about his impressions of Hollywood industry executives and their ability to predict what works and doesn't work. Take heart.)

3. There isn't always an Act II major act break. Indeed, the entire question of whether film stories should be structured around significant act breaks is controversial—some writers insist on them, others just as vehemently deny them. Some films have them, many other films don't. Certainly the start of the story constitutes an Act I major act break; it is obviously a significant event that spins the film around and into a new direction. But an Act II major act break is not necessary. An effective film story only needs accelerating and escalating development crises to hold our attention as it rushes toward the climax.

4. Some refer to this challenge as the Crisis with a capital C, drawing on theater usage. I don't think it is so necessary to make such a distinction but simply consider it as part of the climax event.

5. This is even more crucial than Beginning-Middle-End structure. Experimental film/ video maker Jean-Luc Godard is reported to have said that a film should have a beginning, middle, and end, although not necessarily in that order.

6. Even though we really know the hero will prevail—our favorite action adventure hero is not about to be wiped out—we accept the pretense. We willingly suspend disbelief in order to enjoy the suspense of the story. Knowing that Charles de Gaulle of France was not assassinated doesn't lessen our enjoyment of the machinations and last minute capture of the potential assassin in *The Day of the Jackal.*

7. So emotionally powerful is the anticipation of an event that studies have shown that stress-measured hours prior to a dental appointment is as high for some people as the stress when they are actually in the chair. Psychological testing with films containing stress scenes showed that the emotional response to anticipation of a stressful event was higher than the emotional response to a surprise occurrence of the event. (For example, Markellos S. Nomikos *et al.,* Surprise versus suspense in the production of stress reaction. *Journal of Personality and Social Psychology, 8* [1968], 204–208.) A study found that explicit forewarning of events coming in a horror film actually increased arousal and fright rather than lessened it. (From a study by Joanne Cantor, Dean Ziemke, and Glenn Sparks reported in *Psychology Today,* August 1984, 75.) We get emotionally involved anticipating the outcome of a dramatic enigma.

8. Sometimes the character knows and we don't—we want to find out. In the Who-Done-It, when the detective announces knowing who the killer is but needs just one thing first to prove it, we and the other characters wait anxiously for the revelation. In *Dirty Harry,* Harry foils a bank robbery and has his revolver at the head of a robber. Is it empty or is there one bullet left? The robber wants to know. We want to know. Harry pulls the trigger. There is no bullet.

    Sometimes we know and some characters don't. Then we anticipate the characters finding out what we know. (Dorothy's true gender in *Tootsie,* that the husband and children burned the letter that left the house to Margaret in *Howard's End,* or that *The Fugitive*'s wife was really killed by a one-armed man.)

In many horror pictures we know the terror awaiting the characters although they don't. (Sometimes this simply takes the form of our knowing that when they are too relaxed and off their guard something terrible will strike.)

In *Three Days of the Condor,* we know that the CIA book analysis group has been wiped out, but the hero doesn't. As he returns from getting lunch, we don't know whether or not he'll be attacked. There is dual suspense: how will he react when he sees the carnage and will he be assailed himself?

In comedy, many stories are based on misunderstanding. One character misunderstands whom the love note was meant for and thinks the worst of his or her lover. Since we know what is really going on, we can laugh at the antics of the characters who don't, and look forward to when they learn their folly. A variant of this occurs when we know that two romantic characters are meant for each other but they don't. We wait for them to realize it. This is the basis of many screwball comedies and of *When Harry Met Sally.*

9. Here are highlights of the development of suspense and surprise throughout the film *Witness.* (They are just the highlights. Many, many other micro suspense/surprise points occur as the story develops; these are chosen as illustrative.)

    Surprise and suspense: The boy, Samuel, witnesses the killing and is almost discovered by the killer.

    Surprise and suspense: Samuel identifies the killer as a detective in the police department.

    Surprise: The killer shoots and wounds detective John Book.

    Suspense: Can John keep himself and the boy safe with the police department looking for him?

    Suspense: Will John recover from his wound?

    Suspense: Will John and Rachel—the Amish woman caring for him—realize their love?

    Suspense: Will John successfully survive in the Amish community, which is so alien to him?

    Surprise and suspense: John observes Rachel bathing; he could approach her but he doesn't.

    Surprise: John learns his partner is killed.

    Scene suspense: John puts up with a punk's behavior as long as he can, then he punches the guy out (payoff).

    Suspense: This action leads the local police to realize that John may not be one of the Amish. We realize they will call the Philadelphia police who will come after John.

    Suspense: Killers arrive and chase John to kill him. (This sequence is full of small suspense bits such as John not being able to get the top of a silo door open and almost being discovered.)

    Surprise: One of the killers is "drowned" by grain in the silo.

    Suspense: Will John get Paul to drop the gun he is holding on Rachel and give up?

    Climax: John succeeds, suspense over. But . . .

    Suspense: the Romance Story line: Will John and Rachel get together? They don't, suspense over.

10. Here are two examples that illustrate the extent and variety of conflicts in film stories. For the first, I turn back to the classic western *Fort Apache.* Conflicts visible there include:

> The new colonel's rigid, by-the-book approach versus the more relaxed and realistic fort atmosphere.
>
> The new colonel's destructive authority versus the comparative powerlessness of those who know what should be done.
>
> The colonel versus the captain (who understands Native Americans and how to deal with them).
>
> The colonel versus the young lieutenant (who has romantic feelings toward the colonel's daughter).
>
> The lieutenant's love and desire versus his shyness and uncertainty in wooing the colonel's daughter.
>
> The lieutenant's inexperience versus his father's honored example (his father, once an officer, now a sergeant, was decorated for bravery).
>
> The continual chaffing against army restrictions by the sergeants who love drinking and roughhousing.
>
> The evil Native American agent versus both the Native Americans and the cavalry.
>
> The cavalry versus the Native Americans.
>
> Native American culture versus white oppression.
>
> The coming of civilization versus the vanishing frontier wilderness.
>
> The proper, restrictive Eastern influence versus the more relaxed atmosphere in the West.

For the other example, I chose a complex and disturbing British film, *Sammy and Rosie Get Laid:*

> The father versus Sammy and Rosie; he tries to use his money to control the couple since he wants a grandchild and wants them comfortably set in a house in a better neighborhood.
>
> The father versus their radical friends because of his past political terrorist crimes. (A pragmatic/expedient versus humanist/idealist ideological conflict.)
>
> The father's inability to handle the changing role of women—whether being astonished by Rosie working out with small weights or by calling her lesbian friends "damn dykes." Which is a special case of:
>
> The father's traditional views versus the more contemporary outlook of Sammy and Rosie and their friends; he cannot understand their lifestyle and values.
>
> The father versus Alice, the former lover he briefly takes up with again but can't really connect with.
>
> The father's internal conflict—he can't connect with anyone and finds no place in this London world.
>
> The victim specter (cab driver) versus the father who ordered his torture.
>
> Sammy versus Rosie. Their open marriage versus the strain it puts on their relationship. Their love and need for each other versus how they hurt each other.

The subtle conflict between Sammy and Rosie's lover-to-be Victoria (as when Sammy squirts beer on him).

The squatters versus the land developers.

Sammy's ambivalent relationship with his mistress Annie; he can't keep from talking about Rosie to her.

The ambivalent contradiction of Victoria as a person of color, as a man yet called Victoria. At one point he wears a woman's silly hat in self-parody. He has an affair with Rosie, befriends and aids the father.

The ambiguity of right versus wrong when a neighborhood riot is caused by police shooting an aged woman of color (who raised Victoria), yet being provoked when she threw hot deep fry grease into the face of a policeman when the police burst into her apartment to arrest her son.

The surreal touches of the victim specter, of Victoria's bizarre conduct, of the outlandishly costumed music group that sings "My Girl" outside the trailer where Rosie and Victoria are making love and look directly at the camera, of the grimacing character on the subway versus the reality of a rioting London neighborhood.

Inner city London versus the more genteel suburbs.

Even the music contrasts as when a choral hymn is played during the destruction of the squatter camp.

11. Root, W. (1979). *Writing the Script.* New York: Holt.

12. I use story and plot rather interchangeably. A distinction can be made between them in which story refers to the entire linear narrative while plot is how this narrative is presented and may include such devices as nonlinear flashbacks. Literary theorists may find the distinction useful, but for our purposes I'll use both story and plot to generally mean the same.

13. This model applies to mainstream media storytelling, what is sometimes called the classic Hollywood narrative. It is applicable to the preponderance of what we see on the screens. It is also useful to follow when learning the craft of screenwriting. Even if you later write more experimental and avant-garde works, you'll benefit from mastering this basic media form and the way it works on an audience. Later I'll discuss alternatives to this approach.

14. Andrew, D. (1984). *Concepts in Film Theory.* New York: Oxford University Press, p. 144.

15. Truffaut, F. (1975). *Day for Night* (S. Flores, Trans.). New York: Grove Press.

16. Sometimes from a structure perspective it's necessary to tell the story of a powerful, unsympathetic character through someone else. The story that frames *Citizen Kane* belongs to the reporter whose objective is to discover the meaning of rosebud. *Auntie Mame* is the nephew's story although her extravagant personality overpowers the story.

17. Here's a simple basic story of a film taken from the A. E. Mason historical novel *The Four Feathers* (which has been made into at least three different film and television versions).

England in the 1880s is fighting a war in Egypt and the Sudan. Harry Faversham comes from a family with a proud military heritage of career officers. To please his father, he serves in a regiment with his friends and fellow officers. Even his fiancee is the daughter of a military man. However, Harry would rather settle down to a life of quiet marital bliss than rush off to fight with his regiment. When Harry rejects his marching orders, he is ostracized by his father and other family friends. But the strongest insult is the four white feathers of cowardice given him by his three friends and fiancee. Harry determines to overcome this shame and redeem his honor. (Act I)

Harry steals away alone and incognito to Egypt. Disguised as a mute native, he travels to the battlefield of a British defeat and leads one of his friends, blinded by the sun, across the desert to safety. Trying to rescue his other two captured friends, he is taken prisoner and imprisoned with them. But he leads a prison break that not only rescues his friends but captures the arsenal and helps a British victory. (Act II)

Back in England, his heroic actions have regained his honor. The four feathers are taken back. He is reunited with his fiancee and enjoys the respect and admiration of all. (Act III)

Here's a basic story for a romantic comedy, the original film story *Arthur*.

In this comedy set in contemporary New York City, Arthur, a rich, immature, irresponsible, drunken playboy, is being forced by his family to marry Susan or else be disinherited from a huge fortune that he badly wants. Even though he needs a love he doesn't get from Susan, he agrees to marry in order to get the money. But then he meets poor but exciting Linda and falls in love. (Act I)

Arthur is torn between his options. At times he wants to be with Linda— they are an obvious match. But at other times, having never worked in his life, he can't face the alternative of poverty. Even though Hobson, Arthur's valet and surrogate father, urges Linda to pursue him, Arthur once again gives in to his family and the threats from Susan's violent and ruthless father and agrees to take Susan and the money. Just as they are getting ready to be married, Hobson sickens and dies. (Act II)

Hobson's death wakens Arthur to responsibility and the need to make his own decisions. He backs out of his wedding and chooses Linda and poverty. (CLIMAX) But his grandmother cannot stand the thought of a working class family member so agrees that Arthur can also have the inheritance. He gets both love and money. (Act III)

18. This point is important since it helps you keep your story line on target as well as helps you see that you have a clean and clear story line. However there are definite exceptions, which we'll be discussing later on. Story lines frequently include beats that create a mood, reveal character, develop a theme, or simply give us a breather from the action and suspense. In one sense these are important story elements, but strictly speaking, they may not "advance" the plot. Often a comedy includes segments simply because they are funny, not because they move the story along. Still, unless you have very good reason to do otherwise, ensure that each beat advances the story line.

19. Goldman, W., in T. Sanders and F. L. Mock, p. 18.

20. Arguably we could identify other varieties of story lines to correspond to other types of conflicts, such as socio/cultural thematic story lines. But these are less common and for our purposes would probably confuse things.

21. Rockwell, F. A. (1975). *How to Write Plots That Sell.* Chicago: Contemporary Books.

22. O'Bannon, D., quoted in W. Froug. (1991). *The New Screenwriter Looks at the New Screenwriter.* Los Angeles: Silman-James Press, p. 58.

23. King, V. (1968). *How to Write a Movie in 21 Days.* New York: Harper and Row, p. 61.

24. Field, S. (1982). *Screenplay: The Foundations of Screenwriting.* New York: Delta; and (1984). *The Screenwriter's Workbook.* New York: Dell.

25. Seger, L. (1987). *Making a Good Script Great.* New York: Dodd, Mead.

26. Hauge, M. (1988). *Writing Screenplays That Sell.* New York: McGraw-Hill.

27. King, V. (1986).

28. Pierson, F., interviewed by Holmes, D. C. (September 1986). *Hollywood Scriptwriter,* 385 (76), 4.

29. Mazursky, P., interview in Holmes, D. C. (May 1982). *Hollywood Scriptwriter, 25,* 5.

30. Gelbart, L., quoted in J. Wolff and K. Cox. (1988). *Successful Scriptwriting.* Cincinnati: Writers Digest, p. 121.

31. Froug. (1991).

32. Froug, W. (1992). *Screenwriting Tricks of the Trade.* Los Angeles: Silman-James Press, pp. 61–62.

33. Froug. (1992), p. 63.

34. Froug. (1992), p. 63.

35. Dancyger, K. and Rush, J. (1991). *Alternative Scriptwriting.* Boston: Focal Press.

36. Rockwell. (1975).

37. Vale, E. (1982). *The Technique of Screen and Television Writing.* Englewood Cliffs, NJ: Prentice Hall.

38. Beker, M. (March 1990). Paper given at Screenwriting and the Academy conference, Loyola University, New Orleans.

39. Lucey, P. (August 1987). Paper presented at the University Film and Video Association conference, Loyola Marymount University.

40. Brenner, A. (1987). Talk given at the University Film and Video Association conference, Loyola Marymount University.

41. Dancyger and Rush. (1991).

42. Propp, V. (1970). *Morphology of the Folktale.* Austin: University of Texas Press.

43. Vogler, C. (1991). Interviewed in the videotape *Writing for Hollywood.* Cupertino, CA: Writer's Connection.

CHAPTER 5

Diverse Techniques and Concerns

The writers are the most important single element in this business and we must never let them have any power.

—Irving Thalberg

Here we consider diverse techniques and concerns that don't neatly fit into the chapters on character, structure, scenes, or dialogue. These include:

Title	Openings
Point of attack	Exposition
Preparation	Runners
Forward movement	Credibility
Coincidence	Pace
Tone, Mood, Atmosphere	Big event
Point of view	Ticking clock/Time bomb
Handling objections	Tension relief laugh
Settings	Props
Costumes	Visual elements

Themes   Involving the audience

The active audience

TITLE

Get a *working title* early. Select something that will catch an audience's attention and perhaps has intrinsic appeal. It may be changed by a studio marketing department, but for awhile the script will be known by its working title. Make it striking.

It's been suggested that a film title should be short enough to conveniently fit on a theater marquee. Not a bad idea, but like everything else in this business, there are no rules—think of *Close Encounters of the Third Kind* and *To Wong Foo, Thanks for Everything! Julie Newmar*.

Memorable film titles include: *Adventures in Babysitting, Body Heat, Dances with Wolves, Dr. Strangelove, The Fugitive, The Godfather, Hill Street Blues, Jaws, The Love Boat, Murder, She Wrote, Rebel without a Cause, Repo Man, Robocop, Roots, Sammy and Rosie Get Laid, sex, lies, and videotape, Silence of the Lambs, Star Wars, The Thing, Throw Mama from the Train, 2001, The X-Files*, and *Z*. See what you can come up with.

OPENINGS

The opening is the audience's introduction to the film—location, time period, characters, mood, and tone. It should grab our attention. The opening must also entice the film's "first audience": readers, story editors, producers, and executives. These are people who have mounds of scripts to wade through; the *first ten pages* are crucial to grab and impress them. So keep your opening lean, clean, powerful, and exciting.

The "thrilling grabber opening" is popular with action films; Steven Spielberg and John Woo specialize in it. Think of *Raiders of the Lost Ark* as Indiana Jones enters a hidden Latin American cave to make off with an ancient idol and in the process repeatedly escapes death—from natives, villains, traps, and almost being crushed by a large boulder. In *Indiana Jones and the Temple of Doom* the hero moves from mayhem in an exotic nightclub to a leap from a plane onto a snow-capped mountain while wrapped in a rubber life raft that soon becomes a sled speeding down a slope. *Jurassic Park* opens with a shock as a mysterious creature seizes and kills a workman unloading its crate. These incidents all occur in the first ten or so minutes/pages.

Halloween begins from the point of view of the killer. The audience is looking out from inside a Halloween mask as the killer slashes a girl to death in her upstairs bedroom. We then learn that the killer is the victim's six year old brother! *Sidekicks* opens with a Ninja fight in an exotic temple where a young fighter helps smash the miscreants and rescue the maiden—only to be jarred out of his daydream by the laughter of his classmates. Openings such as these grab our attention and get us involved quickly.

Other stories need time to develop, time to involve us with the characters—their relationships and conflicts. *Arthur* gives us a quieter opening that serves as a fine introduction to the character and situation. The song "In New York City" sets the stage for a romantic comedy. The sound of raucous laughter alerts us that this is a comedy. Arthur and his chauffeured Rolls Royce pick up a hooker—letting us know that Arthur is both rich and dissolute. The comic tone continues as he and his "date" go to a fancy restaurant. The audience likes Arthur and is hooked on finding out what happens to him.

The opening is important in cuing our expectations of the film and thus guiding our response to it. If your film is a comedy, it is important to let us know it early on. The play *A Funny Thing Happened on the Way to the Forum* originally opened with a romantic song, but at the out-of-town tryout, the two-hour farce failed to get the laughs it should have. The opening song was cuing the audience to expect a light romance rather than a comedy. The producers got a new song—"Comedy Tonight"—that cued the audience to expect a comedy, and the laughs came in droves.

POINT OF ATTACK

The point of attack is the point at which the writer chooses to begin the story. Every story is a sort of history, developing over time. Sometimes a writer may want to show us much of that development, as with an historical drama or a biography. At other times the writer wants to show only the most recent part of that history, letting us learn about essential prior events—the *backstory*—through such techniques as exposition dialogue. With any story you make a choice—how much history to show, how much to leave to backstory through exposition.

Films like *Braveheart* and *Indiana Jones and the Last Crusade* show the hero as a child undergoing a significant event, then jump forward to the hero now grown. Other films like *Annie Hall, When Harry Met Sally,* and *Fried Green Tomatoes* trace relationships over a long period of time.

Most films attack the story "in the middle of things," when much has already happened. *Dr. Strangelove* begins with the bombers already at their fail-safe point. In *Jurassic Park,* the dinosaurs are already on the island. In *Silence of the Lambs,* the serial killer has already claimed victims. In *Star Wars,* the empire has already conquered most of the galaxy and is closing in on the rebels, Princess Leia is already on her way for help, and Darth Vader has already discovered where she is and is about to capture her.

Be aware of the "larger story" and backstory, then decide where to attack—that is, begin telling the story.

EXPOSITION

Because most films begin with the story already underway, we need to learn something about certain key events in the past—the backstory—in order for the story to make sense. Similarly, something important may happen offscreen that the audience needs to know about. *Exposition* is the technique for presenting this material (as well as the term used to describe the material presented).

Effectively handling exposition is a thorny challenge. How to provide exposition without seeming awkward and obvious, breaking the continuity of the story, or losing audience interest?

Exposition is most commonly given in dialogue because this is the easiest way to communicate information. Other ways are through a flashback, a narrator, or even a title ("A long time ago in a galaxy far away . . ."), but most exposition is revealed through dialogue between characters—the challenge is to do it as smoothly as possible. The audience should not be aware of being spoonfed information. Here are some suggestions for writing exposition.

Let's begin by looking at a *poor* way to handle exposition—with results that are awkward, obvious, and dull. Consider this classic bad example: the "well-made play" of the late nineteenth century. Such a play might open with a maid and a butler setting the table for a formal family dinner. While laying out the silverware, they gossip together—and thereby inform us about everything we need to know up to this point. "Isn't it exciting about Master Harry returning after ten years lost in India?" "Yes, but what will this mean for his half brother, Lord Paddington, who inherited all when the old lord, Harry's father, died?" "And what about Lady Marion? She was Harry's fiancee, but thinking him lost is now betrothed to Sir Marlowe!" "Yes, and . . . ." And so it goes, piling exposition atop exposition until the table is set and they have said it all. The servents then leave and the family enters, and we watch the characters we have just learned about.

Such exposition is laughable today. Or is it? Do we detect the writer giving us exposition when in a phone conversation the hero lays out his problems while ostensibly asking a friend for help? Or when two characters chat, and blatantly tell us all about themselves and their situation? Or when a TV news program informs us of a major plot development (as when we learn some details of the killing at the beginning of *The Fugitive*)?

A giveaway to flagrant exposition is when the audience is being given information which the characters already know. Why rehash it again if they already know it? Avoid having one character tell another what they both already know; it seems phony to us.

How, then does the writer handle exposition? How can it be made as natural and unobtrusive as possible?

Present Exposition Emotionally.   One unobtrusive way of introducing exposition is to place it within an emotional situation. A couple may be arguing—"Your mother–!" "But if you hadn't–!" We become caught up in the emotion of the exchange while being given necessary information.

If exposition is to come out in dialogue, it is more effective if something else—such as emotional character interaction—is going at the same time. In *Jaws*, the Captain tells his companions a long story about the shark-frenzy carnage during the sinking of the cruiser Indianapolis, in World War II. Thereby heightening the tension since they are out seeking the monster shark.

Present Exposition Naturally.   Although exposition often comes near the beginning in order to give us the backstory quickly and move on with the story, it is best not to give it all in one obvious dose. It is more effective if it is gradually revealed over the length of the story, and at those times *when it is needed.* This often turns out to be the most dramatic time for us to learn something. It's after he falls in love that we might most dramatically learn that a man is impotent. In *Butch Cassidy and the Sundance Kid,* we learn that the Kid can't swim just before he must leap off a cliff into a river. And it is when Butch is facing a gunfight that we learn he's never shot at a man before.

Try to present exposition in a way that seems natural to the situation at the time. This is often when you are revealing something the character has been trying to learn. Or something they really must learn at that moment. In *Chinatown* we realize that a young girl is both the sister and daughter of the female lead character (as a result of an incestuous relationship with her father). It is a powerful, emotional moment as Gittes hears the woman repeating: "my sister . . . my daughter . . . my sister . . . my daughter. . . ."

Present Exposition Appropriately.   Exposition will seem appropriate if we're being told something we want to know, when we, the audience, want to know it. The mental hospital ward in *One Flew Over the Cuckoo's Nest* is an unappealing place, but McMurphy is overjoyed to be there. We want to know why. When we are told that for him it is an alternative to jail, it doesn't seem like blatant exposition.

Some screenplays are based on a horrible past event that is affecting the present. We want to know what the past event was, but usually learn it only later in the film. A typical pattern is the stranger who comes into a town that is trying to cover up something. In *High Plains Drifter,* it's a vicious whipping that took place years before. In *Bad Day at Black Rock,* it's the town's burning out of a Japanese family during the Second World War.

Exposition Examples

Citizen Kane begins with an eight-and-a-half-minute newsreel that gives us information about Charles Foster Kane. We see his palatial home Xanadu, his funeral, shots of his early life, different opinions about the man ("Communist," "Fascist"), his marriage, a love affair, his political life. The reporter's search for information serves as the motivation for others to talk about Kane.

Patton also uses a newsreel to give us information about Patton's background and to cover events that happen offscreen. We receive further exposition from a German captain whose job is to analyze Patton for High Command headquarters.

Annie Hall begins with Alvy Singer talking directly to the camera—and us—about his life and the film; he sets up the problem of his relationship with Annie.

When first meeting Jules and Vincent in *Pulp Fiction,* we get dialogue exposition about a man who was thrown out of a window, seemingly because he got fresh with the boss's wife. Then we learn that the same could happen to Vincent if he isn't careful—the boss has asked him to take the wife out.

PREPARATION

In *Deliverance,* Ed is aiming an arrow at the mountain man who has been shooting at them. Suddenly he begins to shake with buck fever, a nervous response when about to kill. This creates a tense moment, but is it legitimate to bring in buck fever at a life or death moment like this?

In *Duel,* the hero is escaping from a demonic tractor trailer bent on his destruction. He finally reaches an upgrade where he thinks he can outrace the slower truck, only to have his car overheat and slow to fifteen miles an hour. Meanwhile, the truck gains on him. Suspenseful, yes; but isn't there something fraudulently coincidental about his losing radiator water at this crucial moment?

In *The African Queen,* just as the German fort officer lines up Charlie in his rifle scope, the sun glares in his eyes and he has to pull away; the next moment the *Queen* is around the bend to safety. Isn't this too contrived a way to get your hero out of a crisis?

If that were all there was to it, we might well complain about convenience, coincidence, and contrivance in these examples. But in each of these films the events are acceptable because we have been prepared for them.

In *Deliverance,* there is an early explanation of buck fever. Later we see Ed sighting on a deer; but he starts shaking and the shot goes awry. We fully accept his later action when facing the mountain man as probable because of this earlier experience.

Early in *Duel,* David stops at a gas station and is told he needs a radiator hose. He ignores the advice, thinking it is just a sales pitch. At a second station he asks the attendant to check the hose, then rushes off before she has time to do so. It is no surprise when the hose ruptures at a crucial moment—we have been prepared for it.

In *The African Queen,* Rosie mentions that their plan may succeed because the sun will be in the soldiers' eyes. She later repeats this. When it happens, we have been prepared to accept it as probable.

Preparation sets things up by raising events from the merely possible to the probable—and sometimes to the inevitable. It prepares us for certain actions or events, or for the appearance of a special object or person in the story. Later occurrences no longer seem overly coincidental or contrived. Even the most casual reference can unconsciously prepare us for the ready acceptance of a later development. Typically, it is the key beats—important plot twists and developments—that are set up through preparation.

One form of preparation is the *plant*—an object, person or bit of information established in order to be used credibly later. To paraphrase Chekhov, if you're going to use a gun in Act III, show it in Act I.

Another form of preparation is *foreshadowing*. Foreshadowing resembles suspense. Suspense foreshadows—the audience is cued to expect something, and anticipates the payoff. Preparation foreshadowing is somewhat different because the intent isn't so much to have the audience anticipate the payoff as to make the payoff credible. Suspense foreshadowing cues a payoff; preparation foreshadowing sanctions one.[1]

Hitchcock uses both forms of foreshadowing to increase suspense in the following scene from *The Birds*. An earlier assault by sparrows through the chimney has left the room in shambles. We see the mother picking up pieces of broken crockery while conversing. Merely some piece of business to keep her involved while the scene dialogue goes on? Not likely! We are being set up.

Later the mother visits a neighbor. Getting no reply to her knock, she enters the house. There are pieces of broken crockery everywhere. Our suspense quotient takes a leap. We know what this means! It is followed by her finding the neighbor killed by the birds—the payoff.

There's a similar mixture in *Silence of the Lambs*. When we see Hannibal Lecter looking at the doctor's pen, this might be merely preparation foreshadowing, although if we are sharp enough to be cued by it, it can also create suspense. When the doctor can't find the pen, we realize Lecter has managed to steal it—the preparation foreshadowing is paid off and additional suspense is created: how will he use it? Later we see him use it; the suspense foreshadowing is paid off.

The following examples of preparation, plants, and foreshadowing illustrate the technique and indicate its importance.

In *Tootsie*, the producer announces that due to technical difficulties tomorrow's show must be done live. This sets up the live broadcast in which Dorothy reveals she is really Michael. The problem was set up by the videotape technician's spilling soda on the tape, which was in turn set up by an earlier shot of him drinking soda while the tape rolls.

In *Arthur*, Susan's father tells how once when he was eleven years old he killed an intruder with a kitchen knife. Later, when he is upset because Arthur is backing out of the wedding, the father suddenly grabs a knife. Because of the earlier story, both Arthur and the audience expect the worst.

In *Harold and Maude*, Maude mentions a couple of times that eighty years is old enough. Once she says, "It'll all be over by Saturday." It is never clear what she is alluding to. When she says she's taken the suicide pills, we are astonished—yet we accept it. We've been well prepared.

In *Jaws*, the shark is finally destroyed by exploding the compressed-air diving tanks in its mouth. We've been prepared for this because earlier the professor had criticized the police chief for filling the tanks too full, warning him they could explode. Later, when they're about to tow the shark, the tanks shake and the chief rushes to hold them, underscoring the danger.

In *The Third Man,* Anna tells Holly that the cat liked only Harry. Later, outside, at night, we see the cat go up to a darkened doorway and rub against the shoes and pants leg of a mysterious figure hiding there. Ah-hah!

At the beginning of *Raiders of the Lost Ark,* Indiana hops into a plane only to be unnerved by a snake he finds there; he says he hates snakes. Later he must climb down into a snake pit.

At one point in *One Flew Over the Cuckoo's Nest,* McMurphy says he will escape and tries to lift a heavy sink from the floor. He can't. The Chief is watching him. At the film's end, the Chief exerts his strength, rips up the sink, throws it through the barred window and escapes. (And a marvelous moment it is.)

While we don't learn the meaning of "Rosebud" until the end of *Citizen Kane,* we've been prepared for the revelation both by the snow scene paperweight Kane is holding when he dies and by scenes showing young Kane playing with the sled in the snow.

Early in *Rosemary's Baby,* we see her playing Scrabble with her husband. At the time this seems to be merely some background business. Later, when she tries to figure out an anagram, she gets out the Scrabble game and arranges the letters until she sees they spell out ALL OF THEM WITCHES. Another bit of preparation occurs when the witches give Rosemary a charm with a distinctive smell. Later at her obstetrician's office, the nurse comments on how the obstetrician often wears some aftershave lotion with the same smell. Rosemary realizes he is one of them.

In *The Shawshank Redemption,* we don't think too much of Andy's requesting a rock hammer to carve with, or a pin-up poster to hang on the wall. Only near the end do we learn that he used the poster to cover the hole he knocked out with the hammer in order to escape.

After Gittes and Evelyn have made love (in *Chinatown*), he mentions meeting her father. She crosses her arms over her naked breasts, subtly preparing us for the later incest revelation.

Don't make your preparation too obvious. There's a subtle, unconscious quality to making the preparation work. Let it merge with another plot development or seem like incidental business while something else is happening in the scene.

RUNNERS

A runner is a bit of action, dialogue, or perhaps a visual or sound that recurs throughout the story. It's not usually part of a story line, but rather some additional zest added for interest. A runner (there can be more than one) is typically "run" three or more times over the course of the film.

In *The Hunt for Red October,* Ryan is bothered by turbulence when flying. We learn this in the beginning, it comes up again when he rides a navy plane, and a third time when on a helicopter. In *Clerks,* various customers and friends who come into the store comment that Dante smells like shoe polish. Periodic cutting to Brenda's estranged husband sitting in the car watching the goings-on at the gas station/restaurant and making wry comments is a runner in *Bagdad Cafe*, as is the periodic cutting to a New York disc jockey making comments about the gang's progress in *The Warriors*.

Runners shouldn't be confused with secondary story lines; runners aren't as substantial, nor do they have a story line pattern. You don't actually need a runner; most films don't (they are more common in television). If you do use runners, don't overdo it. One or two, used about three times each, is appropriate.

FORWARD MOVEMENT

Forward movement is the audience's subjective impression that the film is moving along without dragging. It is not a matter of short scenes, fast cutting, or terse lines. Forward movement depends on our being suspensefully involved. If the audience is continually engrossed as the character moves from one crisis to another, the film will appear to be moving briskly. Keeping us involved in crises keeps the forward movement going.

CREDIBILITY

A film must be credible within the parameters of its narrative domain, however unusual or surreal that filmic reality may be.

Credibility depends to a large extent on the characters' behavior—who they are, what motivates them and the circumstances and relationships to which they respond. It also refers to real-seeming characters, events, settings, and the cultural world of the story. A film that takes place in New York's garment district should capture the feel of the city and that particular milieu. Dining at the Plaza should reflect that hotel's ambiance. Mardi Gras on Bourbon Street has an atmosphere all its own. Extensive research can help achieve a believable setting.

But credibility doesn't necessarily mean authenticity. Credibility is a sense the audience has and may not reflect actuality. It is more important to be credible than authentic, better to convey a sense of verisimilitude and maintain the story's dramatic flow than to conform to history and reality. It's your dramatic license—as long as it works.

Patton doesn't give us an accurate picture of the general. *The Verdict* is full of legal errors. Many of the events in *Chariots of Fire* simply didn't happen that way. Yet these films still work.

This only works to a point. Caught up in the tense action of *Die Hard 2*, we may overlook some of its inaccuracies, but the film has become infamous for the number of incredible incidents. For example, the passenger's having a stun gun on the plane. It's illegal to take them on board; she would have been stopped at the security check.

Halloween opens with a young boy killing his sister. He then spends the next dozen or so years in a catatonic state. Then he escapes from a mental hospital, steals a car, and drives back to the town he left. How did he learn to drive?

Because a false note will quickly turn off an audience, a sense of credibility is essential to a script. Be sure that we believe your characters would act the way they do.

COINCIDENCE, CONVENIENCE, AND THE CONTRIVED

Using incidents that seem coincidental, convenient or contrived strains credibility and makes the audience feel manipulated. The audience is inclined not to believe these things.

Coincidences happen by chance rather than logical plotting. They include overheard conversations, chance sightings, and items like wallets forgotten or found. A man trapped behind enemy lines who needs a parachute runs into a building that just happens to be a parachute factory. Such a development is too convenient for the character—and the writer. They ring false.

One type of blatant convenience is the *idiot plot* in which the plot develops as a result of a character's doing something completely stupid and idiotic. Think of all those B-movie thrillers in which the stereotypical ingenue is told to "stay here where it's safe, don't move," so naturally she goes off to investigate and is captured by the villain. In *Bird on a Wire*, in spite of nearly being killed everywhere they go, Mary Ann sneaks a phone call that gives the killers their next location. Later apologies don't excuse her inanity. The heroine in *Hard Target* is told to go call the sheriff; instead she follows the hero, thereby enabling the villain to make her a hostage for the final showdown.

There are times when coincidences are more acceptable. Acts of God such as earthquakes, hurricanes, or forest fires are generally acceptable ways of getting your hero into trouble. What we don't want to see is one of these used to get him out of it. He needs to do that for himself. We just don't want you to make things easy for your protagonist.

Coincidences are more acceptable if we are properly prepared for them or if we are so engrossed in the story that we ignore the improbabilities. This happens with the typical last-minute rescue. At the end of *The Day of the Jackal*, the police inspector bursts in just in time to save de Gaulle. The entire film has built to this climactic moment, and the coincidence of the split-second timing doesn't bother us. We accept the established dramatic convention of the last-minute rescue.

PACE

Pace refers to the rhythm and tempo of the film.[2] It comes from the lengths of scenes and of dialogue within scenes. It comes from the action on the screen, from camera movement, and from editing. Fast pacing comes from short scenes, from beginning and ending scenes abruptly (even in mid-sentence), and from bringing us into scenes as late as possible. Slow rhythms develop conversely. Music can do a great deal to set the pace.

Consider using *breather* or *reflection scenes* between moments of intense action. Such scenes give us time to process what we've just experienced. Quiet moments make the exciting ones all the more effective.

Music is often an important part of breather scenes. The bicycle-riding scene in *Butch Cassidy and the Sundance Kid* unfolds to the accompaniment of "Raindrops Keep Falling on Your Head." Or the song break in *Sammy and Rosie Get Laid* in which a group performs "My Girl" outside the trailer as Rosie and Victoria make love. *Bagdad Cafe* makes extensive use of musical breaks—music accompanies shots of trucks on the highway, the wind sweeping the landscape, and minor characters throwing boomerangs.

Horror films need breaks since much of their action is at a high tension level. A tense encounter with threatening creatures is often followed by a break moment.

TONE, MOOD, ATMOSPHERE

Tone, mood, and atmosphere form the emotional climate of the film. It's what we mean when we apply to a film such adjectives as lively, sparkling, violent, erotic, racy, florid, warm, obscure, taut, crude, lyrical, delicate, heavy, somber, sordid, mysterious, scary, forceful, bright, cynical, and campy.

While many elements contribute to the overall tone of the film, it is set as much as anything else by the screenwriter's attitude.

It is important to decide how much *humor* you want in the script. Even serious films often contain a good deal of humor. (During a showing of *Witness*, I counted over thirty loud audience laughs in what is a rather serious action/romance.)

Many recent action/adventure films (*Die Hard, Lethal Weapon, 48 Hours, Beverly Hills Cop*) mix humor with action. The *Star Wars* and *Indiana Jones* films owe much of their success to characters who don't take themselves too seriously. Television, too, has had a number of serio-comic heroes: Jim Rockford, Columbo, McCloud, McMillan, and the Mavericks.

Atmosphere is the look of the film. The sweeping panorama of many westerns. The lushness of *Out of Africa*. The comic book, 1930s look of *Dick Tracy*. Or the postmodern techno-world of *Blade Runner*.

THE MOMENT, THE BIG EVENT

These are the events that stay with us. They are the memorable moments of inspiration and uplift, of the "yeah, yeah!" response, or of something unforgettably funny.

They are moments like the shower scene in *Psycho*, Harold's exclamation "What!" when he realizes Maude has taken the suicide pill; sneezing on the cocaine incident in *Annie Hall;* standing-on-the-desk scene in *Dead Poets Society;* the overconfident swordsman in *Raiders of the Lost Ark* (who arrogantly shows off his skill only to have Indiana Jones draw his gun and shoot); "play it again, Sam" in *Casablanca;* and the end of *Sweet Movie* when we go from newsreel footage of German soldiers in WW II unearthing the Polish officer bodies from the Katyn Forest Massacre to the scene of the dead boys lying on the river bank. They begin to rouse and sit up. The picture dissolves from black and white to color. A train goes by in the distance. Freeze frame.

These are only a small sampling. We can all recall such moments from films we've enjoyed. If you can place such a moment in your film, it will be richer for it.

POINT OF VIEW

Point of view describes the perspective(s) from which the story unfolds. Choosing a point of view is an important part of telling the story.

There are a number of different ways to speak of point of view. There is the filmic view of the recording camera—the unseen, unacknowledged, outside observer of the action that can take on the perspective of a character through close-ups, eyeline matching, and subjective and near-subjective shots. More germane to the screenwriter, however, are *narrative points of view*.

One possibility is to have the story told directly by a *narrator*. This character is typically identified in the beginning by a voice-over introduction. In the opening of *Annie Hall*, Alvy addresses us directly and in person, and his voice-over recurs throughout the film. The narrator of *Stand By Me* initially greets us as an adult, although the film consists primarily of his childhood experiences. At the end of the movie we again meet him as an adult.

The Big Red One is narrated by one of the platoon soldiers. Author Jean Shepherd narrates *A Christmas Story* in which the protagonist is himself as a boy. *The Shawshank Redemption* is narrated by one of the prisoners who befriended the hero.

While it is rare for a film to have an outside narrator (the literary omniscient point of view) this technique is used successfully in *Tom Jones*.

A narrator can provide continuity, linking a series of events that otherwise might lack cohesiveness. A narrating character may also give the story the intimacy of personal biography.

Most films dispense with a narrator altogether, recording the action from a third-person point of view. But how you use this can vary widely.

An *objective* narrative point of view shifts the focus—both visually and psychologically—from one character to another to another. No single perspective dominates.

A *subjective* narrative point of view focuses on a single character. Events happen from the character's perspective. We may be restricted to knowing only what happens in the presence or immediate surroundings of the character.[3]

As you write, decide to what extent the story will focus on the protagonist. Will he or she be in most of the scenes? Will everything happen around him or her or will events occur at which the protagonist is not present? How strongly do you want the audience to identify with the character? Will the attitude of the protagonist guide the scenes in which he or she appears?

Benjamin's perspective dominates the narrative of *The Graduate*, making it a narratively subjective film—almost all the action occurs in his presence. With most films, however, it is a matter of degree; while many scenes are structured around the protagonist, still others may be focused on the villain or another character. There are likely to be shifting narrative points of view as the film develops. Even within a scene or sequence the focus between characters will shift.

Witness is John Book's story, but Rachel plays a vital part and we frequently share her point of view, especially before John enters the picture. At other times we are closer to the boy Samuel's point of view. At the end, some scenes are from the villains' points of view.

While Schindler's perspective dominates *Schindler's List,* we frequently follow events that occur when he's not around.

Rashomon is the classic experiment in narrative points of view. It tells the story of a rape and homicide (or possibly suicide) as perceived by four persons. Three are participants: a notorious bandit accused of the crimes, the dead Samurai warrior husband (as told through a priestess medium), and the victimized wife. The fourth is a woodcutter who alleges to have witnessed the event—although his version, too, is questionable. While none disputes the basic facts—the violation of the woman and death of the husband—each has a different version of how it happened. These are shown in flashbacks as each gives testimony before an (unseen) police magistrate. The episode is told and shown four times, once from each character's perspective.

In part your material will prescribe the degree of subjectivity or objectivity in narrative point of view, but it is also up to you—to what degree should the story and its scenes center around the protagonist?

TICKING CLOCK, TIME BOMB

A useful device for increasing suspense is time pressure. Something is going to happen in five days, or three hours, or. . . . If your hero is struggling to get over the mountains, then increase the pressure by predicting a snowstorm. If he doesn't get to the church by noon, she will marry instead someone she doesn't love (*The Graduate*). The clock is ticking, time is running out, and we are in suspense.

In *Goldfinger,* a nuclear device is counting down; it's finally stopped with seconds to spare. *Die Hard 2* created time pressure by putting planes in the air that are running out of fuel. The pressure at the end of *Star Wars* is the Death Star preparing to blow up the rebel planet. *The Man Who Knew Too Much* builds to a climax involving a villain who is about to shoot when the cymbals clash. We anxiously watch the cymbalist readying himself.

The ticking time bomb is activated in *Star Trek IV* when we learn that the whale has been removed to a sea where there is whaling activity. In *Outbreak,* time pressure depends on the hero's locating the immune host in time to prepare a vaccine. If he doesn't, the town will be destroyed and the epidemic will spread out of control.

The pressure in *No Way Out* comes from the suspense as the computer reconstructs the out-of-focus face on the photograph. With each pass, the screen inexorably reveals more and more clearly the face that the audience—and the protagonist—knows will identify him as the prime suspect.

The ticking clock or time bomb is a useful way to escalate tension in your script.

INFREQUENTLY USED TECHNIQUES

Raise the Objection and Shoot It Down

Also referred to as *pointing an arrow,* this technique can help solve a credibility problem. If there is something in the script that isn't credible yet it is needed in the story, what do you do? One solution is to anticipate the objection of the audience, raise it, and shoot it down. Even if the explanation is unconvincing, acknowledging the problem works to disarm the audience.

In the ABC Children's Special *The Ransom of Red Chief,* two bumbling con men kidnap a boy and hold him for ransom. But it turns out he's a terror who enjoys playing Indian and tormenting his captors. At one point, one of the kidnappers goes to town. He returns to find his harried partner tied to a tree. But the boy is still there! Why didn't he escape back to town? For one thing, we know that he's not happy at home. But that might not be reason enough. The writers deal with it by having the boy say that an Indian never leaves his campsite. This is enough to disarm possible audience objections.

We've already mentioned one problem in *Halloween:* the young boy who spent fifteen years in an asylum in a catatonic state couldn't have learned to drive a car the 150 miles back to his home town. This objection is raised when one doctor tells another that the character couldn't drive a car, then shot down when the other sarcastically responds that the kid did a pretty good job last night, maybe someone at the asylum taught him.

In *Star Trek IV,* Scotty—back in the twentieth century—gives a plastics company the formula for transparent aluminum. Come on! How can the future present something to the past? Someone asks him this very question. Didn't they interfere? Scotty's disarming reply is "Maybe he invented it."

The Tension Release Laugh

The tension release laugh is another infrequently used technique, but useful when you may want the audience to come down emotionally in order to be ready for the next crisis. In such cases, you need a quick way to discharge audience tension. Occasionally an event embarrasses the audience and causes discomfort, or something embarrasses a character with whom we empathize, or something is so close to being hokey that one laugh or comment in the audience could push it over the line for everybody.

For example, at the end of *Fingers* there's a bloody killing in which the hero shoots out another character's eye—a difficult scene to watch. It is followed by the final shot of the film, which shows the hero seated naked and distraught at the window of his apartment. He slowly turns to look directly at the camera. The juxtaposition of the previous high tension scene with this one with his nakedness—an unusual choice—and his direct look at the camera—which borders on being too melodramatic—produced a large laugh from audiences both times I saw the film. They were releasing their tensions, but the laugh detracted from the intended serious impact of the film's ending shot.

If a moment in your script risks this response, consider consciously including some slight, appropriate comic touch just after such an awkward, intense, or embarrassing moment in order to give the audience something to laugh at and drain away their tension. The audience will then laugh with the film—not at it.

In *Scarface*, a big boss kills two guys; what about the third one? The boss looks at him. We (and he) wait anxiously. "Offer him a job," says the boss, thus setting up the tension release laugh.

SETTINGS

The camera photographs places—the environment—as well as characters. The setting of a film is more than just a stage for the actors—it is the *arena* for your action, and an interactive element of the story.

Settings express meaning. Regions have characteristic modes of architecture. Cities, neighborhoods, and houses say something about the people who live in them. The rooms we inhabit, the way we decorate and arrange them, as well as our clothes and adornments, reflect who we are. So it is with film settings.

Many films are intimately connected with a setting. *Roma* reflects that city. *Amarcord* is about remembered life in an Italian village. *Taxi Driver, Mean Streets,* and *Manhattan* are New York City films in style and atmosphere. *The Warriors* presents a New York City setting, but it is a special, "make-believe" New York. *Annie Hall* humorously contrasts the New York City that Woody Allen loves with the Los Angeles he hates. Westerns reflect the wide open spaces of the frontier, Tara and the old South live perpetually in *Gone With the Wind*.

Decide early on how big a part the setting will play. In some films it functions almost as another character.

Settings can provide stimulus for character action and interaction. Talky, character stories such as *The Big Chill, The Breakfast Club,* and *Clerks* put their characters in an enclosed space—one that invites conversation, interaction, and involvement.

Settings help define the style of a film. Think of the futuristic design of *Blade Runner* or the gothic architecture of *Batman*.

Mood, tone, and atmosphere are all influenced by the environmental context. The beauty of nature, of eternal change and growth, highlights the beauty of old age in *On Golden Pond* and *Strangers in Good Company*. The steamy, South Florida atmosphere of *Body Heat* becomes a strong sexual metaphor for the passion of that film. The *Cheers* saloon is a refuge for its denizens, a place "where everybody knows your name."

Decide the *scope* of the setting. Some subjects need a grand-scale arena: *War and Peace, Lawrence of Arabia, Dr. Zhivago, Braveheart.* Other stories need more intimate settings to throw characters together (*Reservoir Dogs*). But avoid writing a script that reads like a theatrical play, with all the action in enclosed settings. The mobile camera can go out and film the world. Use this freedom.

Alternate interiors and exteriors, open and closed settings, lush and sparse environments. Find unique locales in which to play scenes. A strongly interactive dialogue scene between three friends in *Husbands* takes place in the toilet stall of a public lounge during a drinking party. *The Third Man* sets one of its notable scenes in a large ferris wheel compartment high in the air; the exciting climax occurs in the sewers of Vienna. *Five Easy Pieces* contrasts a pop-culture Los Angeles setting of mobile homes and traffic jams to a cultured, isolated family home in the Pacific Northwest with its lush foliage, classical music, and illusory detachment from the outside world.

We've seen certain settings so often that you might consider doing something different with them. Such familiar scenes include using the phone, and being in offices, apartments, bars, and restaurants.

Consider the deli scene in which Annie Hall orders pastrami on white with mayonnaise— a New York no-no. Or the outdoor Los Angeles health-food restaurant where Alvy Singer has to struggle with alfalfa sprouts and a plate of mashed yeast. In *The Producers,* Zero Mostel takes his accountant to lunch—at a hot dog stand. *When Harry Met Sally* stages Sally's orgasm imitation in a restaurant. *Pulp Fiction* puts a scene in Jackrabbit Slim's, a 1950s diner where the booths are made out of cut up 1950s cars and the waiters look like replicas of 1950s movie icons.

Exercises

Pick a scene from your story and describe the contents in minute detail. Include locale, sounds, lighting, even temperature, but no dialogue or action. What's the atmosphere? the tone? the scope of the location? Focus on detail. Then, how do these elements contribute to (contrast with, counterpoint) the action and dialogue?

Be in a place and observe what's going on. Observe the details, then describe them. Leave and see what you can recall. Describe your responses—how the place made you feel.

Attune yourself to your surroundings. Contact them, listen to them, get their meanings. If your room were viewed by a stranger, what impression would that stranger have of you?

Observe some object without comment or note-taking. Take some time. Then leave (or tune out the scene), and write down all the details you can recall. Then return and see what new elements you can observe.

Look at familiar surroundings—your living quarters, street, town, work arena—as if for the first time. Become aware of those things that through familiarization and habituation you no longer notice.

Notice a setting of any sort, anywhere. What sort of scene could be played out here? With what characters? What would be likely to happen? Think of these things again, but this time work against the obvious. See what the contrast might contribute.

PROPS

Properties—objects that are handled and carried by the characters—can, like adjectives, individualize and personalize your characters or they can become important elements in their own right. Consider these examples: Captain Queeg revealing his instability by nervously clicking the steel balls in *The Caine Mutiny;* the laser sabers in *Star Wars;* the turn-on metal spheres in *Sleeper;* the jigsaw puzzle in *Citizen Kane* that becomes an expression of the ennui and banality of their lives. Guns assume special significance in many westerns; as they do in *Yojimbo,* which takes place just when guns were first being introduced to Japan. The sword was still the honorable weapon, but the gun was devastating.

COSTUMES

Costumes say something about the characters who wear them—about their social status, their taste, their sophistication. Costumes should fit the characters, the culture and historical period. Chaplin's little tramp outfit beautifully reflects poverty and alienation, yet also gives a sense of pseudo-aristocracy to the character.

In *A Clockwork Orange,* Alex and his droogs dress in white, as do the Teutonic knights in *Alexander Nevsky* and the storm troopers in *Star Wars* (in contrast to the black outfit of archvillain Darth Vader). White is the color worn to the murdered writer's funeral by his woman friend in *The Player;* it makes her stand out.

Odd Job, the villain's henchman in *Goldfinger,* wears formal dress and a bowler hat that is also a weapon. Mr. Wolf is dressed in black tie when he appears in *Pulp Fiction* to help clean up a bloody murder scene. In *Smoke,* a woman wears a black eye patch.

Mirrored sunglasses are an important symbol of anonymity, separation and authority in *Cool Hand Luke.* The silent comic Harold Lloyd never really became effective until he hit on the idea of wearing glasses with no lenses. In *Harold and Maude,* Harold dresses formally for most of the film, but the more he gets involved with Maude, the more he appears in sweaters.

Except for the framing scenes, *Schindler's List* is shot in black and white. But at one point we see a young child dressed in a muted-red coat. When we later see her body being disposed of, we identify her by the muted-red coat.

In Zeffirelli's *Romeo and Juliet,* the Capulets are dressed in reds, yellows, and oranges—loud, aggressive colors that reflect the family's position. In contrast, the Montagues—a more established, perhaps declining, family—appear in blues, deep greens, and purples. Color reflects the character of each family and helps identify them in the duel scenes.

The writer is not often concerned with costumes; the director and the producer, working with the costume designer, do that. However, if there's a particular effect you want, be sure to describe it in the script.

OTHER VISUAL ELEMENTS

What is true of costume similarly holds for any unusual color, lighting, or makeup effects that are intrinsic to the script. (In *A Clockwork Orange,* Alex wears a single long eyelash.)

Time of day can be important. Night is the realm of terror in horror pictures, the time when vampires and other creatures wander—the children of the night. In other films it may be a moment of safety: "They never attack at night." Time of day and time of year have connotations. Each season has its own mood. Holidays can provide a special atmosphere, as many Christmas-season films attest. Nor should a writer forget to use temperature and weather conditions where they are appropriate.

Don't over-describe. Avoid unwarranted forays into the domains of director, director of photography, producer, production designer, and costume designer; but, if there is a specific effect that is important to the script, express it.

THEMES

We define ourselves and our society by our myths and stories. The media are the great myth-making, story-telling machines of today. They tell us who we are and what others around us are like. Some of these messages are ideological and largely unconscious. They pervade our screenplays because that's how we have been taught to see the world. Other messages are deliberately placed into stories because they represent something we want to say about the human condition. A theme is best expressed as an intrinsic part of the story rather than as a message laid on top of it. Let the theme come out of the situation, conflict, setting, and characters; otherwise the film can become preachy, pretentious, or propagandistic. Let the theme be expressed by the story rather than the other way around. We are—above all—storytellers.

Themes generally express universals such as love, courage, greed, freedom, death, the dehumanization of modern society, the corruption of power and ambition, and the nature of our responsibilities to others. Themes are often summarized with pat statements (often clichés) such as love conquers all, we are all brothers and sisters, crime doesn't pay, war is hell. Sometimes a similar but more sophisticated statement becomes the movie's slogan, as in *Platoon*'s: "The first casualty of war is innocence."

A film can be entertaining while lacking a strong theme, but it will never be considered "great." Most academy award–winning pictures have had strong themes.

Because they are such a part of our society and our media, possibly harmful ideological messages can quietly infiltrate a script. The continuing exploitation of sex and violence is a prime example. And even though we are becoming more conscious of such, negative stereotypes persist regarding minorities, genders, the elderly, the disabled, foreigners, and anyone else who differs from us.

Often filmic messages are conveyed through symbols, metaphors and archetypes. The sleigh in *Citizen Kane* may represent his lost innocence. The huge flag at the beginning of *Patton* announces his hyperpatriotic views. In *The Grapes of Wrath*, the Joads leave their dust-bowl farm for California in a rickety old truck that totters precariously down the road, beautifully symbolizing the uncertain condition of the family.

The cat is a common symbol of evil. In several James Bond movies the arch villains have a pet cat. In *Viva Zapata!*, Zapata's horse is emblematic of his leadership.

In *Shane*, the dog leaves the room when the villain enters. There seems to be an extended dog metaphor in *Yojimbo*, reflecting the dog-eat-dog world of the film. Dogs bark intermittently on the sound track. In one scene a dog runs by, holding a human hand in its mouth. There are frequent references to dogs in the dialogue: "the smell of blood brings the hungry dogs"; "not even a dog fight" describes a peaceful moment; "lucky dog" characterizes an escaped enemy.

Music takes on a symbolic aspect in *A Clockwork Orange* when the central character is aversively conditioned to Beethoven's Ninth Symphony. It is his singing of "Singing in the Rain" that identifies him as one of the marauders. The tuba in *Mr. Deeds Goes to Town* is linked to goodness, integrity and honest rural values.

The cryptic neon sign in *Blow-Up* suggests the elusive truth that eludes Thomas. Chinatown is a symbol of all that is corrupt, unfathomable and frustrating: "Forget it, Jake, it's Chinatown."

INVOLVING THE AUDIENCE

A film does not unfold solely on the screen; it is simultaneously and interactively taking place in the minds of the viewers. The excitement and emotion of a scene needs to be felt by the audience—not just by the characters on the screen.

This is especially apparent when characters are expressing emotions that we can't empathize with. We recognize what they are supposedly going through, but we don't feel that their emotions are justified. We find this unpleasant and overly melodramatic. We need more than mere recognition of a character's emotion, we need *involvement* with it.

Imagine a character feeling an emotion that is painful to the point of tears. If the character is overreacting and the tears are gushing while we are unmoved, we'll find it excessive and be put off. Better for the character to fight back those tears, and let the *audience* feel it first.

If there's a principle regarding the expression of heavy emotion, it's undoubtedly the caution: don't overdo it. It's better to *underplay* than overplay. Avoid pontificating. Express relevant messages subtly, not overtly.

Another way to involve the audience is to make sure they know what's going on. Caught up in the flow of writing, it's easy to forget that you may know something that you haven't communicated to the audience. They know only what you show them or tell them. A script that begins with a description of "an assassin cleaning his rifle," may not be read that way by an audience who simply sees a man cleaning a gun. How do we know he's an assassin? Do we need to know at this point? If so, make it clear.

This problem is the *COIK fallacy*—Clear Only If Known. With your privileged knowledge of the story and its developments, you will know how to read a scene. Be sure the audience does as well. Keep a running check on whether or not the audience will understand what is happening and if they can read screen action as it is intended.

Avoid frustrating *audience cheats,* such as setting up a disaster about to happen, which too conveniently doesn't. An audience is likely to feel manipulated by a television drama that ends an act with the discovery of a bomb about to explode, breaks for the commercial, then comes back for the next act only to reveal that it wasn't a bomb after all.

The Active Audience

Audiences are active. We involve ourselves in myriad ways while watching a film. We are involved emotionally. We get hooked on enigmas and anticipate developments. We come with expectations about genres and compare them to what we are seeing. We project ourselves into characters and situations; feeling along with them, caring about them, showing empathy and sympathy. We "read" looks and reactions to discover what a character is feeling and thinking.

At the same time, we are involved cognitively in the ongoing process of sense-making, of producing meanings. As screenwriter, encourage this by writing *suggestion* and *connotation* rather than explanation and denotation. Iser speaks of this as writing blanks for the audiences to fill in.[4]

This is one reason why *character reactions* are so important. We read meaning in close-ups. As in the classic Kuleshov experiment that featured a single close-up of an actor with a neutral expression intercut with shots of a bowl of soup, a coffin, and a child playing; audiences read the unchanging close-up as subtly expressing hunger, sorrow, and happiness.

Dialogue subtext is another example of active audience involvement. The meaning lies beneath the spoken words. (We'll discuss subtext when we consider dialogue.)

Dmytryk[5] presents a choice example of the active production of meaning in a short scene from the Edward Anhalt script for *The Young Lions* (although the scene does not appear this way in the finished film). Hope is a young woman anxious about the reaction her small-town, conservative New England father will have to her New York Jewish boyfriend. While the two men are taking a walk around town, she nervously stops in the local drugstore.

```
INT. DRUGSTORE - DAY

Mr. Graham puts hot chocolate on the counter. Hope
looks at it unenthusiastically.

                    HOPE
          Mr. Graham, you know what I
          could really use?

                    MR. GRAHAM
          What?

                    HOPE
          A slug of whiskey.

Mr. Graham looks at her sternly, then takes a
medicine bottle from under the counter, pours the
contents into a coffee cup. Hope looks dubiously at
the label.

                    HOPE (CONT'D)
          It says liniment.

                    MR. GRAHAM
          Don't worry. It ain't
          liniment.

Hope picks up the cup, drains it, takes a deep
breath.
```

It's obvious that we, along with Hope, supply the meaning that what is in the liniment bottle is some sort of alcoholic spirits. Well and good. But then Dmytryk takes us a step further with another possible version of the scene.

```
INT. DRUGSTORE - DAY

Mr. Graham puts hot chocolate on the counter. Hope
looks at it unenthusiastically.

                    HOPE
          Mr. Graham, you know what I
          could really use?

Mr. Graham looks at her sternly, then breaks into a
sympathetic smile. He knows what she's going
through. Reaching under the counter, he brings out a
medicine bottle, pours the contents into a coffee
cup. Hope looks dubiously at the label.

                    HOPE (CONT'D)
          It says liniment.

                    MR. GRAHAM
          Don't worry. It ain't
          liniment.

Hope picks up the cup, drains it, takes a deep
breath.
```

It's a better scene. Hope doesn't have to tell us what she needs. We can figure that out. And get pleasure thereby.

This short scene of three dialogue lines asks the audience to actively produce meaning. Such an audience is not simply sitting back receiving information. It is actively involved in enjoying the pleasure of sense-making.

Still another way to actively involve the audience is working with *shared knowledge,* as we discussed earlier. Working the pattern of knowledge between characters and audience can keep the audience actively involved in the unfolding story.

Remember the audience's point of view as you write your script; be aware of audience response and involvement.

SUMMARY

This chapter considered a variety of diverse techniques and concerns to keep in mind when writing a script. It includes such topics as title, openings, and point of attack. Exposition dealt with how to provide audiences with the information they need. Preparation is a way of raising the possible to the probable. Also considered were runners, maintaining forward movement, problems of credibility and coincidence, pace, tone, mood, atmosphere, the big moment, point of view, the ticking clock, raising the objection and shooting it down, and the tension relief laugh. Setting, props, costumes, and other visual elements were discussed, as was the importance of actively involving the audience.

A CHECKLIST FOR STORY TECHNIQUES

Do you have an intriguing title?

Do you have an engrossing opening?

Did you choose an appropriate point of attack?

Have you handled the exposition smoothly?

Have you prepared us for events that might otherwise seem improbable?

Could you make use of a runner?

Do you maintain forward movement?

Is the script credible?

Have you adequately researched the material?

Do you avoid coincidence, convenience, and the contrived?

Have you made things difficult for the hero?

Does the pace fit the subject matter and treatment?

Are the tone, mood, and atmosphere appropriate?

Does the film have a big moment?

Have you consciously chosen points of view?

Have you considered building suspense through a ticking clock, time-bomb technique?

Are settings used effectively?

What have you done with props? costumes?

What is your theme? How is it expressed?

Is the audience involved in the character's emotions?

Do you underplay rather than overplay?

Are you aware of how the script works on an audience?

ENDNOTES

1. In this sense, preparation foreshadowing bears an interesting, almost inverse, relationship to suspense foreshadowing. In one sense, any kind of foreshadowing prepares us for what is to come. But with suspense foreshadowing, we understand the implication of the action or object and anticipate the coming payoff. With preparation, the significance isn't immediately apparent. We unconsciously register the action or object. Only later, when the preparation payoff occurs, does the circuit complete. The earlier event is retrospectively perceived—perhaps unconsciously—to support the later action. The payoff is accepted as a prefigured logical outcome, probable and hence credible. Suspense foreshadowing cues a payoff; preparation foreshadowing sanctions one. The payoff completes the suspense cue, it justifies the preparation.

2. We can distinguish *rhythm,* which is the pulse or cadence we feel as we view the film; *tempo,* which is the rate of the rhythm—how fast or slow it moves; and *pace,* which refers to the various changes in tempo and rhythm. But in practice such fine distinctions are academic. We'll subsume them all under pace.

3. Although a totally subjective camera that is literally the eyes of the character didn't work well as the total perspective of *Lady of the Lake,* it has been successfully used in movies. The beginning of *Dark Passage* presents the world largely as seen through the eyes of an escaped convict. We never see his face, except for a newspaper picture, until after he undergoes plastic surgery, gets a new face (Humphrey Bogart's), and the subjective camera is abandoned. The television series *M*A*S*H* had a very powerful episode that was filmed entirely through the eyes of a wounded soldier. In the opening of *Halloween* we see through the cut out eyes of a Halloween mask.

4. Wolfgang Iser has written in the critical area known as reader response, or reception theory. His well-known work is *The act of reading: A theory of aesthetic response.* (1978). Baltimore: Johns Hopkins University Press.

5. Dmytryk, E. (1985). *On screen writing.* Boston: Focal, pp. 54–59.

CHAPTER 6

Television Narrative

*The actors are important, the director is important, yes, but without that
writing—good writing—it doesn't work.*

—Bill Moyers

While there is much demand for television writers—it's a fine market for good
writers—breaking into the business can be a problem. Getting an agent is important,
of course, as we'll discuss in a later chapter. And you'll need a number of
script samples to show what you can do. If television writing is your ambition, write
some episodes for an existing series as writing samples. Pick a top-quality, challenging
series that shows your range. Decide whether you'll concentrate on comedy or
action/drama and know thoroughly the shows you plan to write for.

TECHNIQUES AND GUIDELINES

Should you become a television writer you will most likely write for an existing episodic
series either as a staff writer or as a freelancer. (Opportunities to suggest original
series or movies-of-the-week [MOWs] are reserved for well-known, established
writers.)

What we've said about story-structure development applies to television as
well. Television writing also involves viewer expectations of established genres (such
as the situation comedy), and keeping in mind the commercial breaks that structure

American television. In this chapter we'll discuss writing the one-hour and half-hour (sitcom) series.

Due in part to time constraints and the presence of commercial breaks, television is a more tightly structured medium than film. A script must hook the audience quickly. The set-up happens very fast—within the first few minutes. Viewers will already be familiar with series characters and typical situations; don't take a lot of time establishing these. Familiarize yourself with the characters, typical situations, and usual development pattern of any series you write for.

A series must maintain a certain consistency from week-to-week to meet viewers' expectations. This familiarity is comfortable for the audience, but may also become overly predictable. So look for twists, cliff-hangers, and unexpected plot turns to make your stories fresh and involving. Try to surprise us with unexpected developments even as you keep your stories clear enough that we understand what's going on and know who to root for.

Indisputably the most significant attractions in a series are its characters; their appeal most contributes to the series' success. We enjoy watching characters we like, find intriguing, and are willing to invite into our homes week after week. Television sitcoms rely on a character "family"—an ensemble of characters thrown together for fun and adventure. This may be a literal family (*The Bill Cosby Show, Family Ties, Fresh Prince of Bel Air*), a work family (*Murphy Brown, M*A*S*H, Wings, Law and Order*), friends who spend time together (*Seinfeld, Friends*), who share a gathering place (*Cheers*), or who live in the same unusual town (*Northern Exposure*).

Other series emphasize a single major protagonist (*Murder, She Wrote; Walker, Texas Ranger; Matlock; Millennium*). When a series has a dominant central star character (or duo as in *Mad About You* and *The X-Files*) let the action center around them; it is their series, therefore their story. A guest star should never dominate the episode.

Particularly with television, it is important to keep the central character proactive. Let their actions move the story forward; they have the problem, their efforts lead to its resolution.

If you're freelance writing a series episode, be consistent with the series. Don't have anyone behave in a way that would be out of character (and maybe alter the future of the series). Don't introduce a long-lost relative, get the character a pet, or take the character to some exotic (and expensive) locale. The producers and staff set the future of the series; as an outside writer you need to keep within established parameters.

Here are some general guidelines when writing for television.

Write to your television act endings, that is, the endings of the television acts that precede the commercials. (To differentiate television acts from three-act structure—Act I, Act II, Act III—I'll refer to television acts as act 1, act 2, and so on.) Television stories have a beginning-middle-end structure; continue to plan the story and various story lines this way, but lay them out within the television act structure.

Writing to your television act endings means that there will be a dynamic close just before the commercial break. It could be a strong *jeopardy beat*—a suspenseful cliff-hanger that makes us want to see how a character will get out of the jeopardy. It could be an unexpected threat or problem, some new and challenging information, or some other surprise. Make it something that hooks us so we don't switch channels during the commercial break. A comedy will often throw in a large laugh at the act break—a promise of things to come. Try to have the act break escalate tension and suspense either physically or emotionally (or both).

Scenes will end with a definite close, a punch, a *button*. Don't let scenes trail off inconsequentially. Make sure to get that definite close.

In addition to the story lines, television series episodes often have a *runner* or two. This recurring bit might be a topic discussed by the characters, or it could be a character's recurring appearance, or some distinctive visual or sound. For humor, it could be a running gag that appears (runs) during the show. You'll typically play out a runner a few times during the program.

Some series episodes feature *teasers* and/or *tags*. Teasers precede the regular story, tags follow it. Each lasts from one to three minutes in length. A teaser can have nothing to do with the main story (as in *Wings* or *Mad About You*), or it can set up the story as when we see a crime committed. It is usually followed by the credits and first commercial break, and then the main story begins.

A tag typically follows the last commercial break, just before end credits. Generally a tag isn't part of the main story line but functions more as a denouement to wind things up. In a comedy, it may be an added joke.

Series and episodes don't need teasers or tags; some use them, some don't. (Recent custom tends to use the terms teaser and tag for any event that seems to tease the audience early in the story or that closes the story off, even if these are not placed outside the first and last commercial breaks.)

Bear in mind that television series have budget considerations. Don't be extravagant. Be wary of writing anything that will increase costs, such as special effects, international locations, animals and children, excessive destruction of sets or props, exterior night shooting, and widely separated locations that involve a lot of production travel time.

To write an episode for a particular series, watch a good number of shows. Tape them. Analyze them (as we'll be doing in the examples). Know the characters thoroughly; determine how each character is typically involved in the story lines. Lastly, be able to answer the following questions:

How does the series use act breaks?

How many story lines does the series use and how are they typically apportioned among the acts?

What are the typical story patterns?

How many beats are there in each act?

How quickly is the audience hooked?

Is there a runner or two?

Does the series use teasers or tags?

What are the standing sets?

How many additional sets are typically used?

How many locations are used? Where are they?

If it is a situation comedy, is it shot on film or live-on-tape before a studio audience?

If it is a comedy, how fast do the jokes come? (Time them.)

Know the series thoroughly, *then* write for it.

HOUR SERIES

The one-hour series is often an action/adventure program, but may also include other types of shows ranging from prime-time soap operas (*Dallas, Beverly Hills 90210, Melrose Place*) to other dramas and lighter fare (*Murder, She Wrote, Northern Exposure, Touched by an Angel, The X-Files*).

A one-hour episode is structured around four television acts (each will be about twelve minutes long). The hour script will usually run fifty-five to sixty pages. Typically each of the first three acts ends with a physical or emotional jeopardy beat—a cliff-hanger. Generally the strongest of these comes at the half-hour break that ends act 2. The end of act 4 is the denouement.

Often each act is patterned with a self-contained beginning, middle, and end—rising from a problem to an act climax.

Remember the importance of the star; often they will appear in the first and/or last scene of each act.

Don't lose sight of the villain; try to introduce a threat from the villain in each act.

Try to make the settings interesting and unusual. Use establishing shots when switching to unfamiliar locations.

Television needs to move quickly. Scenes don't run long. Begin to get nervous if a scene goes more than two-and-a-half pages. Any scene longer than three pages would be the exception in most filmed television writing. Much longer than that is considered poison.

Television episode story lines are commonly referred to as the A story (for the main story line), the B story, C story, and so forth. Outline the story lines separately, then integrate them. And consider a runner or two.

LA Law often has four story lines (the main story line, an alternate main story line, a subplot, and an alternate subplot), plus multiple runners.[1] The fast-moving *Hill Street Blues* at first contained many involved story lines. One or two story lines would begin and end in a single episode. Some of the previous episode's story lines might be resolved, others might not be resolved until a later episode. Audiences found this hectic pace confusing, so later episodes cut back on the number of story lines. *Hill Street Blues* was known for its unbridled pace and quick cuts; other series have a more leisurely pace. Have a good sense of the *pace* and *tone* of any series you write for.

Even though you write with television acts in mind, be sure to retain a beginning-middle-end underlying structure. To illustrate how you might lay out a one-hour episode, here is typical action/adventure structure.

The *Beginning* sets up the problem: some trouble or disruptive situation personally involves the central character and activates the story.

The *Middle* attempts to solve the problem, but unexpected developments cause the situation to deteriorate. The hero is in deeper trouble than before. Just when things look as though they have been solved, it turns out they are really getting worse.

For example, a space station is threatened with destruction due to the malfunctioning of a crucial electronic component. Throughout the Middle section, the crew's attempts to repair the part or improvise other methods to solve the problem are unsuccessful. When they hear a space shuttle is bringing a new replacement part, the crew believes that they are out of trouble. But then the Middle concludes with their optimism shattered as they realize that if the shuttle tries to land on their crippled space station it will throw them out of orbit to certain destruction. An added complication is that the transmitter is also malfunctioning and they can't send a message to the shuttle not to land (which might be an interesting crisis for the End section).

The *End* sees their problems become even worse despite the extreme measures taken to try to solve things. Finally the thrilling climax arrives, and the problem is solved.

Once your story is outlined this way, put it into the four-act one-hour TV structure, being sure to build to your first three-act endings, and giving these some sort of jeopardy or other striking beat.

A one-hour television episode traditionally has four to six beats per act. However, recent programs move faster and may have seven, eight, or even more beats per act. Find out how this is handled by any series for which you intend to write.

Here is a typical four-act outline for a detective action/adventure episode.[2]

Act	Beat	Description
1	1	Teaser. Hook audience, set up problem. For example, a murder is committed.
	2	Commitment of the hero (or perhaps the adversary).
	3	Adversary clarifies his steps, or hero clarifies what is going on.
	4	Investigation by hero. Discovers some clues, some suspense. Things develop a step further.
	5	Antagonist realizes hero is on his back.
	6	End act with a problem, a jeopardy beat.
2	1	Resolve jeopardy beat from end of act 1. That problem is solved, but there is more investigation, with conflict.

Act	Beat	Description *(continued)*

	2	Villain has unforeseen problems, maybe a confederate wants more money.
	3	Hero is getting closer to villain. Maybe contacts villain or person who can lead them to antagonist.
	4	Major jeopardy beat. Perhaps another killing increases the stakes. Even better, the villain becomes a major threat to the hero, perhaps trying to kill him. Hero may be driving down a steep mountain road when his brakes fail due to villain's tampering. This is a major dramatic high point.
3	1	Resolve previous beat. Out of jeopardy, hero tries something new, discovers something important—perhaps a new body or a disappearance. Or hero may be lost; things look bad. This is also a good time to re-explain what the hero is up against. In part to remind new viewers at the half-hour what the episode is about.
	2	Things look good for the villain—all he or she has to do is . . . . Or villain is uncertain, begins to panic.
	3	Hero very close to solving crime; gets a lead, but still needs one more piece of evidence.
	4	Jeopardy scene for either hero or villain, such as being run off the road.
4	1	"Collection scene" in which hero figures out what to do, plans final action, fits that last piece. Tells us what the plan is. Can catch villain if only can do this last thing.
	2	Antagonist about to achieve success, often moved to fight or flight.
	3	Chase scene.
	4	Confrontation and climax—hero catches villain.
	5	Tag wraps things up, maybe gives moral.

This beat outline generalizes the development of the story in terms of the objective—to catch the criminal—and the hero/villain conflict. Do a similar analysis of programs you watch. Detect how the story develops through its beats. While the example is very much a formula, it shows the value of a clear story line. (This example presents a single story line episode, many series episodes have additional story lines as well.)

Below are a number of story line beat analyses one might make as part of a series analysis. First, an illustration of structure for a single story line episode of *Remington Steele*, an amusing action/adventure series featuring Laura, a woman detective, and Remington, her male assistant. She does the real work; Remington is the titular head who often messes things up. But they do investigate as a team. They have a receptionist (Mildred). This episode also features two "singing-telegram girls," and relatives and business cohorts of Myron Flowers, a breath freshener company owner: Brenda (the wife), Chip (the son), Marjorie (ex-wife), Fitts (a colleague), and Nancy (a colleague). Note especially the twists and turns in the plot and the false leads. The story line is: to catch the killer.

Act	Beat	Description
1	1	"Killer" shoots Myron Flowers at his desk. Seen by singing-telegram girls. (SHOW CRIME)
	2	Girls sing for Laura and Remington. Girls get shot at. (NEW DEVELOPMENT)
	3	Laura and Remington investigate girls' previous customers, discover Flower's body, realize girls saw murder. BUT girls can't describe killer. (NEW DEVELOPMENT)
	4	Security guard steals gold breath-atomizer from office, inhales from it and dies. (STRONG ACT ENDING WITH NEW PROBLEM AND SUSPENSE)
2	1	Laura and Remington discover guard's body, leave with atomizer, not knowing it's poisonous.
	2	Laura and Remington visit Marjorie, learn gold atomizers are given to business inner circle executives. (EXPOSITION) Remington says find atomizer owner and will find killer; Laura not so sure. (CHARACTER INTERPLAY)
	3	Laura and Remington visit Brenda and Chip, learn they and Fitts have atomizers, so drop atomizer theory. (TWIST, REMINGTON'S THEORY WRONG. NOW WHAT?)
	4	Fitts concerned girls could identify him as one who shot Flowers, needs to do something. (VILLAIN THREATENS, WE KNOW WHAT LAURA & REMINGTON DON'T)
	5	Laura and Remington discover girls are gone from apartment, fear the worst. Laura looks in the closet: end act on shocked look on her face! (JEOPARDY BEAT SINCE LOOK ON HER FACE IMPLIES THE WORST, ALTHOUGH WE DON'T KNOW WHAT IT IS)
3	1	Girls and Mildred tied up in closet, learn masked man searched their clothes. Laura and Remington realize he was after atomizer. By spraying flowers that then die, Laura and Remington learn atomizer is lethal. (RESOLVE PREVIOUS BEAT, EXPOSITION OF WHAT HAPPENED)

Act	Beat	Description *(continued)*
	2	At laboratory to analyze poison, overhear Chip and Nancy make love, learn Chip had fight with father and almost cut out of will. (NEW SUSPECT)
	3	Fitts after girls, tries to lure them away with a job offer, but Mildred is not falling for it. Fitts gets gun and goes after girls. (VILLAIN TAKING ACTION)
	4	Remington accuses Chip, but girls say he wasn't the one they saw. (PLOT TWIST, FALSE IDENTIFICATION, THINGS MURKIER)
	5	Girls go out on a phony audition that Fitts sets up. (GIRLS IN JEOPARDY)
4	1	Laura and Remington take off to rescue girls. Fitts shooting at girls. Remington catches Fitts. (RESOLVE JEOPARDY BEAT, CHASE, LOOKS LIKE KILLER CAUGHT)
	2	Learn Flowers poisoned to death, not killed by shots. (NEW SURPRISE TWIST, CLEARS FITTS)
	3	Reveal Chip poisoned Flowers because he's Brenda's lover. (TWIST, KILLER IDENTIFIED)
	4	Remington chases and captures Chip. (CHASE, CLIMAX)
	5	Wrap things up for girls.

While having only a single story line, this illustrates the standard development in an action/adventure episode, complete with some plot twists to keep us guessing.

Here's another example of a single story line episode from *The X-Files*. This series about the paranormal spawned a host of imitators. It started with a cult following and then hit mainstream. FBI agents Mulder and Scully work together, often with humor, and take us into scary adventures of the weird, supernatural, and extraterrestrial. In this episode, Scully plays the skeptic doubting Mulder's early concerns. One unusual characteristic of this episode is that the two are constantly on the phone with each other.

This is the notorious killer-cockroaches episode. The story line: figure out what's happening with these roaches and stop them.

Act	Beat	Description
TEASER		An exterminator spraying the basement of a house is attacked and killed by awesome cockroaches.
1	1	Investigating a UFO sighting, Mulder learns of the attack. He calls Scully, but she is skeptical and refuses to join him.
	2	A cockroach crawls under the skin of a partying teenager.

	3	Mulder again calls Scully, but she attributes it to kids on drugs cutting themselves.
	4	Mulder catches a cockroach; it has a metal exoskeleton.
2	1	Mulder learns nothing from a doctor or the sheriff.
	2	Another man is killed by the roaches. Mulder learns from the sheriff that the government has been doing secret experiments nearby.
	3	Mulder just misses catching another roach; when he calls Scully, she dismisses the man's death as natural causes.
	4	Scully meets a USDA scientist who's studying roaches to show that supposed UFO sightings are the roaches nocturnal swarms.
	5	Another man is found dead—covered by roaches.
3	1	On phone. Scully still thinks it's improbable, but is coming to join Mulder.
	2	Mulder finds a metal roach in a roach motel (trap), the scientist refers him to a designer of robots.
	3	But designer can't figure it out.
	4	Panic! People are fleeing the town. Scully tries to calm them.
	5	Act ends as Mulder finds a roach, and as we see him through the multi-lensed eye of the roach, he says to it: "Greetings from the planet earth."
4	1	But Mulder's cockroach is a normal one. Scully then calls about investigating the research facility.
	2	They go to the research facility and find a deranged researcher with a gun; he is frightened by the roaches. The place is filled with methane gas.
	3	Mulder and Scully manage to get out just before the facility explodes.
	4	The town is still chaotic, but there are no more reports of cockroach attacks. The scientist suggests that perhaps the roaches died when they couldn't moult.
TAG		Writing at his computer, Mulder notices a cockroach nearby. He looks at it, then smashes it.

Now for a change of pace. Here's a complex analysis of the *Northern Exposure* episode, "Spring Break."

The important characters in this episode are Dr. Joel Fleishman, Maggie O'Connell (potential romance), Ed Chigliac (half Native American and, therefore, untouched by the craziness), Holling Vincour (saloon owner and older husband of

Shelly), Shelly Tambo (wife to Holling), Maurice Minifield (ex-military hero), Barbara Semanski (visiting state patrol sergeant) and DJ Chris Stevens. (Ruth Anne Miller and Marilyn Whirlwind have brief appearances in this episode.) The characters are locked together in Cicely, Alaska.

There are four story lines, all centering around the craziness that infects non–Native Americans just before the ice breaks up in the river, signaling the start of spring. In this sense, all the stories (except Ed's) are a turnaround since the people involved are waiting for the ice to break in order to lose their temporary lunacy. The story lines are:

1. Joel and Maggie to resolve their mad sexual passion for each other. (eight beats) (Relationship)
2. Ed to uncover the thief who is stealing radios. (six beats) (Task)
3. Holling to find someone to fight. (four beats) (Task)
4. Maurice to get romantically involved with Barbara. (six beats) (Relationship)

Each story line climaxes in the last act, with the first and major one—Joel and Maggie—climaxing last. (Marvelously, the tag uniquely climaxes the spirit of the entire episode.)

There are two or three runners. Shelly is normally openly sexual, but under the influence of the pending-ice-break craziness, she's compulsively reading a sexually explicit D. H. Lawrence novel without understanding its sexual content—Joel tells her one passage is erotic, but she can't see it.

A second runner is the three radio comments of Chris, the deejay, announcing the coming ice break and the wildness it causes. A third runner might be the sound (and shake) of the ice breaking up, which occurs a few times throughout the episode.

The program is interesting in that it features a number of dream sequences: Maggie dreams she and Joel are Adam and Eve in a lush garden. Joel dreams of performing in a suit with five attractive dancers who want to have sex with him. But he's embarrassed about having an orgy in so much light, so they turn the lights off for him—screen goes to black, and after a pause goes to a commercial break. This dream is especially intriguing because Joel knows he's dreaming and he argues with the women as to whether he can consummate sex in a dream. In another dream, Joel imagines that Ed fixes him up with a Native American woman in an igloo—and the woman is played by the same actress who plays Maggie.

Northern Exposure is a fine series for memorable moments. In one episode, a catapult is built to fling an old piano through the air—what an ending! This particular episode also has a great ending. It revolves around the Running of the Bulls, a ritual event that occurs when the ice breaks. The men run naked from the saloon to the river. At first hesitant, newcomer Joel joins in too. The men run out and down the street. Women line the street cheering them on. Spring has arrived. They celebrate together.

The music track comes up with new words to a wonderful classic folk song: The Wild Mountain Thyme. The words sung are: "If we go . . . go insane. We could all go together. In this wild wanton world. We can all break down forever." Yes, "insane" and "break down" are mentioned, but so are "together" and "forever." It's as though this weird group of characters will continue together forever. Like so many television series, the message is that life always goes on. It's a strong close.

Here's the structure breakdown and graphic representation of the episode.

Act	Beat	Description
TEASER		This is a TEASER beat occurring before credits and commercials. Maggie dreams of sex with Joel as Adam and Eve fantasy.
1	1	Visiting the post office/store, we learn that both Joel and Maggie are feeling sexually aroused. Ruth Anne explains that it's that time of year—the ice is about to break up, spring is coming.
	2	Joel finds his truck radio stolen.
	3	Maurice tells Joel about the temporary insanity.
	4	Saloon keeper Holling wants to pick a fight with someone, anyone.
	5	Joel having seductive dream and aware of it.
2	1	Maurice upset since his boom-box radio is stolen, wants investigation.
	2	Ed investigating theft. Says can get woman for Joel, who declines.
	3	Barbara, tough sergeant cop, arrives to investigate theft of Maurice's radio.
	4	Holling tries to get Steve to fight, Steve declines.
	5	Joel and Maggie overcome with passion in kitchen, embrace.
3	1	Joel and Maggie abashed, embarrassed, apologize.
	2	Maurice attracted to Barbara, serves her tea, urges her to work out with his weight set.
	3	Joel dreams he visited Ed's girl, who looks like a Native American Maggie.
	4	Maurice impressed by Barbara's strength. Getting more attracted to her, but she's not interested.
	5	At saloon, Holling asks Barbara to fight, she agrees.
4	1	Maurice irons Barbara's uniform while she trains for the fight. He says he wants to turn control over to her as she makes him feel safe.
	2	Joel again fantasizes about sex with Maggie. (Short mini-beat)
	3	Ed still investigating. (Mini-beat)

Act Beat   Description (*continued*)

	4	Boxing match at saloon. Suddenly, ice cracks. Holling no longer wants to fight, Barbara decks him.
	5	Ed confronts the deejay Chris who took the radios; Ed has recovered them.
	6	Maurice asks Barbara out. She turns him down—couldn't be attracted to someone who ironed her uniform. Maurice protests that wasn't him, he's no pantywaist—it was the ice breaking. But she still turns down a date.
	7	Joel visits Maggie. They are both still sexually attracted. They start to embrace. Then suddenly the change kicks in and they are back to normal again.
TAG		The Running of the Bulls.

GRAPHIC BEAT OUTLINE

```
Acts:              1              2              3              4
S  ┌──────────────┬──────────────┬──────────────┬──────────────┐
t  1  **│ **      ** │        ** │ **   ** │      **      ** │ T
o  2     │ ****        │ ****      │           │  **   **      │ a
r  3     │      **     │      **   │        ** │      **       │ g
i  4     │        ** ** │      **   ** │ **   ** │ **        ** │
e     │              │              │              │              │
s     └──────────────┴──────────────┴──────────────┴──────────────┘
```

(Each single beat is shown by two asterisks: **)

From this you can see the distribution of the story lines over the length of the story. There's a double beat in the first beat of act 2. (Mini-beats are very short beats; they may be combined in the same scene.) I counted Maurice's trying to get Joel to calm down over the radio theft as a beat in the theft story line. The double beat involved both the theft of Maurice's radio as well as the motivation to have Barbara travel the 500 miles to Cicely to try to clear up the theft.

From the graph you can see not only the number of beats in each story line, but the number in each act (1-5-5/6-5-7-1), including teaser and tag. I have not indicated the placement of the runners; they are spaced throughout the story.

Picket Fences takes place in another small town and centers around the Sheriff and the Doctor (husband and wife), their three children, and others in the town. This particular episode is unique for a number of reasons. It was the most popular episode in the first years of the show, and it deals with a topic that traditionally has been avoided by television series as taboo: religion. There are two story lines. The primary one deals with the issue of whether the pregnancy of a teenage virgin might be a divine act. The second story line, thematically relating to the first, concerns the youngest son finding out that Santa Claus is a fake. Here is the outline.

Act	Beat	Description
TEASER		A teenage girl (Dana) is in a car accident and presumed dead.
1	1	Doctor discovers Dana is alive, but in a coma with a dead forebrain. She's four months pregnant, but a virgin—she's never had sex! (SURPRISE)
	2	Older son tells his younger brother there is no Santa Claus. (SECOND STORY LINE)
	3	How could the girl, a religious person, be pregnant?
	4	Two clergymen—Roman Catholic and Protestant—pressed to take a position on this. Could this be another virgin birth? (SUSPENSE)
	5	Sheriff will try to match the DNA of the fetus with everyone she knew. (STAYING ACTIVE)
2	1	The car left no skid marks, this might have been a suicide attempt. In a vegetative state, the girl may not live. Clergymen hire private investigators to prove this a hoax.
	2	Boy visits store Santa, pulls off his beard, calls him a fake.
	3	Girl getting pneumonia; important to terminate pregnancy for chance to survive. But need a court order for this. (NEW COMPLICATION ESCALATES SITUATION)
	4	Courtroom. Attorney for church says can't abort because might be a divine pregnancy. (RAISING STAKES)
	5	Parents tell son real North Pole Santa still coming. Boy asks: if girl has God's baby, why is Santa coming instead of God? (TYING TWO STORY LINES TOGETHER, RAISING ISSUE OF FAITH AND MYTH)
3	1	Boy asks his sister how could Mary conceive Jesus without having sex? (FURTHER QUESTIONING RELIGION)
	2	Courtroom. Attorney says can't abort; girl wouldn't impregnate herself, so might be a divine pregnancy as it was with Mary and Jesus.
	3	Jewish attorney says Mary's virgin birth only a myth. (FURTHER CHALLENGE TO RELIGION)
	4	Older brother tells younger brother that parents lie about Santa Claus; how could Santa know all the kids in the world?

Act	Beat	Description *(continued)*

5 — Smoke bomb in court. Judge is threatened if he rules against the supernatural. Jewish attorney challenges the possibility of a supernatural verdict. (ESCALATING)

6 — Doctor and Sheriff wonder if they really believe in God. They can't help girl, can only pray. Judge is in church praying. (CLARIFIES ISSUE FOR ALL)

4 1 — Courtroom. Choices: (1) terminate pregnancy or girl dies; or (2) since DNA didn't match any of the men she dated, admit this could be divine intervention. (DEFINES ISSUE)

2 — Coroner finds one hair sample in car that isn't girl's; Sheriff pushing to find another answer. (SURPRISE POSSIBILITY OF A NEW DEVELOPMENT)

3 — Courtroom. Warning that a divine birth might cause the world order to crumble, especially if such a birth claimed by the United States.

4 — Judge enters, about to read the verdict. (THE CRUCIAL MOMENT!) Suddenly a deputy bursts in saying girl regained consciousness and might be able to speak tomorrow. (SURPRISE, SUSPENSE)

5 — At hospital, another doctor (male) is arrested as he tries to get at girl. The announcement of her recovery was a hoax to unmask villain doctor whose hair was found in car. He had impregnated girl with a syringe to provide hope for Christianity, then attempted to kill her in a car accident when she found out. (SURPRISE)

6 — Judge gives permission to terminate pregnancy. Says he will never tell his original ruling.

7 — At hospital, doctors say girl will never recover, but then suddenly she speaks, recovered! (SURPRISE) Such a recovery has happened before, but it is extremely rare. Doctors look at each other amazed. (HINT THAT MAYBE THERE IS SOMETHING MIRACULOUS GOING ON AFTER ALL)

8 — Father (Sheriff) tells his children that Santa Claus lives forever making glad the hearts of children. (SORT OF TYING UP BOTH THEMATIC ISSUES)

Law and Order is unusual since it has two clear halves—the first features the police who investigate a crime, the second shifts to the district attorneys who prosecute it. This particular episode is interesting not simply because it deals with child abuse, but because it ends with a question mark and the strong hint that an abuser may have gotten off, that the wrong person may go to jail, and that justice has not been served.

There is only a single story line although it is divided between the program's two parts—identifying the alleged criminal and trying the criminal in court.

Act	Beat	Description
TEASER		A seven-year-old girl is kidnapped from her nanny in a department store. Her father is a divorced Tony Award–winning producer.
1	1	The father is upset and pushes police to find his daughter.
	2	No kidnappers call for ransom. A check of the store security videotapes show the girl talking to an employee who is a convicted sex abuser. (A LEAD)
	3	Police trace down suspect at night job.
	4	Suspect has alibi. (LEAD FAILS) But mentions seeing a woman buying an expensive stuffed animal.
2	1	Woman who bought stuffed animal was seen with a girl. Woman's fancy car got a parking ticket. (NEW LEAD)
	2	Find woman. She works at an abused children's shelter, lies about where bought stuffed animal.
	3	At shelter, those who run it imply the girl was taken to protect her from an abuser.
	4	Detectives arrest shelter psychologist, but girl's mother is there and claims the child told them her father repeatedly molested her. (SURPRISE!)
3	1	Prosecutors doubtful can make a case of child abuse against father; little evidence against him.
	2	Learn father was having an affair with nanny.
	3	A man tells prosecutors that he was falsely accused by shelter psychologist of molesting his son which led to his ex-wife getting custody. (PSYCHOLOGIST UNTRUSTWORTHY?)
	4	Girl questioned and draws pictures of her father as a monster, but won't talk about where he might have touched her. Evidence is ambiguous.
	5	Talking with father's other (grown) daughter from previous marriage, they learn she has some strange memories but nothing definite. But learn father pays for her apartment. (TO ASSUAGE HIS GUILTY CONSCIENCE? STILL NO CLEAR ANSWERS)
	6	Prosecutors now think the father is guilty, but how can they prove it?

Act	Beat	Description *(continued)*
	7	They get a tape made by the psychologist in which the girl talks of abuse, but they think this "homemade evidence" may be thrown out of court. (A CHANCE?)
4	1	Judge can't allow tape as girl may have been coached, but will let girl testify in chambers via closed-circuit video.
	2	The trial. Father's attorney attacks psychologist's testimony.
	3	Wife testifies that ex-husband was too possessive with first daughter, takes nude naps with nanny.
	4	Pediatrician testifies that he saw physical evidence of abuse, but his testimony is besmirched when he admits to testifying in twenty-seven such cases, thirteen of which ended in acquittal.
	5	Girl testifies in chambers. She claims father touched her, but then says that the psychologist and her mother say he's bad. Then she says she forgot what she's supposed to say. She's upset since her mother promised to take her to France and get her a pony. (IT APPEARS SHE'S BEEN COACHED AND BRIBED)
	6	Mother withheld that she wanted custody so could take girl to France.
	7	Verdict: not guilty.
	8	Mother has hidden girl and won't reveal where. Since father has a court order for girl, the mother may go to jail. Prosecutors (AND WE) are left with the disturbing notion that justice was not served.

HALF-HOUR SERIES

The half-hour series virtually mean situation comedies (sitcoms), so called because the comedy grows out of characters caught in situations. Sitcoms can either be shot single-camera, filmic style (*M*A*S*H*) or, as with most, multi-camera, often in front of a live audience. The live, multi-camera sitcom uses a different script format than a filmed show (see Format section).

A half-hour episode runs about twenty-two minutes actual playing time. Because it is live, scenes run longer than in filmed television: three to seven pages on average. Each of the two television acts will have four to six scenes. With the different script format, live, multi-camera program scripts time out at about half-a-minute a page; a live sitcom script runs forty to fifty or more pages.

The number of sitcom beats varies. Some have as few as three per act because more time is spent on comedy—jokes and comic bits. Generally, three to five is considered standard, but many contemporary comedies move faster and may have up to twice that (for example, the *Seinfeld* episode discussed later). *The Simpsons*, an animated series, follows the guideline that animation moves faster than a live series; it is likely to have up to ten beats in each of its three acts.

Some sitcoms have three television acts (two middle commercial breaks). Still, the two-act model remains the industry standard at this writing.

Even though it is a comedy, a sitcom may have a serious story. A strong character problem or objective makes for a stronger script. Present the problem in the first few minutes. Build to a strong act break—possibly a jeopardy beat—and break for commercials. Often a major complication will be resolved just before the appearance of a still larger problem that closes act 1.

You are likely to have a B story line, and maybe even a C. Start the A story early in act 1, and the B story shortly thereafter.

Definitely go for surprise twists. Strong plot twists are important in a sitcom; most shows have at least one.

Give the story to the star; keep the major series regulars involved in the action. Let the stars deliver the best jokes; keep them in the action and on screen as much as possible. Try to use all regular series characters at least once in the episode.

Let much of the comedy and action grow out of character interactions. Don't bring in too many outside guest characters. Sitcoms often have a strong "family" of characters; use them.

Know the standing sets used in the series and use these. Keep additional sets (called *swings*) to a minimum.

Try for four to six laughs a minute—two to three or more per page—one every ten to fifteen seconds. As we'll discuss when we talk about comedy later, the best humor comes from the characters and situations, rather than from set-up jokes.

Carefully study any situation comedy you plan to write for. Know the characters, situations, sets, typical structure, preferred type of humor, and number of laughs per minute. Don't depart too much from the sense of the show. As DiMaggio so aptly puts it, "Rules are broken, but staff writers break them."[3]

Here are the story outline analyses of some situation comedies.

I'll begin with a complex *Mary Tyler Moore Show* episode that has three story lines:[4]

1. Mary's story line to audition for the new announcing job and risk the disappointment of not getting it. This includes both a task component—will she get the job? (although this is downplayed)—and a personal component—how will she handle not getting it?

2. Lou's story line to deal with Mary's disappointment.

3. Sue Ann's subplot story line to audition for the job herself.

There's a runner with Ted showing interest in the job, but it doesn't go very far. There's a definite plot twist reversal when Lou's attempt to avoid his responsibility backfires. Here's the analysis.

This group works at a television station. Mary is the young producer in the newsroom. Murray is a writer there. Ted is the clown character/newscaster. Lou is their boss. Sue Ann does a cooking show for the station. Georgette is Ted's wife. Enid is a guest trying out for a job.

This episode is included as it shows that even a half-hour show can have a number of story lines.

Act	Beat	Description
1	1	Lou wants a woman newscaster like Mary, but not Mary.
	2	Mary is urged by Georgette to audition, Mary not sure.
	3	Mary is urged by Murray to try, but she's still reluctant.
	4	Mary decides to audition. Lou reluctantly okays her trying, but he doesn't want to hurt her feelings if she fails. (BEATS IN BOTH LOU'S AND MARY'S STORY LINES)
2	1	Sue Ann to audition, criticizes Mary for doing so.
	2	Sue Ann auditions and does badly. (THIS SHORT STORY LINE IS DEVELOPED THROUGH JUST TWO BEATS)
	3	Mary auditioned poorly; Lou is worried about telling her that another woman got the job.
	4	Lou tries to weasel out of it by asking Mary to decide based on a tape of the other woman; to his chagrin, Mary picks herself.
	5	Mary learns other woman (Enid) got job. Lou is sorry for lying. We learn Mary placed fourth. Fourth?! Sixth!
TAG		Mary and Enid go off for a drink together and become friends.

Whose main story is it? I've said Mary's but a strong case also could be made for it being Lou's. (Doing an analysis is as much an art as a science.) In this episode there are A, B, and C story lines.

This *Bill Cosby Show* episode has a single story line. Theo, the son, has the story. He wants to wear a fancy designer shirt for a date, but it costs so much that his dad, Cliff, won't let him keep it. As the story develops, Theo's sister, Denise, tries to help by making him a copy of the shirt, with peculiar results. There's a strong act-break and a definite twist at the end when the shirt turns out to be a hit. The show has one runner—Cliff has a cold, but he keeps denying it; only at the end does he admit it. The characters are Cliff, his wife, the two children Theo and Denise, and some guest teenagers.

Act	Beat	Description
1	1	Theo has a problem when his dad won't let him keep the expensive designer shirt he bought even though his date expects him to wear it.

2		His sister Denise says she'll copy the shirt for the smaller amount of money their dad is willing to give Theo; the parents have doubts, other things Denise has tried haven't turned out too well.
	3	Theo is concerned, but Denise tells him it's coming along well—only it isn't!
2	1	Denise gets more money for material.
	2	Theo tries on the shirt; it's a mess. He hates it.
	3	Cliff tries in vain to persuade Theo to wear the shirt. Finally, he gives Theo permission to wear the expensive shirt. But Theo—wearing the homemade shirt—walks into another room, where he runs into his date and another couple.
4		They love the shirt, calling it a new look. Theo comes out okay.

This *Cheers* episode is the one in which Sam and Diane first sleep together. It is Sam's story. All the characters work or hang out at the saloon.

Act	Beat	Description
1	1	Sam and Diane finally decide to sleep together, only we see that Sam has casual sex in mind while Diane wants more romance. (WILL THEY SUCCEED TOGETHER?)
	2	As they leave the bar, Sam comments that he'll have to "work a little harder on this one!" (HE STILL ISN'T IN TUNE WITH DIANE'S NEEDS; HE WANTS THINGS TOO MUCH HIS WAY)
	3	Arriving at her place, Sam is ready to go, but Diane just doesn't want it this way and kicks Sam out of her apartment. (THE MAJOR JEOPARDY TO END ACT ONE)
2	1	Sam returns to the saloon, sulks, but then gets Carla's advice that to succeed he needs to show Diane who's boss. Sam goes to try it. (BUT OF COURSE THIS IS JUST THE OPPOSITE OF WHAT HE NEEDS TO DO)
	2	Sam breaks Diane's door down, acting dominant. She goes into her bedroom to "put on something flimsy," and then is heard making a phone call from the bedroom. When she comes out she tells Sam she called the police on him.
	3	Sam breaks down. He doesn't want her to let them take him away. He agrees with her that hostility and destructiveness don't belong in a relationship. (THIS SHOW OF WEAKNESS ON HIS PART—HE STOPS TRYING TO HAVE IT HIS WAY—GIVES US THE REVERSE THE STORY WAS BUILDING TOWARD)

Act   Beat   Description *(continued)*

They head for the bedroom. Sam gets his objective, but only after giving up his power play.

4   As a tag, Diane tells Sam she never really called the police, so he dumps her stuffed animals out the apartment window.

Notice a few things from this development. There's a definite surprise twist when Sam (and we) think Diane called the police, the power shifts from him to her (a reversal). (The episode is entitled "Power Play.")

The runner is Diane's stuffed animal collection. First Sam discovers the animals, then he removes them from the bedroom as he and Diane get ready to spend the night together, and when he hears she didn't really call the police, he dumps them out the window (thereby letting us know there will be future conflicts in this relationship).

Even though this is Sam's story with Diane, the beginning of act 2 opens with banter and humor among the regulars in the bar, allowing these prominent regular characters to keep active in the episode.

Some contemporary sitcoms play with looser structure and development as *Seinfeld* does. Jerry Seinfeld is a stand-up comic. Elaine, George, Kramer, and Newman are his rather unique friends, although Newman is more of an antagonist to the others. The series takes place in New York City. The *Seinfeld* episode that follows interestingly intermingles story line beats and runners. There are two story lines. The A story is about Seinfeld and his friends trying to make sure their accountant is not on drugs, and that the money they've invested with him is safe. The B story is: can George get a job at a brassiere company?

One runner centers on the action of feeling and asking about the fabric someone is wearing. Notice how it becomes a plot beat. It first appears when Elaine says that her new boyfriend met her by feeling her suit's fabric. But when George tries it later on a woman who turns out to be the head of the brassiere company, she takes affront and fires him from the job he just got. When Newman is going to mail their letter to the accountant, he tries it with a woman at the mailbox. She blows up at him and the letter isn't mailed. At the episode's end, a woman does it to Seinfeld's shirt.

The second runner is even more involved in the story. It concerns the use of exclamation points in writing. Elaine's new boyfriend walks out on her because she badgers him about not putting an exclamation point after the telephone message he took for her about a friend having a baby. A scene later shows Elaine at work being told by her boss that she must remove the many exclamation points she put in something she edited. And toward the end of the episode Seinfeld comments about how the letter they wrote the accountant had all those exclamation points in it. These function both as runners and important plot elements.

Act Beat Description

TEASER   Seinfeld's stand-up routine.

1   1   Elaine has a new boyfriend. When Seinfeld's, Elaine's, and George's accountant stops by, he sniffs continually, says he doesn't have a cold, then goes to the bathroom. They suspect he may be using drugs, and they begin to worry about their money.

     2   George's father gets him a job interview with a brassiere company.

     3   Kramer is told about the accountant's sniffing and also suspects drugs, increasing their concerns.

     4   Elaine's boyfriend walks out over her hassling him about not using an exclamation point in a phone message.

     5   They call and learn the accountant has gone to South America for a week. This increases their suspicions. They decide to test him.

2   1   In a bar, Kramer pretends to be an underworld denizen to draw out the accountant, who is still sniffing. When the man goes to the bathroom, Kramer follows (suspecting drug-taking) and takes his picture while he's on the commode.

     2   George gets the job at the brassiere company by doing a great interview. But then he loses it when he tries the feeling-the-fabric bit on an attractive woman who turns out to be the company boss.

     3   Elaine's boss confronts her about something she's written and asks her to remove the excessive exclamation points.

     4   Jerry, Elaine, and George prepare a letter to the accountant demanding their money back.

     5   The pizza delivery boy starts sniffing; says he's allergic to the mohair sweater. Since the sweater was always worn when the accountant was around, the group begins to think this is why the accountant was sniffing. If only they could get the letter back.

     6   Newman has a confrontation with a woman at the mailbox when he feels her fabric; she chases him away before he can mail the letter.

     7   Later they learn the accountant has gone bankrupt. Had the letter been mailed, they might not have lost money.

          Seinfeld makes a final comment about all the exclamation points in the letter. A woman feels the fabric in his shirt.

TAG   Seinfeld's stand-up routine.

Some sitcoms have even less plot than those described above. The following two examples from *Mad About You* use the plot primarily as a vehicle for the interaction of the two characters Paul and Jamie. (Lisa is Jamie's sister; Selby is Paul's friend; Fran and Mark are their married friends.) This is another New York show.

The first example is from the first show of the series.

Act	Beat	Description
1	1	Jamie wants more sex. They plan a romantic evening but then remember Fran and Mark are coming over and it's too late to cancel the visit.
	2	Lisa comes over upset about having broken up with someone. This interferes with Paul and Jamie's romantic night, so Paul invites Selby over in retaliation.
	3	Fran and Mark arrive; Paul and Jamie each thought the other would call it off, but they forgot.
2	1	Jamie is mad at Paul. They get together alone in kitchen in order to fight, but it turns into lovemaking.
	2	The guests wonder what's going on in the kitchen, with all those violent noises; Lisa stops Fran from checking.
	3	Later, the guests leave.
		Still later, Paul and Jamie are in bed and much in love.

The following is another example from *Mad About You.*

Act	Beat	Description
1	1	It's Sunday. Paul wants to go to a movie, Jamie prefers a quilt show. They start arguing—does he find her boring?
	2	They decide to do it all—lunch, movie, quilt show.
	3	But when they decide to go out, a parade is blocking the street.
2	1	They start to go out but Lisa calls; she's having a trauma.
		It's now too late to go to lunch so Jamie puts a casserole in the oven.
	2	They flip a coin and are about to go out when Mark calls and gives away the movie ending; now Paul refuses to go.
	3	Paul and Jamie decide to go out separately—he to movies, she to quilt show. But they can't; they love each other too much to be separated. They head for the bedroom, ignoring a ringing phone.

This episode has a runner about Jamie deciding to wear a hat, although she has hardly ever done so—not since Paul has known her.

Both episodes have the simplest structure. The humor comes primarily from the interaction of the two central characters, as well as their interaction with their friends. As long as it's humorous and enjoyable to the audience, why not?

As a final example, here's a *Frasier* episode that develops its comedy from misunderstanding—a common humor technique. Frasier is a psychiatrist with a call-in radio show. He lives with his father and Daphne, their housekeeper. His brother Niles is also a psychiatrist; they are often in conflict with each other. Roz is Frasier's acerbic assistant on the radio show. Tom is the new station manager.

The single story line is Frasier's attempt to comfort a distraught Daphne. The cigarette smoking is a runner as well as part of the plot.

(The analysis was done from the script "The Matchmaker" rather than from the aired episode.)

Act	Beat	Description
1	1	Frasier catches Daphne smoking—against house rules, and is bothered when he learns she is upset because of her bleak love life. The scene ends with him beginning to smoke because he's worried about her.
	2	Still worried about Daphne, Frasier manages to insult Roz before vowing to find a man for Daphne. This upsets Niles since he has a crush on Daphne himself. This scene ends with Niles reaching over to the next table (in the cafe), taking a burning cigarette from the ashtray, and beginning to smoke it.
	3	Frasier meets Tom, the new station manager, and invites him over for dinner (as a possible date for Daphne). Tom accepts.
	4	But then Tom mentions to Roz that he's gay and believes Frasier wants to date him. And Roz, still smarting from Frasier's insult, doesn't tell.
2	1	At the apartment dinner, Daphne is attracted to Tom. Frasier encourages her, but when she asks for help in the kitchen, hoping Tom will join her, Niles rushes in instead.
	2	Tom tells Niles he thinks Frasier is dating him, and Niles keeps the information to himself, continuing the misunderstanding.
	3	But when Tom asks for some alone time and Frasier mistakenly thinks this is to be with Daphne, Niles explains the whole misunderstanding. Frasier then explains to Tom what happened and they part friends.

Act	Beat	Description *(continued)*
	4	Later that night, Frasier and Daphne bond—and both smoke cigarettes.
	TAG	Later, still smoking, Frasier reads the warning on the cigarette package and both he and Daphne vigorously snuff out their smokes.

MOVIE OF THE WEEK

These are virtually out of reach for all but an established writer. They are usually developed with writers who specialize in them so it isn't an advisable course for a novice, even as a spec script (that's a script written on the speculation that someone will be interested in it or in you as a writer). If you have an idea that you think will be dynamite for an MOW, write it as a feature film and it might be picked up for TV.

MOWs run 120 minutes; less commercials this makes for about 96 minutes of screen time. The scripts average 100 to 115 pages. They typically have seven acts. The first act usually runs long—about twenty-five minutes. The last few acts are among the shortest at around ten minutes each, but there is no set length for them.

The set-up usually comprises the first act; the last one or two acts are the resolution. MOWs are usually high concept, something that can be condensed into a *TV Guide* log-line and look appealing.

MOW story ideas tend to be trendy, capitalizing on current concerns. Stories with "heart" are preferred (such as an adoptive mother having to give up her child). Recently, true stories have gained popularity. Anything that will attract a star (a popular television star or a movie star) is a good bet.

Ideas for MOWs change rapidly. Years ago the trend was "disease of the week"; that's now dead. Even networks differ as to what they want and the sort of viewers they are appealing to. It's a specialized arena for reputable writers.

DAYTIME SERIALS, THE SOAPS

The daytime serial, or soap opera, is a specialized television writing area. This is a unique form in which stories develop slowly, day by day. They lack the tight build to the climax of other dramatic television narratives. A typical soap might have five stories going, each of which will run for weeks and have major plot points, one or two each week.

There is a market for soap writers (it's steady work), but it is a very specialized field that requires skill in writing dialogue and creating relationships between characters. If you wish to know more about the field, study the soaps, do some sample scenes for the show for which you would like to write, and then try to get them to someone on the show to read. Having an agent helps—but it helps even more if you enjoy the soaps yourself.

Television is always looking for talented writers. And there are additional opportunities in cable and series written for syndication. It's a fine market for new talent.

SUMMARY

This chapter discussed writing for television. It emphasized the importance of considering the presence of commercials and writing to television act breaks. Since so much of the attraction of television is the characters and the television character "family," it pointed out the need to focus on series stars and regulars when you write. A number of analyses of hour shows and half-hour sitcom episodes were included.

A CHECKLIST FOR WRITING TELEVISION SERIES

Do you thoroughly know the series you want to write for?

Do you know how many story lines it typically uses?

Do you have a sense of its pace and tone?

Is there a proactive protagonist who advances the story?

Does the story belong to the star character?

Have you written to act breaks?

Do the acts end with physical or emotional jeopardy (or both)?

Do most scenes end with a definite button?

Have you considered a runner?

Does your episode have strong act endings?

Does your one-hour episode have four to six (or more) beats per act?

Does your half-hour sitcom have three to five (or more) beats per act?

Does your half-hour sitcom have at least one strong twist?

Does your half-hour sitcom have lots of laughs?

ENDNOTES

1. This particular analysis is described in DiMaggio, M. (1990). *How to write for television.* New York: Prentice Hall. This is a recommended book for television writing. Other useful texts are Kaminsky, S. with Walker, M. (1988). *Writing for television.* New York:

Dell; Brenner, A. (1985). *The TV scriptwriter's handbook.* Cincinnati: Writer's Digest Books; Wolff, J. (1988). *Successful sitcom writing.* New York: St. Martins.

2. This outline is a modification of one presented by Terry McDonnell in Miller, W. (Summer 1984). An interview with Terrence McDonnell, *Journal of Film and Video, 36,* 51–57. It is related to what is known as the Quinn-Martin outline. Quinn and Martin were television producers of a number of successful series decades ago; presumably they gave an outline to their writers who simply plugged in different elements and that produced the programs.

3. DiMaggio, p. 58.

4. I analyzed this episode in my earlier book. At that time I identified five story lines. Reconsidering, I think that might have pushed things a bit. Now I've combined some of these and present it as having three story lines.

CHAPTER 7

Alternative Structures: Adventures in Innovation

Stop making sense.
—Talking Heads

The techniques of screenwriting that we've discussed apply to most films and television programs, and for good reason—they work. And they permit a great deal of freedom and flexibility in their use. But imaginative filmmakers are always looking for ways to stretch the mainstream envelope and explore the innovative. The result has been some unusual narrative treatments.[1]

Dramatic structure works because it structures the story and our experience of that story in a way that captures our attention. This process doesn't require typical story line or three-act patterns. An effective screenplay must simply keep the audience suspensefully anticipating developments and dazzled by unexpected turns of events. If these are working in your story, you have a wide latitude to try alternative approaches to narrative.

PATTERNING TECHNIQUES

For some films, a clear narrative story line may never be established. *Amarcord* is a mosaic of stories from an Italian village. *Roma* is a collage of loosely connected incidents. *Small Change* consists of linked vignettes about children's experiences grow-ing up. *Slaughterhouse Five* jumps back and forth in time and place while interweav-ing events through strongly stylized transitions. The surreal *If. . . .* has tension and conflict but not a clear story line; the surprises it presents keep us involved. *Clerks* is about some generation Xers stuck in dead-end jobs and wondering what to do with themselves.

Films with a less pronounced story line structure often use other patterning techniques. A simple (and limited) one is to frame the story in some meaningful way. *Blow-Up* begins and ends with student mimes whose illusory tennis game at the end symbolizes the meaning of the film. *Pulp Fiction* is framed by the incident of two characters robbing a coffee shop. These characters don't appear at all in the rest of the film (although two of the film's main characters get involved with them in the last frame sequence).

A Clockwork Orange patterns with cyclical events. The tramp who is beaten at the film's beginning returns near the end to attack Alex. Violence against Dim is repaid in kind when Dim takes revenge on Alex. Similarly, the attack inflicted on the inhabitants of The Home cycles back when Alex later finds himself a guest there and is violently made to suffer. The operating room scenes and the continual loud-speaker messages in *M*A*S*H* give it continuity.

Some films don't establish their main story line until late. In *Blow-Up*, it is some time before Thomas notices the crime and attempts to investigate it; prior to this we are more involved with him as a character than engrossed with a strong plot line. *Full Metal Jacket* divides into two stories: the first half is about basic training, and two of the main characters are killed off at its end; the second half is about Viet-nam combat.

Instead of a strong story line, our interest in a film often comes from interesting characters. *Strangers in Good Company* is a moving film about a group of elderly women whose bus breaks down in the Canadian wilderness. As they share their sto-ries, the audience begins to care very much about these people.

While a conventional approach stresses clarifying the character's motivations, this need not be the case. Often we just accept that characters are there doing their thing and are less concerned about motivation.

Some films feature strongly symbolic elements that ask us to make connections that aren't spelled out. *Sweet Movie* intercuts its two story lines with tinted old news-reel footage of German soldiers discovering the mass grave of Polish officers slaugh-tered in the Katyn Forest Massacre. These powerful visuals are strikingly juxtaposed against the comic (and often violently black comic) events of the film.

Stories don't have to be told in a linear manner. Real-time chronology matters less in films that feature extensive flashbacks and flashforwards. *Slaughterhouse Five*, *Last Year at Marienbad*, and *The Conformist* are three films that play with time tenses.

A story may abandon continuity for a more elliptical approach. There are eli-sions (. . . .) where we might expect story narrative. Scenes we would expect to see are omitted while scenes less directly important to the story are presented. Intervals assume greater importance than would be expected. An important scene may not be shown. Fewer things are explained. Connections between story elements are omitted, giving the film an episodic quality.

In conventional screenwriting, any event or scene that doesn't advance the story is suspect and likely to be eliminated. But this doesn't have to be the case. Scenes may serve other purposes—create a mood, further explore a character, develop a theme, or simply present an element of style to be appreciated for its own sake.

Other traditional film conventions can be broken, or at least bent to new shapes. Sequences can assume greater independence from the plot; the development within each sequence and the relationship between sequences can be as important as the relationship of the sequence to the overall story.

The single-shot scene, using deep focus and compositional staging (rather than intercutting within the scene) is available, although it is not as common today as it was a few decades ago. Scenes may deliberately start before they would be expected to and continue after we would normally expect them to stop.

Many of the films we've already referred to feature surreal elements—they depart from expected reality. (Of course the surreal is common in broad comedy—think of *Airplane!* and the Zucker/Abrahams films it spawned; it's a tradition that goes back to the Marx Brothers and before.)

PRESENTATIONAL FILM

A film may be presentational rather than representational—it "breaks the fourth wall" and directly addresses the audience. Early experimenters did this frequently. In Godard's *Weekend* the husband and wife grumble about not liking the film they are in because all the characters they meet are freaks. In *Pierrot Le Fou*, Ferdinand says a line directly to the camera. Puzzled, Marianne asks to whom he's speaking. He replies, "To the audience."

At various points in the Canadian film *Les Ordres*, the narrative is interrupted when the actors introduce themselves and discuss the characters they play. Sometimes this is done by voice-over; at other times the actors talk to the camera.

In *What's Up, Tiger Lily?* two fingers appear on the screen as if grabbing the film at the projector gate. Then we cut to an office where executives ask Woody Allen if he can tell them what the film is about. "No," he replies, and the film continues.

Tom Jones places his hat over the camera to keep the audience from ogling a half-dressed woman. Later he turns to the camera and asks us if we saw anyone take some missing money. Looks at the camera appear in films as wide ranging as *Harold and Maude* and *Airplane!*

INNOVATIVE TELEVISION

The television series *Moonlighting* frequently had the central characters address the camera with some wry comment, or otherwise break the realism of the scene. The program often played with narrative and language. In one episode, Maddie takes an imaginary journey to a future in which everyone talks in rhyme. In another, David dreams he has been convicted of a murder and sentenced to death. In the dream he says that you can't dream your own death, only to have the guard tell him, "They changed the rules." One episode is introduced by a TV critic who mentions he isn't being paid for this, only to have a pay envelope handed him by a crewperson. When it starts snowing in their office, David wonders if it's the Christmas episode.

Characters often refer to the fact that they are in a fictional television episode. David speaks of feeling a plot twisting. He challenges another character by asking if the man has stopped to figure the consequence of mauling a major television star. Another time he urges Maddie to wrap this up in twelve minutes because another show is coming on. In one season's final show, David and Maddie are getting passionate in his car's front seat. When she wonders what has come over them, he replies, "Anything to avoid the seven P.M. Sunday time slot." Another character once mused on how she could keep up the show's ratings while the lead actress was on a maternity leave. *Moonlighting* was quite a playful and innovative television series.

An episode of the television series *M*A*S*H* takes a presentational approach by having a war correspondent interview the M*A*S*H personnel. The characters talk directly to the camera; they say hello to the folks back home, discuss their views on the war, and their thoughts about the future. The episode was filmed in black and white to simulate a 1950s TV newsreel documentary.

Some films are successful in spite of structural weaknesses because they have other elements—interesting characters, powerful themes, exciting production values—that attract us to them. Having a strong, workable structure is always a plus, but it doesn't guarantee success. Here are some very enjoyable films that do not fit the traditional structure model.

EXAMPLES IN FILM

Gregory's Girl

Gregory's Girl is a charming Scottish comedy about a high school student's first romance. The story line is: Will Gregory, a likable but nerdy guy, get a girl? The film runs only eighty-six minutes (including credits). Although it is in most respects a mainstream film, it doesn't follow typical story development—as this analysis of its major beats will demonstrate.

Mins

15   Gregory falls in love with Dorothy, the attractive beauty who tries out for the soccer team.

30   Dorothy loves Italy; to impress her, Gregory wants to study Italian.

40   Gregory and his two nerdy friends are impressed when a graduate—now window cleaner—says he's "done it."

45   Gregory's younger sister Madeline buys him clothes and advises him on how to impress girls.

55   Things look up when Dorothy asks Gregory to help her kick goals; but he's so oversolicitous of her that he messes up.

60   Gregory asks Dorothy out and can hardly believe it when she accepts.

64   Gregory waits for Dorothy; she doesn't show.

67   Dorothy's friend Carol arrives with the message that Dorothy can't make it. Carol and Gregory go out for chips. Then Carol leaves on a date.

70   Margo arrives to lead Gregory on a mysterious walk. He's confused. Margo takes him to Susan.

73   Susan and a confused Gregory agree to go on "a kind of a date."

80   Gregory and Susan have fun. She walks him home. They kiss. Gregory is happy—he's got a girl.

84   Having heard that in Bogota the ratio of women to men is quite favorable, one of Gregory's nerdy friends is hitch-hiking with a sign that reads, "Bogota."

While its structure is hardly exemplary, the film works. Describing the major beats can't capture the film's charm. There is a bit about photographing a nurse who leaves her window shades up when undressing, Gregory's father as a harried driving instructor, Gregory's worldly wise younger sister, a fellow student who runs a bakery operation at the school, a runner featuring a wandering character in a penguin costume, and generally a set of delightful characters.

Fried Green Tomatoes

For another example, consider *Fried Green Tomatoes*, whose unusual structure may be due in part to its being adapted from a novel. There are three story lines.

The first is: Did Idge murder a man? The question is posed by the opening image, which shows the murdered man's truck being removed from the river. About six minutes in, the question is raised directly by the elderly woman who narrates the story, but it isn't until forty-five minutes in that we learn the victim was Ruth's husband. And it's only seventy minutes into the two-hour film that we see the murder (but not the murderer). Idge is tried for the murder, but released at ninety minutes in. Only at the end of the entire film do we learn what really happened. (Some 11 beats comprise this story line.)

A second story line is: Will Idge and Ruth live happily together? This begins about 25 minutes in when Ruth visits Idge to help her over her brother's death. Ruth then gets married. At 52 minutes in, she leaves her abusive husband to live with Idge.

At 102 minutes, Ruth dies of cancer and this story line ends. This is the story line we're most concerned with because we like the two strong women characters, yet it doesn't continue for very long—the film ends about 28 minutes later at 130 minutes (12 beats).

The first two story lines take place in flashbacks, as stories told by the elderly woman. The third story line is in the present. It belongs to Evelyn, who is being told the story. The third story line is: Will Evelyn gain confidence in herself, take control of her life, and get her husband's attention? This story line develops more typically and is a humorous counterpoint to the other story lines. It is also a useful frame for the other story lines (7 beats).

If it gets the audience involved, a film doesn't need a tight classical structure. *Fried Green Tomatoes* is a powerful film.

Pulp Fiction

Another powerful film is Quentin Tarantino's *Pulp Fiction*. It is an effective model of alternative filmmaking. Let's see what it does and does so well.

Pulp Fiction has a modular feel to it. It consists of a set of episodes and sequences rather than classic story lines. These episodes nevertheless develop with suspense, surprise, and dramatic structure and at least one fits the story line designation. There are four basic episodes.

The first episode is the frame event—it opens and concludes the film and features the robbery of the coffee shop by Pumpkin and Honey Bunny. These two frame sequences help pattern the film and give it a feeling of completeness.

The second episode concerns the adventures of Vincent and Jules when they are sent to recover a mysterious attache case for their boss, Marsellus. Vincent and Jules go to an apartment, recover the case, and kill everyone there (except for one of their own—Marvin). The shootings offer suspense and surprise.

In the long dialogue between Vincent and Jules as they head for the apartment, a suspense element is introduced—Vincent has been assigned to escort Marsellus's wife Mia. He is worried because it appears that a guy who once gave Mia a foot massage was thrown off a balcony for his impertinence.

The date becomes the third episode of the film. Vincent and Mia hit it off. There is a hint of mutual attraction, but nothing untoward happens. We are, however, immediately thrust into a strong surprise and suspense moment when Mia snorts pure heroin thinking it is cocaine and Vincent has to rush her to a friend's house and give her heart an injection of adrenalin. If she dies, he dies. It's a tense dramatic build to a mini-climax.

The fourth episode—which has the most fully developed story line—belongs to Butch, a boxer. Just after the brief-case recovery, there is a short scene in which Marsellus tells Butch he has to take a dive in an upcoming fight. We don't see Butch again until after the episode between Vincent and Mia. Rather than take the dive, he wins. In fact, he kills his opponent in the ring, sneaks out of the gym, and is about to skip town with a woman friend, Fabian.

Fabian, however, has forgotten to bring Butch's grandfather's watch from the apartment. He goes back to get it, giving us a suspenseful moment because we know Marsellus wants Butch killed. Sure enough, Vincent is in the apartment, waiting to kill him. Instead, Butch surprises Vincent and shoots him dead.

But leaving the apartment, Butch is spotted by Marsellus. Surprise! This leads to a chase that climaxes in a pawnshop where they are both captured by a pair of sadistic hillbillies who proceed to abuse Marsellus. Butch breaks free, but rather than escape, he returns to rescue Marsellus who forgives him for the earlier double-cross. Butch and Fabian are now free to leave town. Butch's story is over.

We then jump back in time—to where the second episode left off. Vincent and Jules have just shot the guys who stole the case, only now we discover that another man was hiding in the other room! He bursts in with drawn gun, shoots at Vincent and Jules, but miraculously all the shots miss.

This sets up a major character reversal. Jules believes the shots missed for supernatural reasons. He takes this as a sign that he should reform, and decides to quit the rackets. But as they drive away, Vincent accidentally shoots and kills Marvin. (Surprise!)

This gives us a new suspense sequence—as Vincent and Jules must find a way to clean up the car and dispose of the body, which they do at a friend's house with the help of the efficient Mr. Wolf. This has the added suspense of a ticking clock because they must do all this before the friend's wife returns from work.

Vincent (whom Butch killed earlier, remember?) and Jules drive to the coffee shop, and the film ends with the frame story of the robbery. The surprise twist here is that the reformed Jules lets Pumpkin and Honey Bunny take the money and go rather than kill them.

Although it doesn't fit the traditional dramatic structure model, *Pulp Fiction* is filled with suspense and surprise—and that is what holds our attention.

It is hard to say whose story it is. Butch has the most story line-like episode, but it occurs primarily in the middle of the film and is more of a subplot. Vincent is the character we most identify with, especially because of his interlude with Mia. Yet he is killed off almost casually, and he does not play a major role in the climax—the confrontation in the coffee shop. Jules is the one who goes through a major change; it is he who grants the coffee shop robbers their lives. But Jules doesn't fit the role of a traditional protagonist with conflict, objective, and a series of crises to overcome.

Pulp Fiction has a number of other innovative stylistic elements. It is clever, funny, and quite stylish. The characters are appealing; we identify with them at moments, but not in any long story lines—which may be what allows us to like them despite their violence. Humor is used to distance us from the violence, and to keep us from being put off. The dialogue often involves long speeches. At times characters discuss trivia, but it has a special quality to it—we like its rhythm and the way the characters interact.

We never see the boxing match in which Butch kills his opponent. Butch only learns he killed the guy when a cabbie says she heard it on the radio. Most films would have shown the fight. Not *Pulp Fiction*.

The film works. We like the way it keeps us guessing, keeps surprising us with clever and unexpected touches: the extravagance of Jackrabbit Slim's 1950s diner, Mr. Wolf's black-tie attire, the gimp's total encasement in black leather bondage gear, the cabbie's bare feet, Jules's reciting a passage from Ezekiel before he kills, and not seeing Marsellus's face during his early appearances in the film. It all adds up to an interesting viewing experience.

Clerks

While *Pulp Fiction* made a strong mainstream impact, this was not true of *Clerks*, an off-beat, very contemporary film about the frustrations of teenagers stuck in dead end jobs, and a society that offers them little to get enthusiastic about. Yet because it rings true for so many youth today—and does so with quirky humor—it has found a strong cult following.

If there is a story line, it is: Will Dante decide whom he wants for a girlfriend? But only by the wildest stretch can this be called a story line. And as a protagonist, Dante is much more whiney than proactive.

There are some strong themes mixed in with the humor. The film makes a strong social critique. Dante tries to be a responsible clerk; Randall thinks this is crazy because the job sucks.

So many things—such as the presence of Jay and Silent Bob—are never explained. And they needn't be; we simply accept them.

The film is characterized by frequently intercutting short shots or segments of Dante in the store, Randall in the video store, and Jay and Silent Bob. It uses frequent vignettes such as the singing Russian and the guy checking the eggs.

Does the film work with suspense and surprise? Arguably these exist, but only at a very low-key level. That's okay. The suspense seems to come simply from our identifying with Dante. We want to see what happens to him.

The film makes more use of surprise with the vignettes and Caitlin's unfortunate sex experience. The surprise holds our interest, provides humor, and helps the film flaunt conventions.

I think one of the attractions of the film is that in its low-key way it is about social rebels. They are only clerks, but they strike a resounding blow for clerks everywhere—and there just might be a little clerk in all of us.

Here's a structural analysis of *Clerks*.

Mins

00   Dante, a teenager, is called to work at the Quick Groceries store in spite of having a hockey game that afternoon. Someone has to be there, and that's him.

05 In the store, Dante is bothered that a guy is preaching non-smoking to Dante's customers, urging them to chew gum instead. The guy is revealed to be a gum company representative.

07 Jay and Silent Bob hang out in front of the nearby video store.

12 Dante is upset that his new girlfriend, Veronica, admits to having given a lot of oral sex. She says it's no big deal, not like having real sex.

18 Dante shares this with his friend Randall who clerks the video store. Dante is further upset when he reads that his former girlfriend, Caitlin, is engaged.

24 Insensitive, Randall orders X-rated video titles over the phone in front of a woman and her young daughter.

26 A Russian who wants to sing heavy metal shows off his singing; it's terrible.

27 Dante continues to be upset that Caitlin is getting married.

33 Randall is doing a terrible job clerking, giving customers in the video store all sorts of trouble.

35 Dante and Randall watch a guy sitting on the floor of the store, checking all cartons for the perfect egg. A customer tells them that guidance counselors do this as they go crazy from their meaningless work. She says her job is masturbating caged animals for their semen. Dante continues to be upset about Caitlin.

41 Veronica brings Dante some lasagna.

42 Since Dante's replacement never shows, he has the hockey game on the store roof, but then they lose the ball down a sewer—and they forgot to bring extra balls.

49 An older man comes to the store and asks to use the toilet; he takes a soft-porn magazine with him. Dante is still upset about Caitlin.

51 Dante and Randall close the stores to go to a funeral, but are chased out. We learn they knocked over the coffin, spilling out the body. Dante defends his commitment to being a responsible clerk, while pointing out that Randall is anything but.

58 A muscular trainer who comes to the store tells Dante that he had sex with Caitlin while Dante was dating her—the whole school knows about it.

60 Dante gets fined by an inspector for selling cigarettes to a four-year-old girl—it was actually Randall who did it.

62 Caitlin arrives and says she is no longer engaged; she was never planning to get married—it was something the boy and her mother announced on their own. For a moment Dante is happy; she seems ready to take him back.

Mins (*continued*)

70   Caitlin goes to use the toilet. She is gone a long time. When she comes back she is excited that Dante snuck in and had sex with her in the dark (the light is broken). But it turns out that her paramour was the older guy who went in there earlier with a sex magazine and died (with an erection). Caitlin becomes catatonic after learning she had sex with a dead guy.

80   Jay and Silent Bob tell Dante he should stick with Veronica since she takes such good care of him. Dante agrees and says he loves her. But Randall tells Veronica about Caitlin; Veronica gets upset.

84   Now Dante is angry with Randall. They have a fight that tears up the store. Randall blames Dante for making his job bigger than it is. They both have lousy jobs; why should they commit to them?

87   Dante and Randall finish cleaning the store, friends as always.

Annie Hall

As a final example of innovative techniques, I turn to Woody Allen's *Annie Hall*, made at a time (1977) when filmic experimentation was more prevalent than it is today. It is mainstream in overall structure, but innovative in many of its techniques. Comedies seem to lend themselves more readily to experimentation. This one certainly does.

The film is introduced by Alvy talking directly to the camera. He sets up our expectations by telling how the film will show us how he got involved with, then separated from, his former girlfriend Annie.

As Alvy tells us (voice-over) of his early school experiences, the camera trucks across nasty, nagging teachers instructing at the blackboard. As a classroom teacher berates little Alvy for kissing a classmate, Alvy the man replaces Alvy the child in the now-cramped classroom desk seat and defends his healthy sex drive. When he wonders whatever became of his classmates, they appear beside their desks—still children—and address the camera as if they were now grown up: "I run a profitable dress company"; "I used to be a heroin addict, now I'm a methadone addict"; "I'm into leather."

Getting to know each other, Alvy and Annie share some wine and routine, intellectual-sounding, first-meeting conversation while subtitles showing what they are really thinking flash on the screen—what sort of sex partner the other would be, whether or not they are making a good impression.

In a quick bit, a sailor and his date run by; she breaks the fourth wall by throwing a kiss to the camera. Waiting in line for a movie, Alvy is irritated by the remarks of an opinionated man who is pontificating to his date about the theories of Marshall McLuhan. Alvy breaks out of the scene to tell us he can't stand the stupid things the man is saying. The man joins him and defends himself to the audience. Alvy reaches behind a billboard in the theater lobby and magically brings out McLuhan, who tells the guy he doesn't know what he is talking about.

In bed together, Alvy complains about Annie's being sexually distant. A spirit doppelganger image of Annie rises from her body and they discuss the spirit as "distant."

In a dinner scene at Annie's house, Alvy must deal with her anti-semitic grandmother and her critical family. One shot shows Alvy made up to look like an orthodox rabbi, reflecting his self-consciousness.

A split screen simultaneously shows this dinner and an earlier dinner with his family to point up the contrasting lifestyles. The two conversations go on simultaneously, then consecutively. The families talk to each other across the split screen.

A split screen is also used later to show Alvy and Annie talking to their psychiatrists. Their conversations interrelate and blend.

In a flashback to an earlier event with Annie and a date at a party, Alvy and Annie appear in the scene as invisible viewers—as if they had been transported back in time. In another scene they go back in time to an episode in Alvy's childhood home.

Talking of his childhood, Alvy says he liked the wicked witch in *Snow White*. The film then becomes a cartoon showing a cartoon-figure Alvy with the wicked witch. Then Alvy's friend enters, also as an animated cartoon figure, and says he's lined up a date for Alvy. The next scene is back to live action, and we see Alvy with the date.

Near the end there is a scene in which two actors we haven't seen before are rehearsing an ending scene for the film—one in which Annie comes back to Alvy. Alvy addresses the audience: "Wouldn't it be great if real life was like this?"

Done badly, such innovations can seem self-conscious, gimmicky, irritating, even infuriating. They risk flaunting differences for their own sake, or of being obscure under the pretense of innovation. Done well, innovations expand the horizons of narrative and produce exciting and challenging films. Be open to stretching the boundaries of film narrative even as you realize that the principles of narrative film structure are grounded in both filmic and dramatic storytelling traditions. They are also part of our media traditions and of audiences' expectations and marketing considerations. But there is always a place for the new and unique.

SUMMARY

This chapter presented alternate ways of approaching screenwriting. While most films follow the mainstream techniques discussed earlier, there is always room for the innovative and experimental. Examples were given from both film and television, and included detailed analyses of four diverse films: *Gregory's Girl, Fried Green Tomatoes, Pulp Fiction, Clerks,* and *Annie Hall.*

ENDNOTE

1. For further discussion of some innovative approaches to scriptwriting, see Dancyger, K., and Rush, J. (1991). *Alternative scriptwriting: Writing beyond the rules.* Boston: Focal Press.

CHAPTER 8

Scenes/Sequences

In my opinion, the writer should have the first and last word in filmmaking, the only better alternative being the writer-director, but with the stress on the first word.

—Orson Welles

Butch and Sundance are trapped on the edge of a fifty-foot cliff. Far below is a raging mountain river. Above them, going for shooting position, is the super posse. Is this the end? Then Butch has an idea—they'll jump. The posse won't dare follow, and if the river is deep enough, they just might survive. It's their only chance. But Sundance refuses. They argue. "We got to." "No." "Yes." "No." "What's the matter with you?" Finally Sundance blurts, "I can't swim!" Butch laughs, "You stupid fool, the fall'll probably kill you." They jump.

I like to show this scene in class because here in about a minute and a half is dramatic development in miniature. There is a beginning *set-up of the problem*: trapped between the super posse and the tall cliff, how will they survive? (*Objective: to survive.*) The middle section is their argument about jumping, and includes a new suspense element—why won't Sundance jump? We're hooked on two *suspense enigmas*: How will they survive? Why won't he jump? Then comes the humorous *surprise twist*—he can't swim. And then the *climax* as they jump (although in this case we don't really know they've survived—the resolution—until after the scene).

It's all there in one compact scene. And that's what you're now ready to write—scenes and sequences. This means, of course, that you've successfully outlined your

story. Beginning, middle, end, major plot point beats, acceleration to climax—
you've got it so it all works.

Now go back and devise the *scene action* that will realize the story beats in the
most interesting and engaging way imaginable.

Take a rather prosaic boy-meets-girl story beat and turn it into Rick meeting
Ilsa to the strains of "As Time Goes By" (*Casablanca*); Arthur rescuing Linda after
she steals the tie (*Arthur*); Annie and Sam finally meeting at the Empire State Building observation deck on Valentine's Day (*Sleepless in Seattle*); and the delightful way
Romeo spies Juliet at the dance and their later meeting in both Zeffirelli's *Romeo and
Juliet* and Luhrman's modern day transformation (thank you, Shakespeare). All express the classic boy-meets-girl beat; each is done with its own unique scene action.

WHAT IS A SCENE? WHAT IS A SEQUENCE?

A *scene* is a unit containing a single and continuous dramatic action unified by time,
space, content, concept, character, theme, or motif. While it could conceivably be a
single shot (such as some scenes in *Annie Hall*), a scene is usually a cohesive series of
related shots.

A *sequence* is a longer segment made up of a series of closely related scenes that
together form a unified whole. Sequences need not be continuous; their events may
occur at different times and places just as long as they are related to each other. A
montage of battle scenes would constitute a sequence, so would intercutting between the pursuer and the pursued.

Typically, a film has between thirty to fifty or more scenes and some eight to
fifteen sequences. Of course, this depends on your material. Contemporary action
films can easily have twice that number of scenes. The fast-moving script of the
opening episode of the one-hour television series, *Hill Street Blues*, had 120 scenes
crammed into its 59 pages befitting the machine gun pace of the show.

Fast pace is a hallmark of most Hollywood films, so scenes rarely run long. A
dialogue scene typically runs three pages or less. In filmed television (not live
sitcoms in which scenes run longer), two to two-and-a-half pages is about the limit
before producers start getting nervous. Sequences take more time to develop, and
may well run seven to fourteen minutes (the final chase/confrontation sequence in
Witness goes about fourteen minutes and comprises virtually all of Act III).

PLANNING YOUR SCENES

Consider the following characteristics of scenes and sequences before beginning to
write. For each scene, you'll want to decide its:

Purpose

Internal Scene Structure (suspense and surprise)

Characters, including what each character wants in the scene and whose scene
it is (that is, whose point of view leads the scene)

Tension/Conflict

Relationship to Other Scenes

Setting and Staging

Purpose refers to how the scene functions in the story. This usually means how
it realizes a story beat, but it can also characterize, set a mood, introduce a locale.

Internal scene structure points to an important quality of scenes—they are as
carefully structured as a story line, and include a beginning, middle, and end.

Characters appearing in the scene interact with each other. Each character
wants something in the scene; tension comes from conflicting objectives. Typically
one character's perspective leads a scene; the scene develops from their point of view.

Tension/conflict is significant because it can make most scenes more effective.
This also applies to tension that is friendly or humorous (such as the sparring banter
between two lovers).

Relationship to other scenes includes the rhythm and flow among the scenes and
transitions between scenes.

Setting and staging can do a lot to add interest and atmosphere to a scene.

Now let's consider each of these in detail.

WHAT SCENES DO

What is the purpose of the scene within the overall story? It is worth being clear
about this because in the tight construction of a screenplay if a scene doesn't have a
purpose it may well be eliminated.

Most scenes *advance the story*; they realize a beat in the story line. They may
introduce a problem or resolve one, or they may introduce a complication. Because
it is usually so important to keep the story moving, if a scene doesn't realize a story
beat it needs a hard look to see whether or not it belongs. Even some of your best
scenes may have to go if they hold up the story.

Scenes will have other objectives. Especially in the set-up, there will be scenes
that *introduce characters, present exposition* (to fill in the backstory), deliver some
relevant information, establish a setting, create a *mood, reveal character relationships*,
or express a *theme*.

A scene may serve as a *transition* from one time or place to another. Some
scenes provide a pause in the action, a *break* so the audience can catch its breath or
absorb the significance of what just happened. Some sequences present a quick
montage of action that compresses time. Some scenes contain some unusually interesting action; others are there simply because they're funny.

As you determine a scene's primary purpose, think about what else it might do. A scene that advances the story could also introduce a new character, set a mood, prepare us for a plot twist, or reveal more about the characters.

When Jake rips out a page of the county land records in *Chinatown*, he not only gets an important clue about the fraudulent water rights scheme, he reinforces our image of his unprincipled character and—to our delight—puts one over on the snotty clerk who hassled him.

Most scenes you write are scenes that *realize a story beat*. They advance the plot. There's a key moment in *Witness* when John Book, dressed as an Amish, punches out an harassing ruffian. When we watch the young tough accosting the Amish—who are non-violent and won't fight—we want him stopped. When he harasses John, we are glad to see John let out his anger.

Then a citizen complains to a passing police car about such atypical Amish behavior, thus thrusting us into the next major story beat. We know that John has been discovered and the villains will come after him. The scene is the act-break crisis that ends Act II. It spins the story around and sends us into Act III.

Although characters are always revealing themselves, some scenes exist primarily to *reveal character*. The opening of *Harold and Maude* looks like a suicide. Only as the scene ends do we realize—surprise!—it's all been staged. What sort of person is this Harold?

Sometimes we are invited to share an intimate moment with a character. In *The Grapes of Wrath*, Ma Joad sits alone in the deserted shack that the family has long called home, but which they are now forced to leave. Ma is sorting through old postcards and souvenir trinkets that sum up her life over the years. She looks wistfully at each one before throwing it away. The pillar of the family is closing the book on her past only to face an uncertain future.

Can anyone who has seen *Ikiru* forget the scene with the dying old man singing his lonely song while sitting on the swing, in the snow, alone in the park that he struggled to have built for the townspeople as his final act of meaning?

Some scenes *present a theme*, or *thesis*. Toward the end of *Viva Zapata!* there's a scene in which Zapata has been called back to his village where his brother is oppressing the people—stealing their land, possessions, even their wives. Zapata challenges them: they are wrong to always look for great men to lead them. There are no great men; there are only men like themselves.

Pauses or break scenes give the audience time to evaluate previous scenes or to anticipate future ones. Sometimes break scenes are simply a breather from the action. The rise and fall of story development often requires tranquil moments from which to jump into the next crisis. This is especially true in horror films, in which a tense encounter is followed by a temporary lull before moving on to the next thrill.

Hitchcock claimed he put the talky restaurant scene in *The Birds* in order to let the audience catch its breath. The barn raising sequence in *Witness* serves as a break in the tension. So does the scene in which the children and Grant rest safely in a tree and meet a friendly plant eating dinosaur in *Jurassic Park*.

Informational scenes (exposition) are among the most difficult to write. They are often talky scenes that risk being dull. Try laying out the information that you must get across, then edit it as much as possible. Then as you write the scene try to make it as interesting as possible even as you give us the information.

Comic relief scenes are useful to break tense narrative development. The classic example occurs in *Macbeth*. Just after the murder of Duncan there is an unexpected knocking at the gate and the comic porter appears. Many serious films use comic relief to diffuse tension and to highlight the more intense moments.

Short transition scenes bridge the move to another time, place, or action. Often this is done by a montage, such as a car driving the road to a musical accompaniment (shot MOS—"mit out sound").

Time transitions present a special challenge: how to carry the audience over a period of time. We've all seen the stereotypical calendar pages fluttering away, clock hands spinning, candles burning down, or apples rotting on a sill. Transitions covering continuing action are often presented in condensed montage sequences—such as a boxer in training, a bandit committing robberies, or a sports team winning games. In *Tightrope*, we see Wes take some tequila and then suck a quarter of a lime. As he pours another we see a pile of used limes on the table—this tells us that Wes has been drinking all day.

A *money scene* features action that is so exciting it can be run in the promotional trailer to attract audiences—the dam bursting or the skyscraper collapsing in flames. It is usually the most expensive scene in the film, but it might be anything that can be hyped—a noted actress baring her breasts, or a well-publicized sexual encounter between two major stars.

INTERNAL SCENE STRUCTURE

Like story lines, individual scenes have a structure that must be plotted. Many scenes use a *basic dramatic structure pattern* with beginning, middle, and end, including a build to the scene climax. We saw this in the *Butch Cassidy and the Sundance Kid* scene at the beginning of this chapter. Such scenes are laid out much like a story line.

First, determine whose scene it is and identify that character's conflict, problem, or objective. Then identify objectives for the other principal characters in the scene because *every character will want something*. Here again, do so with the active verb form, "to _____."

For example, in a scene from a romantic comedy his objective is "to seduce without commitment" while her objective is "to resist seduction and get commitment." Trace the development and complications of the conflict/problem/objective and determine its climax and resolution.

Here's an example of a dramatically structured sequence from *The African Queen*. It's the moment when Charlie and Rosie attempt to sail the Queen past the German fort overlooking the river. Their objective is to safely get past the fort. The objective of the soldiers is to stop them—by shooting them. It has classic dramatic build. There is a problem—to get by the fort and its gunfire. The problem is exacerbated when a bullet hits a steam line, causing the boat to lose headway. The soldiers gleefully continue firing as the Queen slowly drifts in the water. The final crisis occurs when the German officer draws aim at Charlie, who is trying to repair the damage. Just as the officer is about to shoot, the sun reflects off the eyepiece of his telescopic sight causing him to be temporarily blinded. (We've been prepared for this.) When he looks again to shoot, the Queen has rounded the bend out of sight of the fort. A successful climax and resolution.

The Button.   Well-written scenes don't just abruptly stop, they have a designed end—a *button* that gives the scene a sense of completion. It could be a payoff or scene climax. It could be an action that thrusts us into the next scene or simply a fitting conclusion to the action. But there is usually something that "buttons up" the scene. The "curtain line" that closes a scene with a bang is an example of a forceful button. Don't simply let scenes end trivially; be sure to give them a button.

Twists and Reversals.   A *surprise twist* is always welcome to keep us guessing (as in the *Butch Cassidy and the Sundance Kid* scene that began this chapter). Similarly, a *reversal* of position or fortune adds spice to a scene. In *Dances with Wolves*, Dunbar's intended suicide ride (rather than have his leg amputated) leads to victory in the battle. The leg is saved because the commander notices Dunbar's bravery and has the leg treated. All this leads to Dunbar's being sent West.

Begin Scenes Late.   Quite often the audience enters the scene late—after much of the action has already happened. Imagine a scene that shows a romantic couple breaking up in their favorite coffee house. The entire event would encompass arriving, being seated, and ordering coffee. There might be an obvious strain between them making conversation difficult. Perhaps someone drops over to say a quick hello. Things gradually build until one of them makes the dreaded announcement that their relationship is over.

You might choose to include all of this in the scene so the audience can anticipate what is to happen and watch the stress on the couple as things build to the scene climax. On the other hand, showing the entire action of the event might not fit a fast moving story. It might be best to come to the point quickly and move on. Rather than show all the preliminaries, the screenwriter chooses to "enter the scene late." Perhaps the couple is already seated, and the action begins with one of them announcing the break up.

Screenwriter William Goldman says that he always starts his scenes at the last possible moment. It's something to consider as you write your scenes.

Keep Scenes Flowing.   The *African Queen* sequence described above is quite self-contained. It is a miniature dramatic event with beginning, middle, and end. After they round the bend to safety, there is a momentary breather before the next crisis begins. This is a typical scene pattern—solve one crisis and then begin another.

There is another way to write a scene that keep things flowing without the lull between scenes. Resolve the main crisis of a scene as usual, but have an unresolved element in the scene that *thrusts us directly into the next scene.*

Something is unresolved, and this suspensefully carries us to the following scene. It may be a new crisis, or an element of the previous crisis left unsettled. But the scene ending doesn't close something off so much as keeps something hanging unresolved. This way we always are involved in some continuing crisis, and the scenes flow along.

In *Alien* when the crew members first chase the creature, they think they have it cornered, but what was showing up on their sensor reading turns out to be the spacecraft's cat. It's a tense scene, building to the point when they throw open the hatch to reveal . . . the cat. But then one of the crew lets the cat get away and now must go after it. He does and is killed by the creature. One scene climaxes—only to thrust us into the next crisis.

In a sequence in *The Good, the Bad, and the Ugly*, some villains are sneaking up the stairs toward the room of the hero, who lies on the bed slowly reassembling his six-gun after cleaning it. The sound of marching men in the street outside covers the sound of the villains' creeping footsteps. We intercut back and forth. Then the marching halts for a moment, and the hero hears the jingle of a spur outside in the hall. The villains pause outside the door. One slowly reaches for the doorknob. The hero is hurrying to insert bullets in the gun. Will he make it in time? The door is flung open—and the hero shoots them all! But then his primary antagonist appears at the window and gets the drop on him! A new crisis!

Screenwriter Frank Pierson believes audiences should not be given a chance to breathe; they should be swept along with no time to reflect on what the action is all about.[1] He advocates a series of sequences that never come to a halt. Pierson suggests bringing a scene to the point of resolution—one of the two characters in conflict must win—then cut away before we see the resolution! The next scene tells us what happens in the previous scene's confrontation, then plunges immediately into a new crisis. This pattern of cutting out before the scene resolution continues up until the actual resolution that ends the film.

Pierson sees this as the secret of narrative drive.[2] He admits that not many movies have this sort of thrust, but he mentions two that do: *The Third Man* and *The Maltese Falcon*. Like much of what we discuss, if this approach fits what you're writing, see if you can use it.

Discontinuous Sequences and Scenes.   Sequences are not always continuous in space and time. In an early scene in *Apocalypse Now*, Captain Willard is in his hotel room in Saigon reflecting, thinking, doing a martial arts exercise. It is all shot discontinuously in time.

A scene sequence can similarly develop discontinuously in space. In *Pulp Fiction*, Jules and Vincent have a continuous conversation that moves from a car to an apartment building lobby, into an elevator, and finally to the front door of the men they've come to kill.

Pace.   Consider the pace of each scene. How quickly should it move? How short should the dialogue segments be? Are sentences completed, or cut off before they are finished? Do the characters interrupt one another? Does the pace of the scene increase as it builds? How fast or relaxed is the action? The pace should fit the scene as well as the overall pace of the film.

Sometimes you'll lay out a strong scene of four to five pages/minutes, only to find that this is too long for a moment in the script that can support only two or three pages/minutes.

On the other hand, if a scene is working well, don't rush it. You may want to milk a good scene and play it for all it's worth. With less significant scenes, it's best to get in and out quickly.

Tone and Mood.   The tone and mood of a scene will reflect the film as a whole, as well as the purpose and content of the particular scene. Consider how a particular tone or mood can enrich a scene, and be aware of how mood contrasts help pace the film. In *Pulp Fiction*, even as Jules and Vincent go to kill, their conversation adds a macabre humorous tone to the sequence.

Active Characters.   In dialogue scenes it is a good idea to have the characters *doing* something. This can avoid the problem of "talking heads." For example, if a character is called into the boss's office to be fired, consider having the boss offer the character a drink. Just as she starts to take it, the boss announces, "You're fired." Even this small bit of business is better than two characters just standing there.

SCENE ATTITUDE/POINT OF VIEW

Just as we asked "Whose story is it?" we can ask "Whose scene is it?" Usually a particular character's presence dominates the scene—to one degree or another. Their attitude and point of view leads the scene. But this isn't always the case. As we discussed earlier, it is also possible to have a more objective point of view that favors no particular character. Or you can shift the point of view within a scene or sequence from one character to another.

Shifting a point of view can produce surprise and suspense. Imagine shots of a couple talking intimately, the scene building until they finally embrace and kiss. Cut to a shot of the kiss in a very long shot, as seen through some bushes. This establishes the jealous husband's point of view and completely changes the scene.

Once Upon a Time in the West begins with a trainman writing on a small blackboard. Opening shots concentrate on him, and his attitude leads the sequence. As he nervously watches three gunslingers who await the train, the point of view—the focus and leading attitude of the sequence—shifts to the three gunmen. Titles are superimposed over the waiting gunmen. As the train arrives, there is a shift to longer shots. After the train leaves, we hear the sound of a harmonica. The point of view now includes the new character who is playing the harmonica. He kills the three who were waiting to ambush him. The focus of the sequence has shifted from a lesser character to the three ambushers to the central character.

Some interesting effects result when an event is seen through the eyes of an external observer. We interpret the action from the observer's point of view. In *Paper Moon*, we perceive the con man pulling his Bible-selling scam through the eyes of a young girl. We identify with her as we watch the scene from her point of view.

In *2001: A Space Odyssey* when Dave and Frank sit in the pod discussing how they must disconnect HAL, the malfunctioning computer, we cut to HAL's point of view outside the pod. We can no longer hear Dave and Frank, but when we see their lips moving, we know HAL is on to them.

Subjective perspectives can be striking if not overdone. In Dryer's *Vampyr* there is a subjective shot from the corpse's point of view in a coffin—and then he starts to move!

In *Spellbound*, there is a shot in which the camera is in the subjective position of a man sighting over the revolver he holds on a woman. She talks him out of killing her. We follow her over the sights of the revolver as she goes to the door and exits. The gun slowly turns around until it directly faces the camera—now both the man and the audience—and then fires.

It is important to know whose point of view leads a scene. Be sure to give the scene to the right character.

SCENE TENSION/CONFLICT

Just about every scene benefits from tension or conflict. Conflict plays. It involves us. Tension punches up a scene and adds spice. Try to include some conflict or tension whenever possible. Review each scene with an eye to punching up scenes by introducing tension and conflict.

In a scene from *The Caine Mutiny*, the Captain is leaving his ship for the last time. The sailors give him a watch as a parting gift. He could have accepted it with some sentimental speech, but the scene works better with tension. The Captain points out that gifts are against navy regulations and refuses it, placing it on a small table near the railing. Then as he leaves the ship he sees the watch, acts as if someone has forgotten it, and puts it on, saying he'll set it a half-hour slow so he'll always remember the fouled-up crew. The conflict both moderates and intensifies the sentiment of the scene.

It's a romantic cliché that if a man and woman don't like each other when they first meet, it is guaranteed they'll get together before the film's end. Although overdone, the principle is a good one—get tension or conflict going between them to accentuate the romance to come. It's in all the bickering that goes on in screwball comedies such as in *When Harry Met Sally*, and in television romantic comedies like *Mad About You*.

An exposition scene plays well if two characters are arguing about the information. Or maybe one doesn't want to hear it and the other insists they must.

Many comic scenes contain conflict. Cruelty and grievances are at the root of much comedy. Tension helps even if it's only in jest. In very stressful situations, we often make jokes. Much of the humor in the classic *The Mary Tyler Moore Show* episode, "Chuckles Bites the Dust," consists of the characters making jokes about Chuckles's death.

In *Butch Cassidy and the Sundance Kid*, they didn't simply face the problem of escaping, then jump. By introducing Sundance's rejection of Butch's plan to jump, the scene built tension (and suspense).

A scene from *Murder, My Sweet* illustrates how tensions and conflicts (and the suspense they engender) can make a mediocre scene into a masterful one. The scene is between detective Philip Marlowe and the Moose (referred to in the scene as the Big Man). It is their first meeting and sets up future developments.

The beat of the scene is simple: Marlowe accepts an assignment to search for a missing woman. It could have been played rather boringly. But look how it develops:

It is evening. Marlowe is sitting in his office. He is looking out the window; across the street a neon sign flashes off and on. Uncomfortable, he removes his gun from inside his coat and sets it on the desk behind him. Turning back to the window, he freezes, swallows smoke from his cigarette. The neon light has just gone on. When a moment later it flashes off, we see what he sees reflected in the windowpane—the impassive features of an imposing face. Slowly, Marlowe turns around in his chair.

A huge mountain of a man is standing there. Marlowe glances at his gun, but the man pushes it aside as if it were an ashtray and sits on the desk. He asks Marlowe to look for someone. Marlowe tells him to come back tomorrow, he's closed now (and picks up his gun, returning it to his inside coat pocket). The Big Man continues, saying he can't find her. Marlowe glances impatiently at the phone, expecting a call. The Big Man takes out a roll of bills and shoves some across the desk.

At this moment, the phone rings. Marlowe reaches for the phone, then looks at the money. He replaces the phone, pockets the cash, and says to the Big Man, "Okay. You show me where she worked." Marlowe flips off the light and the two head toward the door.

The beat is simple—Marlowe accepts the assignment to find someone. The scene isn't long, just ten short dialogue speeches, but the way it develops adds suspense: the flashing neon light, the windowpane reflection, the surprise appearance of the Big Man, the suspense of the gun, and the sudden interruption of the phone call.

Without conflict there is no story. Without scene conflict, there is often little interest. See if you can't put tension and conflict in just about every scene you write.

SCENE SUSPENSE AND SURPRISE

Suspense and surprise—so important to a media story—are also important principles when you write your scenes and sequences.

Suspense is generated when the audience is led to anticipate an exciting development or payoff. Suspense frequently follows this cue-delay-fulfillment (payoff) pattern. The audience is cued to some impending action that is then delayed. We are kept hanging and our tension builds. Then comes the payoff, and hopefully it is more surprising than what we expected.

Consider this scene from *The Conversation* in which the hero is searching an immaculately clean apartment for evidence of a murder. We are in suspense that something will be found. But he finds nothing. The place is spotless. Looking in the bathroom, he approaches the closed shower curtain. He hesitates. We expect the worst. He flings the curtain aside to reveal . . . nothing. The delay is maddening. He looks further. Where is the evidence? Where is the body? Then comes the surprise payoff as he flushes the toilet and blood overflows from it!

Hitchcock once defined suspense this way: if a bomb goes off unexpectedly, we get a few seconds of excited response. But suppose we make the audience aware that there is a bomb ticking away under the table. The people in the room talk about football. Or an important character starts to leave . . . but then returns because he has forgotten something. He continues to procrastinate and delay; something always calls him back—telephone calls, a last memo to write. All the while, the bomb is ticking away. The tension is tremendous; we know about the bomb, they don't. This is building scene suspense.

Manipulating Knowledge

Letting the audience know something the character doesn't know is a way to create suspense. We wait for the character either to find out or face the consequences. This packs a two-fold punch: suspense for the audience based on privileged knowledge, surprise for the character when fulfillment comes. (And perhaps surprise for us too—we don't know when the payoff will come, and it may not be what we expect.)

Much of our pleasure is anticipating the character's reaction to finding out what we already know.

In the previously mentioned scene from *2001: A Space Odyssey*, Dave and Frank think they'll be undetected when they go into a space pod and decide to turn off HAL, the computer. But we see HAL watch their lips moving and we know—but they don't—that HAL is reading their lips and knows of their plans. Having been cued, we wait suspensefully to see what HAL will do.

Television crime programs sometimes let us see the crime committed so that we know the identity of the criminal even though the detective doesn't. On other shows, neither we nor the detective know and we both find out together—or one of us finds out before the other.

In a classic Hitchcock suspense scene from *The Birds*, we watch Melanie seated on a park bench outside the schoolhouse waiting for the children inside to finish singing their song. We see crows gather on the jungle gym behind her. Our suspense builds as we anticipate her discovery. Then Melanie notices a solitary bird in the sky. She follows its flight path and discovers the horde of crows behind her. We experience the suspense of anticipating her discovery and empathically share her surprise.

The Payoff

The payoff should justify the suspenseful build up to it. Try including a surprise—something we don't expect. Imagine Laurel and Hardy walking down a sidewalk. Hardy is lagging about a dozen yards behind, trying to straighten his tie. Laurel finishes peeling a banana and drops the peel on the sidewalk. We anticipate that Hardy will step on it and fall. And so he does.

But as he falls, he grabs for a store awning and pulls it down. This knocks over a fruit-and-vegetable pushcart, spilling its produce all over the street intersection. Cars swerve and smash. One hits a fire hydrant, sending up a geyser. In a few seconds, the intersection is pandemonium. The payoff is better than we expected.

A well-remembered payoff occurs in *Raiders of the Lost Ark* when a swordsman confronts Indiana Jones. The swordsman shows off with some fancy sword acrobatics. How will Indiana deal with this formidable adversary? He simply draws his gun and shoots the surprised foe. (And gets a big laugh from the audience as we see the pretentious adversary get his put down.)

A suspense scene can end without such a dramatic payoff and still satisfy us. *Marathon Man* features a powerful scene in which a former Nazi finds himself in New York's diamond district. His action in the scene is simply to walk away, but we can read the tension in his face.

A woman on the other side of the street recognizes him. She calls out for people to stop him, but her English isn't good and the passersby think she is crazy. Finally, the woman tries to stop him. She starts to run across the street and is hit by a taxi. Her pursuit is over. The man walks on, away from the commotion—not a flashy resolution, but it concludes a suspenseful scene (and is a suitable button).

Comedy scenes often build to a comic payoff. We'll discuss this in the chapter on comedy. For now, here's an example from an early sophisticated comedy—*Trouble in Paradise*, directed by Ernst Lubitsch. It's been called the perfect Lubitsch scene. The Baron and Countess are having a romantic dinner.

With perfect elegance, the Countess announces, "Baron, you are a crook. You robbed the gentleman in 253, 5, 7, and 9. May I have the salt?" "Please," he replies, "Pepper too?" "No thank you." "You're welcome."

They eat a moment, then he decorously says, "Countess . . . let me say this with love in my heart. You are a thief. The wallet of the gentleman in 253, 5, 7, and 9 is in your possession. I knew it very well when you took it out of my pocket. In fact you tickled me. But your embrace was so sweet."

The Baron gets up and locks the door. He gallantly helps the Countess up from her seat—then shakes her and recovers the wallet that falls from her dress. They resume eating, always maintaining composure. "I like you, Baron," she says. "I'm crazy about you," he answers. They speak without looking up from their plates.

The Baron then returns the pin that he stole from her dress, saying there is one really good stone in it. She asks him the time, but he finds his pocket watch missing. She returns it to him, stating that it was five minutes slow but she regulated it for him. He thanks her, then tops the sequence by asking the Countess if he may keep her garter. She checks to see if it is indeed gone. He holds it up to her, and she jumps up and embraces him. "Darling!" she says.

Two examples from *The Fugitive* illustrate the interplay of suspense and surprise, as well as the dramatic build to sequence climax. To review the story, Dr. Richard Kimble has been falsely convicted of killing his wife. His story objective is to catch the real killer and clear himself, even as he avoids being recaptured.

In the first example, Kimble is in a police bus, which is taking him to prison. On the highway, one convict feigns acute illness. When a guard starts to help him, he stabs the guard with a pen. In the ensuing melee, a guard shoots some of the escaping prisoners as the bus spins out of control and rolls down an embankment. This makes for wild action and strong visuals.

Because Kimble is a doctor, his wrist irons are unlocked so he can help the wounded guard, but the bus is resting on train tracks and a train is bearing down on them—strong surprise and ticking-clock suspense. The other guard bails out, abandoning his buddy. Kimble takes the time to get the wounded guard out a window as the train speeds closer. (Characterizing him as a nice guy and reinforcing our sympathy for him.) He jumps free just as the train hits the bus.

Then comes a striking visual effect as Kimble tries to run to safety, hampered by the leg irons he is wearing, with the locomotive bearing down directly on him. He jumps into a ditch as the train barely misses him, then crashes and burns.

An added element thrusts us into the next sequence—Kimble discovers that he is injured, which leads to his sneaking into a hospital to fix his wound.

The second sequence follows shortly thereafter. Leaving the hospital, Kimble steals an ambulance for his getaway. But he is discovered. Quickly U.S. Deputy Marshal Gerard in a helicopter and police cars are on to him. He gets trapped in a tunnel and abandons the ambulance. He has no place to run—both tunnel ends are blocked. Is he about to be recaptured? Then he notices a drain.

Gerard and the others are stymied. They can't find Kimble among the other cars in the tunnel. Has he escaped? But then Gerard notices water flowing into the drain and follows Kimble into it.

Now the chase is on foot; they slog through the large storm drain. The drain branches. Gerard goes one way, sends his men another (thus permitting the one-on-one confrontation coming up). But—surprise—Gerard slips in the tunnel and loses his gun. Kimble picks it up, getting the drop on Gerard. For a moment they face each other. Then Kimble proclaims, "I didn't kill my wife." Gerard replies, "I don't care." It is a strong moment and the lines highlight their encounter.

Kimble turns and continues along the drain. Gerard takes out a second gun and pursues him. Kimble runs into a dead end—the drain ends overlooking the immense dam and the water flowing over it. Gerard gets the drop on him; there is no escape now.

But then Kimble does the unthinkable—he jumps into the dam waters. A thrilling climax, and one that creates still more suspense—will he survive?—and shoots us into the next scene.

RELATIONSHIP TO OTHER SCENES

There's a rhythm and flow to the progression of scenes, to how one scene relates to those preceding and following it. Often scenes build in *speed and intensity* as the film builds to its climax. Other films have more thoughtful endings that allow us to reflect on what we have seen and what it means to us: Rizzo's quiet death on the bus at the end of *Midnight Cowboy*, or the sentimental endings of Chaplin films.

Vary the rhythm of the scenes. A series of scenes at the same level—even an intense level—can grow tedious. Especially in the middle section, moments of crisis, confrontation, and climax can be balanced by quieter moments—by those lulls in which characters reveal themselves or a mood is established. The audience catches its breath before being rushed to another dizzying height.

The African Queen moves from one crisis to another, but preceding each crisis is a slight lull—a breather in which Charlie and Rosie enjoy each other's company and laugh at the hippos and other wildlife before being thrust into the next calamity.

You can develop scene rhythms with other elements besides activity and intensity:

Dialogue and action

Fast and slow tempo

Light (or comic) and serious tone

Long and short time duration

Night and day

Interior and exterior

Static and dynamic activity

Intimate and expansive settings

Subjective and objective point of view

Noisy and quiet

Close and distanced

Variations in flashbacks, flashforwards, and real time

Presenting information, mood, or emotion

Theme, character, mood, and plot scenes

Check and Correct Weak Spots

This is something that can be done from the scene outline. If the script seems too active or melodramatic, add scenes that reveal character or relationships. If there are too many action high points bunched together in the middle, introduce a break, a dialogue scene that reveals character or a development from another story line. On the other hand, if the script seems to drag—not enough exciting highs—insert another crisis, a stronger suspense build, or a surprise twist.

In television, it is best to keep the major character in the scenes before and after the act breaks, and to have the villain in every act. In film, one may pace the appearance of principal characters, but don't go too long without a scene featuring the central character. Most likely each major character will have at least one scene with every other major character; observe how these scenes are dispersed over the film.

We've already discussed another sort of scene alternation that's especially prominent in the middle section—the *oscillation of positive and negative developments*. No sooner is one crisis problem solved (+) than another arises (−). While it doesn't necessarily need to happen lock step, it is a useful way to plan story line development.

Check the interaction of the various story lines. Pattern these over the course of the film. You might not want to go too long without playing at least one scene from a B or C story line.

Modular Patterns

Some films have a distinct modular feel to them. They are patterned around chunks of recurring and self-contained sequences.

You get a sense of this in *Harold and Maude* from Harold's series of staged suicides, his three dates, and his recurring visits to the psychiatrist, priest, and military officer. There's a similar pattern in *The Warriors:* the succession of gang battles—each complete in itself, and the periodic cutting back to the radio disk jockey's comments and to the Riffs gang. While not seen in many films, it is an interesting pattern to experiment with.

Scene Transitions

While most transitions from one scene to another simply use straightforward standard devices—the cut, dissolve, or fade—some interesting things can be done with stylized visual and aural transitions. For example, things can be spiced up by *overlapping sounds* or *dialogue* from one scene to the next. The dialogue of the prior scene can continue over the initial visual of the subsequent scene. (While this decision may be made during editing, indicate it in the script if you believe it is important.)

Citizen Kane features a number of interesting dialogue transitions in which a line of dialogue from one scene is completed in another time and place. The banker Thatcher wishes the young boy Kane a "Merry Christmas." Kane replies, "Merry Christmas." Cut to the next scene fifteen years later as Thatcher continues, "And a happy New Year."

There's a scene during Kane's gubernatorial campaign in which Leland tells a street crowd: "Charles Foster Kane . . . entered upon this campaign"—and then cuts to Kane in Madison Square Garden extolling to the auditorium crowd—"with one purpose only . . . ."

The same film gives us some unusual sound transitions. Kane's applause for Susan's singing segues into applause for Kane at a political rally. A scene in Susan's seedy apartment in which Kane is listening to her sing dissolves to a future scene in which Kane, in the fancier apartment he has given her, listens to a richly dressed Susan conclude the song.

In *Clear and Present Danger*, Ryan's being told by the President to go to Colombia overlaps the image of his perplexed face with his friend's laugh in the next scene. At the film's end, the camera holds on the dismayed figure of NSA advisor Cutter as we hear the senate committee calling Ryan to the stand to testify against him.

There are a number of unusual scene transitions in *Slaughterhouse Five* as the film jumps back and forth in space and time. Billy Pilgrim's wife calling him—"Billy, Billy"—segues into a voice calling him when he was in the army—"Billy." As a child, Billy is thrown into a swimming pool to either sink or swim; he sinks. From this envelopment in the depths of the water we cut to Billy under anesthesia in a hospital where he is receiving shock treatments.

In another scene, Billy nominates an army friend for POW leader and the subsequent applause from the men leads into the applause that Billy receives as he accepts the presidency of his town's Lion's Club. Billy walking upstairs with his dog in his arms is intercut with his walking up the bomb shelter stairs in wartime Dresden. On the planet Tralfamadore, Billy asks its unseen inhabitants: "What will I do?" We cut back to Dresden where, as if in reply, a German officer tells him and his fellow POWs to pick up the dead bodies from the air raid.

Fancy match cutting transitions such as a cut from two diamond studs in a glove to an extreme close-up of two eyes in the same position as the diamonds—in Lester's *The Three Musketeers*—are out of fashion, although *Vampire in Brooklyn* features a match cut from the vampire's glowing yellow eye to the yellow sun shining through the sky's haze.

Scene transitions can be smooth or hard. The greater the contrast—visually and aurally—the harder the transition and the more dramatic the impact. Sometimes a smooth transition is preferable. At other times a shock effect is better.

Interesting transitions between scenes can add to the tone, rhythm, and style of your film. Just don't get too gimmicky.

ENRICHING YOUR SCENES: SETTING AND STAGING

When preparing a scene, give thought to where you are going to place it. Also consider the fact that the meaning and feel of the scene are created by where and how you stage it. Imagine the atmosphere of your scene and consider the following:

Is it well-lit or dark?

Sparse or congested?

Full of activity (in the background) or peaceful?

Noisy or quiet?

Colorful or drab?

What is the temperature—hot or cold?

What is the humidity?

Is the space open or confined?

Will there be music in the scene?

Will the action be interrupted by other activity?

Are there symbolic elements that add to the scene's meaning?

How imaginative can you be in staging the scene without getting so contrived that it detracts from the story?

Can a simple scene be spiced up by more fluid staging? Can tension and conflict be increased? Would added action make the scene more interesting?

Here are examples of how you can punch up scenes by giving thought to their staging. They are adapted from a student script.

This part of the story deals with how a United States development worker in a Latin American country befriends the young daughter of a rebel guerilla. She protects the child when soldiers search the town. The two scenes given as examples involve her later meetings with the child's mother, one of the guerillas. In the first scene, the mother comes to thank the worker. In the second scene, the mother warns the worker that they shouldn't be seen together.

As originally staged, the first scene has the woman come to the worker's house, knock on the door, enter and offer her thanks. The second scene has them passing on the street and having a brief chat. Neither staging adds much excitement or tension.

Consider instead if for the first scene the guerilla furtively moves through the village at night, being sure not to be seen. There are night sounds, a loud voice, dogs bark. The guerilla moves in and out of the shadows. Quietly she knocks at the door—too quietly, there's no response. Inside, the development worker is restless, unable to sleep. She thinks she hears a noise. She walks outside and is surprised by the guerilla stepping from the shadows.

The second scene could still happen on the street, but suppose as the development worker and guerilla see each other, the guerilla ducks behind a house. The worker is puzzled. She tries to find out why the guerilla is avoiding her. She searches around some village houses. Finally she catches up with the guerilla and confronts her.

Each of the scene versions might well have the same dialogue, but by giving attention to the staging, tension and atmosphere were added that weren't there before.

Vale gives a fine example of how choice of settings can influence the emotional content of a scene.[3] A father is informed that the hit-and-run driver who injured his small son is his neighbor. Consider the difference it makes if this scene is located in a police station (which can stress the legal issue of prosecution), a hospital (to stress the emotional turmoil of the father), or his backyard where he can see the neighbor's children playing next door. Setting is an important choice.

Here are some imaginative scene stagings:

In *Lethal Weapon 2*, Detective Murtaugh is nearly blown up by a bomb rigged to the toilet. The sequence plays out as he sits on the commode, unable to move since that would trigger the explosion.

The crop-dusting chase and the climax at Mt. Rushmore are two legendary sequences from *North by Northwest*.

The Big Red One, set during World War II, has an interesting sequence that takes place when the platoon assaults German soldiers who are quartered in a mental asylum. A furious fire fight goes on while the "crazies" continue eating their meal, totally ignoring the shooting and killing—even finding it amusing. The contrast between the vicious battle and the indifference of the inmates is striking.

Sweet Movie has two lovers literally get locked in a sexual embrace, unable to free themselves, on the Eiffel Tower. Part of the film takes place on a fantastic boat filled with candies, a suspended bed of sugar, and with a huge head of Karl Marx at the prow.

Pulp Fiction plays the sequence between Vincent and Mia in Jackrabbit Slim's 1950s diner complete with booths made from fifties' cars and waiters posing as entertainment stars from the period.

Staging involves more than the setting; it includes how you have the scene play itself out—how you develop the action. One way to add to a scene is to *have something else going on* besides the primary action. This technique isn't appropriate for every scene, but it can be useful to spice up many scenes. Give the characters some business—cooking, playing pinball, washing a dog, working on a computer—any additional activity that will avoid the stiffness of people standing or sitting and talking.

In *When Harry Met Sally*, Harry talks about his romantic troubles with a friend. The scene is staged at a football game where the two mechanically rise and raise their arms with the other spectators in the "wave" cheer. It's a small bit of business, but adds interest to the talky scene.

Because the SS Commander in *Schindler's List* has a cold, he holds a handkerchief to his face while choosing a housekeeper. Good use of a small prop.

Enrichment can include adding some sort of counterpoint to a scene in order to enhance the meaning, or to keep the audience occupied while they are getting information.

Sammy and Rosie Get Laid has a confrontation scene in which Rosie accuses Sammy's father of torturing many people back in his country. The subject matter is serious, yet the scene is staged in a busy restaurant. They continue eating; their voices rise and disturb other diners. Two violinists come to their table and (quite humorously) play ferociously, trying to drown out the loud conversation. The counterpoint makes for a most intriguing scene.

In the opening episode of the television series *Our House*, Grandfather Gus and the mother are discussing the problem of getting the daughter into school—a lot of information that is counterbalanced by having the younger kids at the dinner table surreptitiously feeding their liver to the dog.

In *SOB*, a character is trying to conduct business over the phone while a woman tries to seduce him—totally distracting him.

When is a car chase not just a car chase? In *Foul Play*, the main characters are rushing to prevent an assassination. After wrecking a car and pickup truck, they commandeer a taxi with two elderly Japanese tourists in it who don't speak any English. The tourists are at first terrified by the wild driving, until one protagonist explains "Kojak—bang bang," which they seem to understand (they must have seen that television show). They repeat it with broad smiles and enjoy the rest of the otherwise terrifying ride.

WRITING THE SCENE

Keep in mind Viki King's admonition to first write a (random) draft in order to discover what you want to write. Don't aim for perfection. Expect that your first draft will be long—the better to be able to go back and prune. Let descriptions and dialogue run long; just realize that you'll trim them remorselessly as you rewrite.

But even for your first draft, it's a wise idea to write each scene twice—once simply isn't enough to do a scene justice. Do a first writing to flesh it out, then go back and smooth it out—still trying to stay much in your creative mode—before adding it to the first draft material.

Without this second reworking, the rough draft may be too rough when the rewrite begins. On the other hand, if you keep rewriting and rewriting a scene you can get too bogged down in details and lose the sense of the script as a whole.

When reworking a scene, add color to settings, characters, and action. Could there be more suspense, an additional surprise, or more humor?

Descriptions. Make the descriptions of characters, settings, and actions a good read. Not excessively flowery, but as interesting as you can. Use action words, active tense, and striking images and metaphors. "So hot your Nikes stick to the road tar!" is more vivid than "It was a very hot day."

Use "to be" verb forms sparingly.

Character description should be kept to a sentence or two and convey just the essentials including their age if it's not clear from the script.

Writing Shots

Beginning screenwriters always wonder how much they should call shots. Should they put in CU, LS, ZOOM TO? The answer is they shouldn't. Calling shots is not the screenwriter's job, let the director do that. But a screenwriter can accomplish much the same thing by describing the scene effectively. Consider the following:

> Half-hidden in the partial shade of the scrub pine, Geer squints to make out the approaching figure. But from here, it is still a dot shimmering in the heat waves of the sand. Geer's hand slowly slides to his holster and releases the strap. The gun sets lightly in the hot leather. He squints again. Has he really seen something in the distance?

This description clearly indicates a close-up, an extreme long shot, a close-shot, another close-up, another extreme long shot. "Write" the shots in the way you describe the scene. Just don't get too literary. Remember that film writing is lean and economic.

SUMMARY

With the story outlined, you are ready to begin writing the scenes and sequences that constitute a script. This chapter looked at how to write such scenes and sequences. It began by discussing what scenes do and examining their purpose.

Quite important is the internal structure of each scene: dramatic structure, beginning scenes late, keeping scenes flowing, twists and reversals, the button that closes a scene, scene pace, tone, and mood.

Just about every scene benefits from scene tension and conflict. Suspense and surprise are fundamental scene elements, and are often derived from manipulating knowledge in the scene and building to a strong payoff. A scene develops with one or more points of view guiding it.

Scenes relate to one another and generate scene rhythms over the course of the script. Interesting settings and staging enrich a scene. The chapter concluded with suggestions for writing a scene.

A CHECKLIST FOR WRITING SCENES

What is the scene's purpose within the overall story?

What other functions does the scene serve?

What scenes will come before and after the scene?

Does the scene flow rather continuously from the scene before and into the scene after, or does it have a more autonomous, discrete, chunky feel to it?

What are the transitions between this scene and those on each side of it?

How does the scene relate to other scenes with respect to rhythm, flow, and pacing?

What characters will be in the scene?

What is each character's objective in the scene? What does each want?

What is each character's attitude within the scene—how does each feel about the events in the scene?

What is the scene's internal structure? Does it follow a beginning, middle, end, climax, and resolution pattern? Or another pattern?

Does the scene have conflict and tension?

Does the audience enter the scene early or late?

Does one scene thrust into the next?

If one scene crisis is resolved, is there another left unresolved to move us to the next scene?

How does the scene begin?

How does the scene end? Does it have an appropriate button?

Does the scene have suspense? A surprise twist? Other surprises?

Does it have an interesting setting (or staging)?

Does the scene need other things going on for additional interest?

How does the protagonist deal with conflict?

Does the scene stress action and visuals (not simply people talking)?

Is the length of the scene appropriate for its place in the script?

ENDNOTES

1. Pierson, F. (September 1986). *Giving your script rhythm and tempo.* (Interview by Douglas Holmes.) *Hollywood Scriptwriter,* issue 76.

2. He similarly suggests avoiding many reaction moments since they slow the story down unless you can give them some sort of twist that changes our expectation, such as seeing the lead character smile when we didn't expect a smile. A resolution of the scene? No, because in the next scene he's strangling somebody as a result of what was in the scene before. We've been caught off balance.

3. Vale, E. (1982). *The techniques of screen and television writing.* (2nd ed.). Englewood Cliffs, NJ: Prentice Hall, p. 61.

CHAPTER 9

Dialogue/Sound/Music

You speak like you write everything down before you say it.
—from *A Thousand Clowns*

This chapter considers the uses and abuses of dialogue, sound, and music. There's a real sense in which film is foremost a visual medium—images predominate. Try to let the visuals tell the story. Yes, there are sections of many films that are dialogue dependent, but in general the best advice is: show, don't tell. Even when writing, *think visually*.

Television is somewhat different. For a variety of reasons, including the smaller screen and manifold distractions, our attention is not so focused with television. We attend to, rather than look at, the tube. Audio carries more weight in television and should be granted more importance.

Thinking visually includes realizing that both film and television communicate through *behavioral details*. Characters don't just stand and talk. They interact. They touch, assume expressive postures, and react with facial expressions and body gestures. In reel life as in real life, characters communicate by intonation, movement, gesture, reactions, pratfalls, looks, shrugs, touch, and all the other aspects of body language.

Be conscious of non-verbal dimensions when developing character interaction and dialogue. Many of these things don't need to be written down—actors and directors are quite good at coming up with them. But if you imagine non-verbal communication—if you leave space for it in beats and pauses and in the rhythm of your dialogue—you'll write stronger scenes, more effective character interaction, and better dialogue. (The term *beat* as used within scene description or parenthetical business means a short pause; it has nothing to do with a story line beat.)

DIALOGUE

> *Of all the gin joints in all the towns in all the world, she walks into mine.*
>
> —from *Casablanca*

Dialogue provides information and advances the story. It manages time through rhythm, tempo, and pacing. It defines characters by reflecting their background, education, occupation, social status, attitudes, and individuality. It reveals character rather than describing it. It reveals emotion, mood, feelings, conflict, and intent. Even more important than the spoken words, we "hear" the intent and feelings that underlie the words.

Dialogue also provides information and exposition, preparing and foreshadowing things to come. It adds to the rhythm and pace of the script. It contributes to the ambience of each scene. It can connect shots and scenes by providing continuity (such as overlapping dialogue from one scene to the other). Offscreen dialogue and sound can suggest the presence of objects, events, and persons that aren't seen. Dialogue should complement rather than restate the visual.

Effective Dialogue

Effective dialogue *sounds natural.* It conveys the sense of real speech, but is more structured than the meanderings of daily speech. Effective dialogue is more economic and direct than real-life conversation. It moves more quickly.

The tone of dialogue is *conversational*—as opposed to literary and theatrical. Its rhythms and diction seem more naturalistic than stage dialogue. In the theater, we listen. In film, we eavesdrop.

Screen dialogue uses all the indirection, pauses, hesitations, and contractions that we use in everyday speech, but it is more condensed. Sentences are incomplete and interrupted. Characters mumble, evade, and exaggerate.

Dialogue development is controlled, but the sense is oblique, as it is in conversation. What is most significant is not what the characters say, but what they mean.

Film writing is *lean and economic.* It contains short sentences of simple construction using simple, informal words. Speeches are brief and crisp. Both dialogue and narration must be easily understood; the audience can't go back and reread a missed segment. Madeline DiMaggio calls good dialogue "a dance of two- and three-liners."[1]

Implicit Dialogue

In film, words are used more for their implicit rather than explicit meaning. What is important in dialogue is the meaning being conveyed in the circumstances of the scene, not the literal meaning of the words used. What is left unsaid can be as important as what is said.

Effective dialogue stresses connotation rather than denotation, it implies rather than explains. (Explanations are one of the deadliest functions of dialogue, to be avoided when possible.) Ernest Hemingway compared words to an iceberg—there are only a few visible on top but many more implied underneath.

On-the-nose is a derisive phrase that refers to dialogue that is too blunt, direct, explicit. While this may seem like a good way to get a point across, it can restrict audience participation in identifying what is going on behind the words. Some call it two-plus-two-equals-four writing. Your dialogue will be stronger if you consciously try to avoid writing on-the-nose dialogue.

Underwrite rather than overwrite. Be subtle rather than heavy-handed. And go easy on the adjectives; they can overload the intended meaning.

Individualized Dialogue

Dialogue should *fit the character*—their mood and emotions in the particular situation. It should have the rhythm and individual form of expression typical of the character. Dialogue should sound like the character and not like you the writer.

Characters' speeches should also *differentiate the characters from each other*. See if you can identify their dialogue styles and rhythms, their voice patterns, their favorite words and expressions, and their non-verbal means of communicating.

Try switching some dialogue around. Imagine one character's lines being spoken by another character. If speeches can be switched without any problem, they probably aren't individualized enough.

One way to individualize characters is to give them favorite expressions and dialogue styles. Rocky expresses his Philadelphia working-class background by continually punctuating his words with: "Ya know." "Ya know what I mean?" "Ya understand?" "Wha'd'ya mean?" "Wha'd'ya think?"

Leo, the comic-relief character in *Lethal Weapon 2* and *3* keeps repeating as part of his singular vocal pattern: "Ok, ok, ok." Inspector Clouseau of the *Pink Panther* series says "beuhm" for bomb, "reuhm" for room, and "leuhr" for law. Alvy Singer in *Annie Hall* is characterized by his neurotic, whiney kvetching (complaining), a pattern often used by Jerry on *Seinfeld*. And consider the unique repetitious rapid-fire dialogue style of Mars in *She's Gotta Have It*:

Is ok? Is ok? But I didn't bring nothin'. Is ok?

The first. The very first? It's good? The very first, huh?

Jamie, you call me sometime. You call me? You call me?

Can you call it in the air? Can you call it? Can you call it? Gonna call it in the air, right? (When a coin is flipped.)

Credible Dialogue

Dialogue *fits the situation and emotion* of the moment. In a time of emotional stress, a character will be less coherent, less able to speak in concise, formal prose. A novice writer's dialogue illustrates the problem of being too verbal when it doesn't fit the character's situation:

> An old woman falls and hits her head, she passes out from lifting heavy crates of vegetables outside her small New York City store. Her collapse is sudden and unexpected. A young woman rushes up to help and asks what happened. The old woman replies: "I don't know. First I got dizzy. Then I broke out in a cold sweat. My hands felt clammy. And then I blacked out. The next thing I knew I was flat on my face in the street."

It is difficult to believe that anyone would talk so coherently under the circumstances. Make sure the dialogue fits the circumstances of the scene.

Context and Intention.   Meaning in dialogue is dependent on both the context in which it is spoken and the intent behind the words. Consider the words "I love you." Depending on the way they are said, to whom, and in what circumstances, they can mean:

> I care for you. I worship you. I want you sexually. I feel protective of you. I want to control you. I want to make you feel guilty. I like you. I don't want to be bothered by you. I want to confuse you. I want to manipulate you. I want to use you. I am trying to trick you. I hate you.

Underwrite.   Dialogue is best when *underwritten and understated.* We can get turned off by characters spouting platitudes or being excessively melodramatic. If a scene is strongly emotional, it helps if the audience has been adequately prepared for it. This is even more important when the material and emotions are potentially embarrassing because of either the content or the intensity.

Here is an excerpt from a scene by an unskilled writer. A college student has just learned that his girlfriend was raped by one of his best friends. The scene takes place with the student and another friend in his college dormitory room. Here's a sampling of the dialogue:

> All I feel right now is anger and revenge—I want revenge because he disappointed me in my trust for him as a friend and roommate and he hurt the girl I love. . . . Rape—an act of violence—an act of violence against my girlfriend—Why someone you love?—Why is it that I am having a hard time accepting what happened? I really trusted him, you know. I guess I've got to face up to it—. She

was raped. Beaten and emotionally torn over what happened last night—. My God—the pain, the torture.

Read aloud, this invariably gets laughs. It is simply too heavy-handed. The speaker expresses emotions that the audience don't yet feel. Besides, do male college students talk this way to each other? Not very likely.

A useful way to deal with a sensitive event like this is to play against the emotion of the scene rather than bludgeon it. By understating you leave room to let the audience feel the emotion rather than simply recognize it.

Screenwriter Paddy Chayefsky doesn't specifically mention emotion, but I think he was on to the same principle when he advised, "First, cut out all the wisdom. Then cut out all the adjectives."[2]

Avoid Clichés.   Try to *avoid tired truisms and clichés.* They are attractive as short-cuts to quickly convey meaning, but they are also stale and will give your dialogue this same feeling.

There are exceptions, of course. You might want to create a character who spouts clichés. In *Arthur,* Susan is meant to come across as well-intentioned but banal. She says things such as, "I've cried over your loneliness" and "I'll love you whether you ever call me or not." We are meant to take her as a jerk.

Such characters are the exceptions. Try to avoid the stereotypical, the hackneyed, the trite (which, because they are such a part of our daily life, isn't always easy to do).

Writing Relationships.   When writing dialogue, keep in mind that you are writing relationships. The relationships expressed by the attitudes of the characters toward each other can speak louder than the words they use.

Character relationships can mirror those from real life. Relationships can be charged with all the emotions we know and express. They can turn outward toward another, then inward to the character's own thoughts. They can show adult characters relating as adults, or regressing and acting as children or parents to toward each other.

Character interaction scenes will be more effective if you focus on the relationship, and let the dialogue develop out of that.

Subtext

What is important in dialogue is what's being communicated—the meaning being expressed. In film dialogue, as in life, the actual meaning often lies beneath the surface meaning. This is the subtext. It may be intentional, it may be unconscious, it may be a hidden agenda that the character is trying to cover up.

A revealing metaphor describes an interpersonal dialogue scene as one in which the text words bounce back and forth like ping-pong balls while the true meaning resounds like bowling balls rolling around under the table.

Subtext applies to actions and behavior as well as dialogue. It is in the smiles and glances that pass between people, the subtle signals of intrigue, artifice, and desire.

In the wonderful eating scene in *Tom Jones*, Tom and Mrs. Waters are eating a sumptuous tavern meal of meat and shellfish. The action is eating, but what is going on through their stares and glances is a rather obvious mutual seduction.

Subtext often occurs in interpersonal "games." Eric Berne describes a flirtation game, which takes place at a suburban party.[3] A man and woman meet. He mentions to her that their hosts have restored an old barn, would she like to see it? (Subtext: he finds her sexually attractive; would she consider a possible romance?) She replies that she loves old barns and would like to see it; let's go. (Subtext: she finds him attractive as well and would like to see what sort of relationship might develop.)

Sometimes subtext is part of a deception. A character says one thing but means another. Another character may or may not sense this subtextual meaning. The audience is aware of the subtext even if the characters aren't. The stereotypical "silver cord mother" tells her son that she only wishes the best for him and that the girl he brought home is "nice"—but is he sure he's ready for marriage? Subtext: Don't get involved with her, stay with me.

There's an interesting scene in *Annie Hall* in which Annie and Alvy are making small talk about art while subtitles on the screen tell us what they are really thinking—how she would look naked, how they are coming across to each other. In the short film *Doubletalk* the actors speak the text while their voice-over commentary delivers the subtext.

A frequent comedy subtext, too often overdone, is the sexual innuendo played for laughs. In *Little Big Man*, young man Jack is being bathed by Mrs. Pendrake. Throughout the bathing and subsequent drying, she is talking about Jesus and resisting temptation, while her tone and actions express her obvious sexual arousal.

Screenwriter Harold Pinter is known for the effective use of subtext in his screenplays. In *The Servant*, Barrett gradually reduces his employer to a dependent wreck. At one point he interrupts a romantic scene between the employer and his fiancee, which creates tension between the two lovers. Later, as Barrett shows her out, he addresses a startling comment to her that seems to refer to the spat: "I'm afraid it's not very encouraging, Miss." She looks shocked. "The weather forecast," Barrett continues with feigned innocence.

Dialogue Techniques

> *The pellet with the poison's in the vessel with the pestle, the flagon with the dragon has the brew that is true . . .*
>
> —from *The Court Jester*

For most films—and there are exceptions—you'll want to make your dialogue lean and economic. This means writing short, uncomplex sentences—made up of words from a small vocabulary.

Because film dialogue is conversational, you'll want to avoid the stilted and literary.

And as characters converse, see if the dialogue can be interactive as the characters relate to each other in words and action rather than an exercise in characters taking turns speaking, which can call attention to the dialogue's written quality.

Most speeches will be short—just a few lines. When you have a longer speech, considering structuring it like a story—with beginning, middle, and end. The beginning will catch interest and perhaps state a problem or conflict. The middle will intensify this. The end is the payoff that convinces. (It's the same with a joke, build to the payoff punch line.)

Try to avoid *handles* that introduce speeches, such as: nevertheless, look, you know, say, by the way, still, anyhow, the point is, as I see it.

Should your characters keep repeating each other's names when they talk to each other? This is not an easy question to answer. Names should be used a few times when we first meet a character, but, beyond that, it depends on the situation and the characters.

In *The Last Detail*, Badass keeps repeating the name of Meadows, and also often uses his partner's nickname, Mule. It's his style of addressing them. In *The King of Comedy*, Rupert continually uses "Jerry" when talking to him; it's a character style.

For the dialogue in most present-time films, make liberal use of *contractions*— it's, I've, don't, there's. We use these in our conversations; so should your characters. Also use words like: gonna, wanna, cuz.

When writing *dialect and accents*, try for the style and rhythm of the speech, but it's better not to try the accent nor to suggest pronunciation. Before a character with an accent or strong dialect first speaks, add a note to this effect in stage directions.

If a speech is to be spoken in a *foreign language*, write it in English, but make a note that it is to be spoken in the foreign language (for scripts written in English).

Voice-Over Narration.   This is sometimes used to set, unify, and illuminate the story. It can supply a certain objectivity if the narrator is not a character (*Tom Jones, Joseph Andrews*) or a personal touch if the narrator is a character (*The Big Red One, Little Big Man, A Clockwork Orange, Dances with Wolves, The Shawshank Redemption, Red Sorghum, The Usual Suspects*). Some stories need a narrator to provide a different perspective or a unifying structure.

Offscreen Dialogue.   Much can be done with offscreen dialogue. At its simplest, it merely conveys the presence of another character, but it can also be used more stylistically. Near the opening of *Mr. Klein*, the dialogue of Klein buying a painting for a very low price from a Jew fleeing Paris during World War II is heard over the visual of Klein's mistress in the next room getting out of bed and dressing.

Overlapping Dialogue.   We usually think of dialogue as alternating between characters, but dialogue can also overlap, producing rhythmic, realistic effects or a comic feel.

In *The Magnificent Ambersons,* as the guests leave the Amberson's ball, the dialogue of one group of characters overlaps that of another, and then another. The dialogue of each group has its own verbal quality—young people speaking rapidly at normal levels, a middle-aged couple talking softly and slowly, the family members shouting. All blend into a harmonious sound montage. Quarrels among the Ambersons are similarly treated, with shouting and accusations overlapping each other, much as they do in real life.

Robert Altman is well known for overlapping dialogue—having characters speak simultaneously. In *M*A*S*H*, Radar and the Colonel often speak simultaneously because Radar is always anticipating everything the Colonel wants.

Modifying Distance.   The way in which we hear dialogue doesn't have to approximate the distance we are from the speakers. Sometimes we see the characters in a very long shot while their dialogue sounds as if they were nearby.

In *Annie Hall,* two characters walk toward the camera from an extreme long shot in which they are so distant they are out of sight. Yet their voices are close and remain so as they approach. This same effect is achieved when we are outside a building looking in, yet hear the dialogue as if we were inside.

In *The King of Comedy,* a conversation between Rupert and the head of building security begins in a reception area, then moves to the hall. As the glass door closes behind them, we continue to hear their dialogue at the same level.

Mit Out Sound Scenes.   Films frequently contain scenes shot mit out sound (MOS, or without sound). This is typical of mood scenes or traveling scenes. Often these are accompanied with a music track.

An unusual use of MOS occurs in *Cries and Whispers* when two estranged sisters briefly reconcile. We see a series of MOS shots linked by dissolves in which the women urgently tell each other everything they have been unable to say for so long. But we hear none of it; it is all MOS.

When Maude is in the hospital, we see Harold talking and arguing with hospital personnel. Finally we see the doctor come and tell him of Maude's death—all MOS.

Entrances/Exits/Closes.   *Tag lines* (which close a scene) and *curtain lines* (which close a television act) are frequently climactic lines that make an impact and project us into the next scene. A television action/adventure curtain line might be: "It wasn't an accident, it was murder!" A tag line can be a strong button. In *The Sting,* Hooker is asked why he wants to pull the big con on the racketeer who had his friend murdered. He replies, "'Cause I don't know enough about killing to kill him!"

In television situation comedy, entrances and exits are often accompanied by comic lines.

The Mechanical.   Tone and voice quality are important not only with human characters, but also with their mechanical counterparts. Much of the impact of HAL, the computer in *2001*, comes from the soothing texture of his voice. There's an individuality, too, in the fussy, "auntie" quality of C3PO in *Star Wars*.

Legends.   Written legends are frequently seen at the beginning of films to set the situation. They can also be used effectively at the end to sum up and provide a final impact.

A legend at the end of *Schindler's List* tells us how many Jews there are now in Poland (relatively few) and how many (more) are the living descendants of those Schindler saved.

Powerful, too, is the dramatic printed and spoken legend that concludes *Z*. A narrated list unrolls on the screen of all the activities and literature barred by the despotic government, ending on a picture of the man the government assassinated, along with a large letter Z, and the narration: "and the letter Z, which in ancient Greek means he is alive."

Dialogue Builds.   Ordinarily, if you have a build of elements in a dialogue speech, you'll want to build upward, from the milder to the stronger: "I was in an accident. I smashed my head. I may die." To build it the other way—a downward build—risks it being humorous, as is this deliberately comic downward build from *Monty Python* when a character is asked if he's seen a Yeti (the Abominable Snowman). "Well, I've seen one. Well, a little one. A picture of a little—. I've heard about them."

Dialogue Absence.   *Harold and Maude* makes interesting use of dialogue—or lack of it—to underscore Harold's relationship with his mother. The first line he speaks to her is in the second scene when he says in a hoarse, artificial voice, "I have a sore throat." The only other line he says to her is near the end when he tells her he is getting married and shows her Maude's picture. They have many scenes together; in most of them the mother is talking incessantly, but not a word from Harold.

The protagonist of *The Piano* doesn't speak throughout the film; she conveys meanings through looks, actions, the writing pad around her neck, through her daughter, and most vividly through her piano.

Improvisation.   *Script everything spoken.* You can't expect the actors to improvise dialogue bits for you unless it is extremely simple—but even here it is safer to write it down. Watch for scenes such as those with a television program or some other activity in the background. The lines will have to be scripted.

On rare occasions, dialogue is developed with the actors through improvisation. This can produce an exciting touch of authenticity, as in the taxi cab scene in *On the Waterfront*: "Oh, Charlie . . . it wasn't him, Charlie, it was you . . . you was my brother . . . it was you, Charlie."

John Cassavetes used an improvisational technique with his near-ensemble group of actors. Robert Altman uses similar techniques with his players. *Secrets and Lies* was reportedly done without a script.

Although it can produce exciting results, many film actors can't handle the demands of improvisation. Attempts at totally improvised dialogue frequently produce long, talky scenes as actors struggle to find the dramatic essence of the scene. The demands of film continuity, rhythm, and pacing require tighter control than improvisation permits. And studios will hesitate to finance a film without having a script they can evaluate.

Dialogue Hooks

> *Forget it, Jake. It's Chinatown.*
>
> —from *Chinatown*

Dialogue hooks are techniques that help smooth the flow of dialogue speeches. Used judiciously they give your dialogue an easy continuity. But they run a real risk of imparting a mechanical, artificial texture to your dialogue. Use them sparingly. Nothing takes the place of natural dialogue. As your characters become increasingly real to you, you will begin to hear their voices.

Question/Answer. A hook refers to how one line hooks into the one preceding. Question/Answer is an obvious type of hook. But it is also one of the most dangerous since you want to avoid an obvious back-and-forth pattern. Too many direct answers to questions will come out sounding stagy. Especially avoid yes/no answers.

If you have one character ask a question, have the second character come back with something unexpected—another question, an action, a change in the subject.

In *Network*, at their first meeting, Max asks Diana what she's doing for dinner that night. Instead of answering him directly, she picks up the phone, taps out a number, and tells the person on the other end that she can't make dinner that night. Max has his answer.

In *Butch Cassidy and the Sundance Kid*, Sundance is trying to get a job as a mine payroll guard. With his gun in his hand and aiming, he misses a tobacco plug target. Then he asks, "Can I move?" The confused foreman responds, "Move? What the hell you mean, move?" Sundance quickly draws from his holster and fires, hitting the target. "I'm better when I move."

There's a wonderful bit in the third film of Inagaki's *The Samurai Trilogy*. The famous Samurai swordsman Miyamoto Musashi—the greatest swordsman in Japan—is staying at a humble inn. There is a crowd of very noisy men outside his room. A boy who has been traveling with Musashi goes out and asks them to be quieter. The leader of the group, a tough horse trader, comes into the room and challenges Musashi. Musashi wishes no trouble and so ignores the man. But the man insists, drawing his knife. Musashi pauses from eating his noodles and plucks a fly from the air with his chopsticks! He flicks it away, then plucks two more off his kimono, then some from the bowl of noodles, all with the tips of his chopsticks. This deft display of skill awes the horse trader and answers his challenge; the astonished man hurriedly backs out of the room.

Agreement/Disagreement.   This is a hook from the previous line to the next by either agreeing or disagreeing with it. Disagreement can be expressed by contradiction, evasion or sometimes by no answer when one is expected. In *Butch Cassidy and the Sundance Kid*, the pair are trying to escape the posse.

> *Butch:* I think we lost 'em. Do you think we lost 'em?
>
> *Sundance:* No.
>
> *Butch:* Neither do I.

In this example from *Network*, Max and Diana are breaking off their relationship. They disagree (in Chayefsky's rather excessive prose). Note also the hook on matched words in the transition from the first to second line.

> *Diana:* I don't want your pain! I don't want your menopausal decay and death! I don't need you, Max.
>
> *Max:* You need me badly! I'm your last contact with human reality! I love you, and that painful decaying menopausal love is the only thing between you and the shrieking nothingness you live the rest of the day!
>
> *Diana:* Then don't leave me!
>
> *Max:* It's too late, Diana! There's nothing left in you that I can live with!

Repeated or Matched Words.   Continuity can be developed by hooking repeated or matched words from one speech to another (as in the previous example). Just don't overdo it. Here's another example from *Network*.

> *Diana:* Well, Max, here we are—middle-aged man reaffirming his middle-aged manhood and a terrified young woman with a father complex. What sort of script do you think we can make out of this?
>
> *Max:* Terrified are you?
>
> *Diana:* Terrified out of my skull, man.

From *A Clockwork Orange.*

> *Dim:* What did you do that for?
>
> *Alex:* For being a bastard with no manners. . . .

*   *

> *Alex:* To what do I owe this extreme pleasure, sir? Anything wrong, sir?
>
> *Mr. Deltoid:* Wrong? Why should you think of anything being wrong?

This hook also answers a question with a question.

* *

Georgie: All right, no more picking on Dim, brother. That's part of the new way.

Alex: New way? What's this about a new way?

Parallel Construction/Repetition. A similar device uses parallel construction of consecutive lines or the repetition of a line.[4]

Peter: Uh, hello, Shade. I bet you didn't expect to see me.

Shade: I bet you don't expect me to talk to you!

* *

Shade: Apologize and I'll *think* about working for you!

Peter: All right, I'll apologize *if* you come and work for me!

Police are concerned about a possible criminal threat and what they might do to prevent it.

First Policeman: What are we going to do?

Second Policeman: What are *they* going to do?

Sharing a Progression. A smooth continuity can be achieved when speakers are sharing a progression. This might be an interrupted build.

Hal: There'll be music and munchies—

Andrea: —and drink and dancing—

Hal: —and we'll have a ball!

Or there might be a building progression.

Peter: I want you to take the job!

Shade: I already told you what you could do with your job.

Peter: I know, I read my door.

Shade: Was there anything there you didn't understand? I'll gladly show you graphically the area I had in mind.

Peter: I want you to have the job because you are highly qualified—

Shade: —not for what you have in mind!

Peter: To make films! You're a good cameraman. I want to hire you.

Shade: It's camera*person*, and I'm waiting for your apology.

Peter: That's not why I came.

Shade: But that's why you're staying!

These are useful devices for smoothing dialogue, but their overuse will call attention to itself and make the dialogue appear artificial.

Slang and Buzzwords

Slang can give a sense of authenticity to your work, but can also go out of fashion and date your work very quickly. It can take up to three years to get a script onto the screen—after it has been bought.

You'll probably want to buy a slang dictionary, as well as a couple of thesauruses—in addition to the one on your word processing program. When writing about a special subculture, try to let the dialogue reflect the jargon of the group. Research is one of the best ways to pick this up. For example, here is some motorcycle slang:

> Hogs were once used pejoratively to refer to Harley-Davidson bikes; now they're used by the riders with pride. Scoot, scooter, putt-putt or iron are affectionate terms for a bike.
>
> Scooter trash is a way to identify a woman picked up by a Harley rider. If a hog is described as dressed, it means it's loaded with accessories. Packin' means carrying a passenger. Cage refers to an automobile.[5]

Almost every occupation has its specialized terminology. Using it will add authenticity, but be sure not to confuse the audience with unfamiliar terms merely to appear modish.

Avoiding Bad Dialogue

> *For one who has not lived even a single lifetime, you are a wise man, Van Helsing.*
>
> —from *Dracula*

Let's consider some of the things you want to avoid in your dialogue.

Generally, *avoid yes/no answers*. If one character asks a question that invites one, vary the reply. For example, instead of "yes" you could use something like "Piece of cake," "No problem," or "You wish!".

Also try to *avoid who, what, when, where, and why* questions. They seem too obviously set up. They act as *feed lines*, feeding a question to a character so that the audience can learn the answer.

Avoid a question/answer series as it rarely sounds conversational. Here are bad and good ways to handle this.

BAD

> *Jill:* So I graduated college and went to LA.
>
> *Pat:* And what did you do there?
>
> *Jill:* I worked in a newspaper morgue and really liked it.
>
> *Pat:* Why?
>
> *Jill:* Because the guy I worked with was cute.
>
> *Pat:* Who was he?

BETTER

> *Jill:* So I graduated college and went to LA.
>
> *Pat:* I bet you had a tough time.
>
> *Jill:* It wasn't so bad, I worked in a newspaper morgue and really liked it.
>
> *Pat:* I'd find it hard to meet people in a new city.
>
> *Jill:* The guy I worked with was cute.
>
> *Pat:* Tell me about it!

You can also find indirect ways to ask questions by having material come out in conversation other than by giving answers to questions.

> *Jack:* After I graduate I'm going to LA.
>
> *Bob:* You always did want to get into the industry.
>
> *Jack:* I figure I'll see Uncle Jim at Universal.
>
> *Bob:* You can write pretty well, I think you'll make it.

Let's review some of the ways to avoid bad dialogue:

Be subtle. Underwrite. Avoid dialogue that's too much on-the-nose. Use sub-text. (For your first rough scene-draft, you might even try to write out some subtext to see what your characters are really thinking and feeling—consciously and unconsciously. Then go back and make it subtextual.)

Individuate your characters. Give each their own voice.

Be sure your dialogue isn't wooden, strained, labored. Let it be easy to speak.

Motivate the dialogue; make sure it is said for a reason.

Here's an example of what a bad-dialogue scene might look like. Read it over, then we'll discuss its problems.


```
EXT. BACKYARD - DAY

Carolyn looks up from her lawn chair to see Feiffer
standing by the wooden fence that separates their
two houses and yards. Near her is a boom box blaring
LOUD MUSIC. Seeing him, she turns it down so they
can talk.

                    CAROLYN
               (surprised)
          Feiffer, what are you doing
          up? I thought you slept all
          day because of your night job
          at the bottling plant out on
          route 75.

                    FEIFFER
               (upset)
          I've had it. I can't take it
          anymore. I'm fed up, Carolyn.

                    CAROLYN
               (curiously)
          What's troubling you,
          Feiffer?

                    FEIFFER
               (pointedly)
          It's you, Carolyn.

                    CAROLYN
          What am I doing?

                    FEIFFER
               (firmly)
          No one can sleep around here
          with all that noise you're
                    (MORE)
```

                    FEIFFER (CONT'D)
making. Don't you think that
I don't know you do it
deliberately, Carolyn? Don't
you think that I didn't see
you deliberately move the
chair from where it was on
the other side of the yard to
right over here by my bedroom
window? You're not fooling
me, Carolyn. You're asking
for it.

                    CAROLYN
                (challenging)
So what are you going to do
about it, Feiffer?

He comes out from behind the fence carrying an axe.

                    CAROLYN (CONT'D)
                (frightened)
Where did you get that axe?

                    FEIFFER
                (strongly)
I'm going to smash that box
to slivers and chips. I'm
stopping this noise once and
for all. I'm through being
nice.

                    CAROLYN
                (desperately)
Feiffer, no!

                    FEIFFER
Here's Feiffer!

                    CAROLYN
Feiffer!—

He chops the boom box into pieces.

Now let's dissect the scene. First, it needs to get rid of all—or at least most—of the parenthetical instructions that precede each speech. These should be used extremely sparingly. The line itself should indicate how it is to be spoken. Don't use a parenthetical unless there is doubt about the delivery—such as some irony or underlying emotion that might be missed.

The characters have an absolute obsession with each other's names. Let each repeat a name maybe once or twice—that's all.

The dialogue throughout is too on-the-nose, too blunt. The entire scene is too melodramatic.

Carolyn's first lines are obvious exposition. What difference does it make that Feiffer works at the plant or where it is located? We need to know that he sleeps all day and works all night but the information must be delivered subtly. Remember that whenever one character tells another something they both know, it's likely to be fraudulent exposition.

Feiffer's first line contains three clichés. Then Carolyn asks him two questions—*feed lines*. She feeds him questions so we—the audience—can get answers.

Feiffer's reply is much too long, and gives us much more information than we need. Explanations make for irksome dialogue. Then Carolyn gives him another feed line. Then she comes up with a *radio line*, so named because it harks back to the days of radio drama when the only way the audience would know about the appearance of an axe (or knife, gun, whatever) was to have it pointed out. But we can see it and the line seems phony.

He then delivers a *downward build* speech. If he must say these lines, they should be reversed so the build goes from through being nice to stopping the noise, to smashing the box.

Finally, let's give him credit for the one redeeming line in the scene—his "Here's Feiffer," which is a parody of "Here's Johnny" from *The Shining*, which is a take off of Johnny Carson's introduction on the *Tonight Show*. Too bad this attempt to play against the excess melodrama of the scene didn't persist throughout.

Working Your Dialogue

Do your scene draft to see what the characters have to say. Determine what has to be said and then say it in the most economical way possible.

Your first draft may be long. Expect it to be rough. Then rigorously rework it. Remember: *Effective dialogue is rewritten dialogue.* Eliminate excess references, repetitions, padding; make speeches shorter. You'll be surprised at how much unnecessary material can go.

On-the-nose dialogue can be eliminated as speeches become more subtle and indirect. Try to do more implying than explaining; work in subtextual meaning.

If most of the speeches run to four and five lines, there's a good chance the dialogue needs trimming. Consider cutting it down to two or three lines. (And be sure to preserve proper dialogue format spacing—don't try to fool yourself by extending the dialogue into the right margin to make the number of lines seem less.)

Check that the dialogue contains conflict, and that it moves quickly, using active verbs and colorful images. Give the characters some business so they're not simply talking at each other. As an exercise, cover the names above speeches and see if you can identify who's talking. If the speeches seem interchangeable, you're not personalizing the characters' voices.

Try to hear the lines as they would be spoken by an actor playing the character. Try reading them aloud. Have them read to you. Tape some of the lines and play them back.

In order to fine tune your dialogue writing, tape a two-person conversation of some substance. Transcribe it. Note the main points that are made. How much extraneous material is wasted getting to these points? Cut out what is irrelevant and see what's left. Try to make it read like dialogue.

SOUND

> *A relationship, I think, is . . . is like a shark, you know? It has to constantly move forward or it dies. And I think what we got on our hands is a dead shark.*

> —from *Annie Hall*

Sound is one of a filmmaker's most useful resources, and one of the most often neglected. Sound is pervasive, it gives the impression of filling the screen. It has no specific direction (except as used in multi-speaker systems). Perhaps because it is less specific than the visual, sound can be strongly suggestive and connotative. And sound—because it's added on top of the visual—can make its contribution without slowing the action.

As you visualize a scene, listen to the sound. What special sounds might the scene contain? How can sound complement or counterpoint other scenic elements?

Perhaps the most common use of added sound is as background ambience—to help establish a locale or set an atmosphere. Such sounds include birds, crickets, dogs, traffic, surf, city noises, the sound of a village festival, and the sounds of war.

Offscreen Sound.   Offscreen sound can be used to expand the frame or suggest an event we don't see. A train whistle has long been used to evoke separation, loneliness, adventure, or an opportunity missed. In *One Flew Over the Cuckoo's Nest*, McMurphy stays to help a fellow inmate rather than escape. As he waits, we hear the sound of a distant train whistle over a close-up of his face. He never does get away. While the FBI agent is searching for the missing girl in *Silence of the Lambs*, the search is accompanied by the yapping of the killer's dog.

Offscreen crashes can be inexpensively substituted for the real thing. In *The Pink Panther*, a bystander watches a wild car chase. We hear the loud sound of an offscreen crash. The camera follows the bystander over to where he discovers all the cars piled up.

At the end of *Airplane!*, an ambulance drives off with the sick girl. Offscreen we hear the sound of a crash and a hub cap rolls into view.

Evoke Emotion.   Sound seems to have a special ability, along with music, to evoke emotion. Consider the effect of a wailing wind or a creaking door in horror films. In *The Birds*, before some of the frenzied attack scenes, a few preliminary screeches and wing flaps cue us to suspensefully expect the terror-filled moments to follow.

At the end of *Duel*, the personified tractor-trailer that has been trying to destroy the central character is forced over an embankment. In slow motion, it falls to its destruction. As it falls, it is accompanied by a strange sound, an almost animal cry like an elephant's call. The truck "dies" like some huge animal.

In *Star Wars*, the archvillain Darth Vader is all the more menacing because of the snorkel-like sound of heavy breathing through his mask. The whirring and humming of the small droid, R2D2, and the whistling way he communicates to the other robot, are clever ways to characterize him. The sound of the laser swords gives the dueling scenes much of their attraction.

At the end of *Harold and Maude*, the sound of the Jaguar's racing engine continues even as the camera freeze frames the car's going over the cliff.

Build Suspense/Shock.   Sound may be used to build suspense, as with the sound of footsteps in the night, or to shock, as with a sudden banging shutter.

Both suspense and shock combine in a scene from *Cat People* in which a woman seems to be pursued by a leopard. Walking at night, her tapping heels alternate with periods of silence during which the camera is on shadows and quietly rustling leaves, strongly suggesting—by the absence of sound—the padded footsteps of the leopard. Suddenly there is a loud, frightening screech that turns out to be caused by a bus.

Sound Transitions.   Sound can be used for transitions. In *The 39 Steps*, a cleaning woman enters a room and discovers a dead body; her scream segues into the screech of a train whistle and a shot of the train tearing along the countryside. A similar effect occurs in *The Godfather* when the screaming of a woman being beaten segues into the sound of a baby crying.

Sound Absence.   Unexpected *silence* has a way of directing attention, perhaps because when we quiet down we become aware of the slightest stimuli. A moving camera shot seems especially suspenseful when accompanied by silence; it is the hush before the expected payoff.

In *Kwaidan*, a Samurai is riding a galloping horse and shooting arrows at a target. A close-up of the horse's hooves is accompanied by the loud sound of hooves pounding on the ground. Suddenly the hoof beats are silent even though they continue visually. The effect is striking.

The horrible massacre of peaceful Native Americans in *Little Big Man* is accompanied by noisy gunshots, screams, and the cries of frightened horses, as well as music. Little Big Man's wife is killed. We go to silence. The massacre continues. Horses mill wildly in the dust thrown up by the carnage. The screen is very active. But there is no sound. Then, fading up gradually, is the sound of "Garry Owen" played on flutes and drums. There is no other sound. It is an eerie scene.

Silence accentuates a powerful scene in *All That Jazz*. There is a reading rehearsal of Joe Gideon's new comedy. He is unsure how good it is. Reading his lines, the cast breaks up in laughter. Then we go to silence. The actors continue reading and laughing, but we hear none of it. Instead, we hear amplified sounds from Gideon. His finger taps on the table. He puts out a cigarette, pulls up his chair, takes another cigarette. He inhales, drops the cigarette, and grinds it out on the floor. He walks, and we hear only the sound of his footsteps. He breaks a pencil and drops it on the ground.

These sounds are greatly amplified. All the while, the actors animatedly talk and laugh, although we do not hear them. Then his sounds fade. We return to the scene and hear the actors applauding his work.

Symbolic Sound.   Sound can have a symbolic function. In *Chinatown*, Jake responds to a call about a woman, goes to her place, and finds her dead. As he moves around, we hear the sound of a dripping faucet which is ironic—she was killed because of the Los Angeles water scandal.

A striking scene from *St. Elsewhere* features a doctor going to the room of a woman who has just received a heart transplant from the doctor's dead wife. He watches her for awhile. The monitors by her bed record her life signs, including heartbeat. Then he removes his stethoscope and puts it over her heart. On the soundtrack, we hear the amplified beat of his dead wife's heart, the heart he must have heard so many times as they lay together. The scene (and that episode) ends.

MUSIC

> *May the Force be with you.*
>
> —from *Star Wars*

Music is one of those important elements in film which we think of as added in post-production by someone other than the screenwriter. True. However, if you have strong feelings about it, you can suggest music for your script, and describe how it can be used to augment or counterpoint a scene. Be wary of suggesting specific musical compositions—they might not be available.

Music Creates Mood and Emotion.   Music can be used to augment (or work against) the impact of a scene.

A Strauss waltz accompanies the space vehicles and astronomical bodies floating across the screen in *2001*. The theme song of *High Noon* explains the concern of the main character—"Do not forsake me, oh my darling . . ." and lays out the story of the film.

The theme song at the opening of *Arthur* sets the mood of a light, romantic comedy. The haunting, animal-like theme music of Leone westerns—such as *The Good, the Bad, and the Ugly*— sets the mood for the tense action. The villains break into the Federal Reserve on Wall Street to the accompaniment of the martial "When Johnny Comes Marching Home" in *Die Hard, With a Vengeance*.

Music evokes emotions because it works beneath the conscious level. Without taking up additional screen time or space, it can cue us on how to respond to a particular scene.

Mood sequences depend heavily on music to create the proper atmosphere and tone. Music can reinforce the intent or emotion of a scene, or it can serve as counterpoint. In *The Birds*, the children's round sung in the schoolhouse as the birds assemble outside contrasts to the mounting danger and increases the tension.

The helicopter attack in *Apocalypse Now* is accompanied by the blaring sound from copter loudspeakers of "The Ride of the Walkeries."

Music Reinforces or Counterpoints.   Music can strengthen a weak scene or moderate a scene that's too strong. Music can help build a scene to its climax—it is essential in chase sequences. Music can reinforce a suspense build, or surprise and shock with a sting chord. (Film composers usually avoid the heightened intensification known as "Mickeymousing," which overscores each move of the film.)

Music Sets Time Periods and Locations.   Music can set a time period or a location and suggest socio-economic or ethnic groups. Drums in a western suggest the proximity of Native Americans. The folk tunes of John Ford westerns suggest that period and place. The music of *Witness* is based on Amish themes. Pop tunes of the period appear in a variety of films (such as *American Graffiti* and *The Big Chill*). The juxtaposing of country and western songs and classical music in *Five Easy Pieces* sets the two worlds that Bobby finds himself suspended between.

Music can originate in a film—*plot music* (also called *diegetic music*)—as well as be added as *background music*. In John Ford westerns, the cavalry frequently sings folk songs or army songs that are used as background music in the film. There's an exciting banjo duel in *Deliverance*. *A Clockwork Orange* features Beethoven's *Ninth* throughout. As the main character falls dead in *Public Enemy*, a phonograph playing "I'm Forever Blowing Bubbles" gets stuck in a groove.

Television series use theme songs both to identify the series and to establish the situation and characters.

The musical score of a film is usually the responsibility of the composer, director, and producer—in large part because the role of music can't be determined until the film is shot and edited. Still, the impact of music on the meaning of a scene is so important that you needn't ignore its potential when writing.

If you are absolutely sure that a certain type of music—a song style, a rhythm—is necessary in a scene, suggest it. But try to do so rarely and in the most general terms. Locking into specific pieces, unless they are in public domain, may not be possible.

DIALOGUE EXAMPLES

Here are some dialogue examples that stretch the principles we've described to create their own unique style. Note how the rapid interchange of short, interrupted dialogue from *Butch Cassidy and the Sundance Kid* develops with conflict between them. Butch and Sundance are trapped on the edge of a fifty-foot cliff. A posse is trailing them. Far below is the rushing river. What do they do?

Butch: We'll jump!

Sundance: Like hell we will.

Butch: No, no, it's gonna be okay—just so it's deep enough we don't get squished to death—they'll never follow us—

Sundance: —How do you know?—

Butch: —Would you make that jump if you didn't have to?—

Sundance: —I have to and I'm not gonna—

Butch: —It's the only way. Otherwise we're dead. They'll have to go all the way back down the way we came. Come on—

Sundance: —Just a couple decent shots—that's all I want—

Butch: —*Come on*—

Sundance: —No—

Butch: —We got to—

Sundance: —*No*—

Butch: —Yes—

Sundance: —Get away from me—

Butch: —Why?—

Sundance: —I wanna fight 'em—

Butch: —They'll kill us—

Sundance: —Maybe—

Butch: —You wanna die?—

Sundance: —Don't you?—

Butch: I'll jump first—

Sundance: —No—

Butch: —Okay, you jump first—

Sundance: —*No*, I said—

Butch (big): *What'sa matter with you?*

Sundance (bigger): I can't swim!!

Butch: You stupid fool, the fall'll probably kill you.

They laugh, then jump together.[6]

The last scene of *Tootsie* is a fine example of underwriting. While disguised as Dorothy, Michael became a soap opera star. He developed a relationship with a co-star, Julie. For Julie, it was a close friendship with another sympathetic and caring woman. For Michael it meant falling in love. When he finally reveals—on live television—that Dorothy is really a male, Julie slaps him and walks away. (The scene preceding this one involves Michael making up with Julie's father, who was romancing Michael as Dorothy.)

This final scene reunites Michael and Julie, and starts them off on a real romance. It would be easy for such a scene to become sentimental. Instead, notice how subtly it develops.

> Julie comes out of the studio, calls for a taxi, then signs some autographs. Looking up, she notices Michael leaning against a van, watching her. She walks off. He follows, then catches up with her.

Michael: Hi. I—uh—I saw your father. I drove up to see him at that bar he hangs out in.

Julie: He doesn't hang out there.

Michael: Oh, yea, I forgot. How's Amy?

Julie: Fine.

Michael: Your dad and I had a coupla beers and shot a good game of pool. We had a really good time together. (Beat) How's it goin'?

Julie: Terry Bishop's back on the show. April's lost her radiology license—

Michael: —I meant with you.

Julie: I know what you meant. (Pause) So you're pretty hot after the unveiling, Michael. What's your next triumph?

Michael: Well, I'm gonna do this play with a coupla friends of mine up in Syracuse—

Julie: —Good. I've gotta catch a cab, Michael.

Michael: Julie, can I call you sometime?

Pause as she reflects on it.

Michael (cont'd): Look, I don't wanna hold you up. I just did it for the work. I didn't want to hurt anybody. Especially you.

Pause as she thinks, then:

Julie: I miss Dorothy.

Michael: You don't have to. She's right here. She misses you. Look, you don't know me from Adam, but I was a better man with you as a woman than I ever was with a woman as a man. (Beat) I just gotta learn to do it without the dress. I mean at this stage in our relationship there might be an advantage to my wearing pants.

Pause. They both smile.

Michael (cont'd): Hard part's over, ya know. We were already good friends.

Pause.

Julie: Will you loan me that little yellow outfit?

MUSIC in, grows louder over the following.

Michael: Which one?

Julie: The Halston.

Michael: The Halston! Oh no, you'd ruin it.

Julie: Michael!

Michael: I know—

Julie: I will not!

MUSIC drowns out their continuing dialogue as song lyrics come in. Michael and Julie walk off together. They put their arms around each other. FREEZE FRAME as END CREDITS roll.[7]

The dialogue of *A Clockwork Orange* is unique in its rhythm and in its use of an idiosyncratic jargon of invented words. We can often guess at their meaning, but their role in stylizing the dialogue is more important than a precise denotative meaning. We understand what is being expressed even if certain specific words escape us.

At one point near the beginning of the film, Alex and his droogs come across Billyboy and his gang in the act of a rape. Alex challenges them to a fight after first introducing us to the situation as follows:

Alex (voice-over): It was around by the derelict casino that we came across Billyboy and his four droogs. They were getting ready to perform a little of the old in-out, in-out on a weepy young devotchka they had there.

Alex (on camera): Ho, Ho, Ho. Well, if it isn't fat stinking Billygoat Billyboy in poison. How art thou, thou globby bottle of cheap, stinking chip oil? Come and get one in the yarbles, if you have any yarbles, you eunuch jelly thou.

After Alex and his droogs terrorize a couple, they go to a milk bar for refreshment, and Alex hears a woman singing a phrase from

Beethoven's *Ninth*, a favorite composition of his. Dim, one of the droogs, gives the singer a raspberry, so Alex smashes Dim across the legs with his stick.

Dim: What did you do that for?

Alex: For being a bastard with no manners and not a dook of an idea how to comport yourself publicwise, o my brother.

Dim: I don't like what you should do what you done. And I'm not your brother no more and wouldn't want to be.

Alex: Watch that . . . Do watch that, O Dim, if to continue to be on live thou dost wish.

Dim: Yarbles, great bolshy yarblockos to you. I'll meet you with chain or nozh or britva anytime. Not having you aiming tolchocks at me reasonless, it stands to reason I won't have it.

Alex: A nozh scrap any time you say.

(Dim slowly backs down.)

Dim: Doobidoob. A bit tired maybe. Best not to say any more. Bedways is right ways now, so best we go homeways and get a bit of spatchka. Righty, right?

Pete/Georgie: Righty, right.

Alex: Right, right.[8]

The Passenger reflects an oblique, elliptical, and ambiguous quality that invites audience involvement, typical of many challenging films of some decades ago. Locke is in a Spanish palace, a tour is passing through. An attractive woman tourist sits on a bench near him. Locke goes up to her, sits beside her.

Locke: Excuse me. I'm trying to remember something.

Girl (very naturally): Is it important?

Locke: No. Do you know what it is? I came in by accident.

Girl: The man who built it was hit by a train.

Locke: Who was he?

Girl: Gaudi. He built this house for a corduroy manufacturer.

(She gets up)

Girl: Come.

(They enter a big room.)

Girl: They used this room for concerts. Wagner.

Locke: Do you think he was crazy?

Girl: What do you think?

Locke: No, he wasn't.

(She laughs easily.)

Girl: How could you come in here by accident?

Locke: I was escaping.

Girl: Wow ... From what?

Locke: I thought there was someone following me, somebody who might recognize me.

Girl: Why?

Locke: I don't know.

Girl: Well, I can't recognize you. Who are you?

Locke: I used to be someone else. But I traded him in. What about you?

Girl (smiles ironically): I'm in Barcelona. I'm talking to a man.

(Locke smiles at her.)

Girl: I was with those people but I'm going to see the other Gaudi buildings alone.

Locke: All of them?

Girl: It depends how much time you've got. They're all good for hiding in.

Locke: I must leave today—this afternoon.

Girl: I hope you make it. People disappear every day.

Locke: Whenever they leave the room.

Girl: Goodbye.[9]

Blow-Up is another film that often uses oblique dialogue. This scene seems to go against earlier advice about not asking too many leading questions. Yet the mood of the scene plays against this. Thomas has gone to tell Bill and Patricia about seeing a murdered man, but finds them making love. Patricia looks up from the bed; she seems remote from Bill—who is on top of her and doesn't notice Thomas.

Thomas then returns to his studio to discover his photographs of the murder have been taken. Patricia comes in. The scene involves not only Thomas's discovery, but Patricia's emotional estrangement from Bill. The tone of the scene is rather detached—hardly fitting considering the subject matter.

Patricia (perfectly normal voice): Were you looking for something just now?

Thomas: No.

Patricia: Oh.

Thomas: Do you ever think of leaving him?

Patricia: No, I don't think so.

  (Pause)

Thomas: I saw a man killed this morning.

Patricia: Where?

Thomas: Shot. In some sort of park.

  (He studies photograph.)

Patricia: Are you sure?

Thomas: He's still there.

Patricia: Who was he?

Thomas: Someone.

Patricia: How did it happen?

Thomas: I don't know. I didn't see.

Patricia: You didn't see?

Thomas: No.

Patricia: Shouldn't you call the police?

Thomas: That's the body.

Patricia: It looks like one of Bill's paintings.

Thomas: Yes.

Patricia (thinks, then): Will you help me? I don't know what to do.

Thomas: What is it? Huh?

Patricia: I wonder why they shot him . . .

Thomas: I didn't ask.

  (She smiles, leaves.)[10]

Earlier, the woman he photographed in the park with the man who was killed comes to get the pictures back. She claims they represent a threat to her personal life (unaware that Thomas knows about the murder). He plays with her, wonders if she has done any modeling work. She says she isn't interested, she's in a hurry and would like the pictures. We enter the scene at this point.

Thomas: You'll get your pictures, I promise. I always keep my word.

  (He falls onto the couch.)

Thomas: Come here. Show me how you sit.

  (Telephone rings. He ignores it, suddenly dives and digs around to find it.)

Thomas (into phone): Who is it? Oh, yes, that's right. Hold on a second.

(He holds receiver out to girl.)

Girl (shocked): Is it for me?

(She hesitantly picks up receiver.)

Thomas: It's my wife.

(Girl hurriedly puts receiver down.)

Girl: Why should I speak to her?

Thomas (takes phone, says into it): Sorry, love, the bird I'm with won't talk to you. (hangs up)

(Girl is impatient.)

Thomas: She isn't my wife really. We just have some kids . . . no . . . no kids. Not even kids. Sometimes, though, it . . . it feels as if we had kids. She isn't beautiful, she's . . . easy to live with.

(He sits down, lights a cigarette.)

Thomas: No, she isn't. That's why I don't live with her.

(Girl shows first sign of interest in him.)

Thomas: But even with beautiful girls you . . . you look at them and . . . that's that. That's why they always end up by . . . (sighs) . . . well, I'm stuck with them all day long.

Girl: It would be the same with men.

(Scene continues, but we'll stop it at this point.)[11]

Pulp Fiction is one of a number of Tarantino films known for the interesting quality of its dialogue. It works even though Tarantino does things contrary to conventional screenwriting wisdom—he often uses long speeches, and frequently has characters talk of trivialities. Here are some examples.

Hit men Vincent and Jules are walking to an apartment building. We track alongside them.

Jules: You remember Antwan Rockamora? Half-black, half-Samoan, usta call him Tony Rocky Horror.

Vincent: Yeah maybe, fat right?

Jules: I wouldn't go so far as to call the brother fat. He's got a weight problem. What's the nigger gonna do, he's Samoan.

Vincent: Yea, I think I know who you mean, what about him?

Jules: Well, Marsellus fucked him up good. Word around the campfire is was on account of Marsellus Wallace's wife.

They get on the elevator.

Vincent: So what'd he do, fuck her?

Jules: No no no no no no no, nothin' that bad.

Vincent: Well what then?

Jules: He gave her a foot massage.

Vincent: Foot massage?

Jules nods his head: "Yes."

Vincent: That's it?

Jules nods his head: "Yes."

Vincent: Then what did Marsellus do?

Jules: Sent a couple of cats over to his place. They took him out on his patio, threw his ass over the balcony. Nigger fell four stories. They had a little garden down at the bottom, enclosed in glass, like a greenhouse—nigger fell through that. Since then, he kinda developed a speech impediment.

Exit elevator.

Vincent: That's a damn shame.

Later, in the apartment, Jules and Vincent confront the guys who stole from Marsellus. At one point Jules takes out his gun and shoots Roger. Then he continues his conversation with Brett (who was in the process of apologizing, but seeing Roger killed just messed his pants).

Jules (to Brett): Oh, I'm sorry. Did I break your concentration? I didn't mean to do that. Please, continue. You were saying something about "best intentions."

Brett can't say a word.

Jules: Whatsamatter? Oh, you were finished. Oh well, allow me to retort. What does Marsellus Wallace look like?

Brett still can't speak. Jules tips the card table over.

Jules: What country you from!

Brett (petrified): What?

Jules: "What" ain't no country I ever heard of. They speak English in "What?"

Brett (near heart attack): What?

Jules: English-motherfucker-do-you-speak-it?

Brett: Yes.

Jules: Then you know what I'm sayin?

Brett: Yes.

Jules: Describe what Marsellus Wallace looks like!

Brett (out of fear): What?

Jules takes his gun and presses the barrel hard in Brett's chest.

Jules: Say "What" again! Say "What" again! I dare ya, I double dare ya motherfucker, say "What" one more goddamn time!

Brett (doing his best): He's . . . black—

Jules: —go on!

Brett: He's bald—

Jules: —does he look like a bitch?!

Brett (without thinking): What?

> Jules shoots Brett in the shoulder. The scene continues, but we'll stop here.

For the final example from *Pulp Fiction* (and a change of pace) here's a bit of the dialogue between Vincent and Mia while they're eating out at Jackrabbit Slim's, seated in a '59 Edsel "booth."

Mia: What do ya think?

Vincent: I think it's like a wax museum with a pulse.

> A waiter looking like Buddy Holly comes to take their order.

Buddy: Hi, I'm Buddy. What can I get'cha?

Vincent: Let's see, steak, steak, steak . . . Oh yeah. The Douglas Sirk steak. I'll have that.

Buddy: How d'ya want that cooked, burnt to a crisp or bloody as hell?

Vincent: Bloody as hell. And, oh yeah, look at this. Vanilla coke.

Buddy: How 'bout you, Peggy Sue?

Mia: I'll have the Durwood Kirby burger—bloody—and a five-dollar shake.

Buddy: How d'ya want that shake, Martin and Lewis or Amos and Andy?

Mia: Martin and Lewis.

Vincent: Did you just order a five-dollar shake?

Mia: Uh-huh.

Vincent: That's a shake? That's milk and ice cream?

Mia: Last I heard.

Vincent: That's five dollars? You don't put bourbon in it or nothin? Just checking.[12]

SUMMARY

This chapter considered the role of dialogue, sound, and music in the script. We examined dialogue functions, effective dialogue, implicit dialogue, how to individualize speeches and make them credible, the importance of context and intention, the value of underwriting and avoiding clichés, and the importance of writing relationships when writing dialogue.

We also discussed subtext—the meaning that lies underneath the written words. Dialogue techniques include voice-over narration; offscreen dialogue; overlapping dialogue; dialogue over distance and obstructions; scenes shot MOS; entrances, exits, and scene closes; legends, how to build dialogue; the absence of dialogue; and improvisation.

Dialogue hooks are techniques to smooth dialogue writing; they include question/answer, agreement/disagreement, repeated, or matched words, parallel construction and repetition, and sharing a progression.

Other considerations discussed were slang and buzzwords, avoiding bad dialogue (including an extended example), and working the dialogue.

The discussion of sound included offscreen sound, evoking emotion, building suspense and shock, sound transitions, the power of the sudden absence of sound, and symbolic sound.

Music creates mood and emotion. It can either reinforce or create a counterpoint, and can help set time periods and locations.

The chapter concluded with some unique dialogue examples.

A CHECKLIST FOR WRITING DIALOGUE/SOUND/MUSIC

Think visually.

Does the dialogue sound natural and conversational?

Is it lean and economic?

Do you use words for their implicit meaning?

Do you avoid tired truisms and clichés?

Do you avoid on-the-nose dialogue?

Does the dialogue fit the character?

Does it fit the situation and emotion?

Is it underwritten and understated?

Do you write relationships, not just words?

Are you using subtext?

If you use dialogue hooks, do you do so judiciously?

Have you rewritten and rewritten the dialogue?

Have you considered how sound could enrich the script?

Have you allowed for music helping your scenes?

ENDNOTES

1. DiMaggio, M. (1990). *How to write for television.* New York: Prentice-Hall, p. 18.

2. Quoted in DiMaggio, p. 18.

3. Berne, E. (1964). *Games people play.* New York: Grove Press.

4. Unless otherwise noted in the text, the examples given were written by the author.

5. Buzzwords. (13 August 1990). *Newsweek.*

6. Goldman, W. (1986). *Butch Cassidy and the Sundance Kid.* In Sam Thomas, Ed., *Best American screenplays.* New York: Crown, p. 369.

7. Taken from the film script credited to Larry Gelbert and Murray Schisgal.

8. Selections from Kubrick, S. (1972). *A Clockwork Orange.* New York: Ballantine Books, (1972), unnumbered pages.

9. Peploe, M., Wollen, P., and Antonioni, M. (1975). *The passenger.* New York: Grove Press, pp. 89–91.

10. Antonioni, M. (1971). *Blow-up.* New York: Simon and Schuster, pp. 101–102.

11. Antonioni, pp. 71–73.

12. From the film. An earlier screenplay version is found in Tarantino, Q. (1994). *Pulp fiction.* New York: Hyperion.

CHAPTER 10

Doing the Rewrite

It never gets any better than the script.
—Barry Diller

YYou've finished your first draft of the script. Congratulate yourself. Celebrate. Take a vacation. Clean the garage. Put the script aside for a bit so you can go back to it with a more detached perspective.

Rewriting can be very rewarding. It isn't always easy, but the payoff is seeing what you've written take on new life and refinement. With a good rewrite, a scene that works only moderately well can be made to go like dynamite.

OVERVIEW

When you are ready to review the first draft, read it all at one sitting. Read quickly in order to get an overall impression; don't be too concerned about details. Avoid making judgments as to whether it is good or bad. Don't take notes during this quick overview—go for a general impression. (It may help if you read it aloud.)

When finished with this reading, reflect on it. Consider:

What are your overall impressions of the script?

Does it work? If not, why not?

Does it hold our attention?

Will it attract a mass-media audience?

Are the stories and characters unique and refreshing or do they sound like something we've seen repeatedly in the media?

Is the story credible?

Is the script a page-turner or is it a difficult read?

Is there a good mix of suspense and surprise?

Is it predictable?

Note any spots where your interest lagged. Punch up those sections.

If a comedy, did you laugh (or at least smile)?

Does the story have a clear beginning, middle, and end?

Does it build to a climax?

What major changes do you think it needs?

Take notes on your reactions and any new directions you think the script might need. Then—barring any need for major overhauls—start your detailed analysis.

THE DETAILED ANALYSIS

Go over the script act by act, scene by scene. Review each scene according to the guidelines we've mentioned above. Be rigorous in your critique. Get that proverbial blue pencil and cut! cut! cut! Can you say it in two lines rather than five? Then do so. Three words rather than six? (This is why you made the first draft long—so you can pare it down to what is essential.)

Check that the major story line carries the film. Be sure that any problem, conflict, or objective we meet early on is climaxed and resolved.

THE STORY

Is there a clean, clear story?

Is something important at stake for the main character? Be sure pace and tension accelerate as you approach the climax.

Check that there is a development by crises, perhaps a strong – + – + build.

Does the story develop logically—with one thing leading to another?

Are there strong act endings (if needed)?

Are we hooked by the opening?

THE CHARACTERS

Are we involved with the characters? Do we care about what they do and what happens to them?

Could you use some of the techniques we've discussed to further endear the characters to us?

Do we meet the major characters early in the film?

Could you eliminate a character by combining that character's function with another's?

Do you need to add a character?

Is there anything that could be done with the characters to make them more effective—change genders, ages, physiques, occupations?

Are the central characters proactive—that is, do their actions advance the story?

Is the central character in most of your scenes?

Is there a strong villain or other antagonistic force?

Do some characters grow and change over the story?

Does the climax belong to the main character?

Is the problem or conflict we encountered in the beginning resolved?

Are secondary characters interesting?

Do all characters have goals?

SCENE ACTION

Have you visualized the action? Does it develop visually?

Could more interesting and significant settings be found?

Have you checked that (with few exceptions) each scene advances the story?

If more than one scene has the same function, could they be combined?

Do the scenes work?

Do we enter them at the best possible moment?

Do they have buttons?

Do they build?

If appropriate, do they thrust us into the next scene?

Could a very long scene be broken into several shorter scenes?

Is there a good balance of scene contrasts?

DIALOGUE

Is the dialogue pared down to the bone (except for stylized exceptions)?

Is it short, concise, simple?

Is it conversational?

Is it unique to each character?

Is it easy to speak and listen to?

Have you visualized the dialogue scenes so they don't seem too talky?

Do you show us through action and business—rather than simply through dialogue?

Have you avoided on-the-nose dialogue?

Have you used subtext?

Do you avoid clichés, feed lines, and the like?

Is exposition presented in an entertaining way?

If there are problems later in the script, go back to Act I and try making changes there.

Expect to do a major rewrite of the opening; it is one of the most frequently rewritten parts of a script. Now that you have a better grasp of character and direction, review the opening and see if it introduces the story effectively.

If you've written a comedy, go back and structure the humor. Build to the punch lines—visual and verbal. Let the humor grow out of the characters and situations. Make it funnier!

Try to work consecutively, from beginning to end. Make sure this is a *major* rewrite. Make the script come alive—scene by scene, beat by beat.

Let others read it and listen to what they say. Don't argue with them, just hear them out. Some of what they say will be valuable. Ask especially what parts they don't understand, what parts are a slow read for them, where their interest flags.

Review some of the points discussed in the first chapter. Review the material on structure, characters, scenes, and dialogue.

You'll probably do more than one major rewrite, but soon you'll find you're doing more polishing than major rewriting—a scene or two here, a section there. Make it something that will jump off the desk—a page turner that the reader can't put down.

And be sure to use proper script format and to print or type it neatly.

Good luck.

CHAPTER *11*

Comedy

Dying is easy, comedy is hard.
—actor Edmund Kean
(on his death bed)

Sullivan is a serious director with a social conscience that impels him to make socially relevant films. After all, it's the 1930s, and Americans are suffering. Preston Sturges's *Sullivan's Travels* opens with the end of Sullivan's latest film—a film in which labor and management symbolically clash as two men fight atop a moving boxcar then fall to their deaths. In order to make his next film even more trenchant, Sullivan masquerades as a tramp and hits the road, panhandling and living in flophouses to experience firsthand the plight of the dispossessed.

But misfortune intervenes. Sullivan wrongly finds himself a prisoner on a chain gang. One night the convicts are given a rare treat; they are shown an early Mickey Mouse cartoon, and for a brief moment they forget the misery of their lives. Watching them laugh, Sullivan has a revelation. If he is ever released, he resolves to make only comedies. He has realized the importance of laughter.

Humans (with perhaps a few higher primates) are laughing animals. We are apparently the only animal aware of non-existence—the starting point of tragedy—but we are also the only animal aware of our imperfections and of the incongruity of life as it is and as it ought to be—the starting point of comedy. Comedy is a mirror of human absurdities; it shows us our weaknesses, albeit in a way that arouses laughter rather than anger. Comedy shows us our pretensions. It says: all humans are fools.

Comedy also entertains us. Laughter is good for the body as well as the spirit. Comedy and comics make the world more enjoyable.

Is comedy writing a gift? Perhaps. But there are comedy skills that can be acquired and polished through practice. These skills are the subject of this chapter.

COMEDY THEORIES

What makes comedy comedy? What is humor? Why do we laugh? It happens so easily—until we try to analyze it. While a comprehensive theory of comedy doesn't yet exist, there are various partial theories. These can be grouped under the headings of disparagement or aggression theories, superiority theories, tension release theories, social function theories, and incongruity-resolution theories.

Disparagement or Aggression Theories

Disparagement or aggression theories see humor as the expression of human aggression, as a socially acceptable outlet for violence. Our laughter distances us from the object of the aggression.

There is a *cruel* element in comedy—a sense of derision permitted by its not-for-real quality. We enjoy watching the misfortunes of others—the pie in the face, the hapless cuckold, the violence of Punch and Judy, Hardy hitting Laurel, or Abbott picking on Costello. There is a certain pleasurable superiority in seeing it happen to someone else (all the while knowing it is comically "safe"). In *The General*, it is funny when Buster Keaton loads a mortar on his train tender and lights the fuse, only to find that the movements of the train have joggled the barrel down until it is pointed at him; to make matters worse his foot is caught in a chain, which anchors him as the helpless target.

Laurel and Hardy shorts are often structured around the premise that Hardy trusts Laurel, only to suffer some terrible calamity. In one film, their open car is stuck in a parking place behind a dump truck. Hardy, behind the wheel, sends Laurel to move the truck. Of course Laurel dumps the full truckload of sand on top of Hardy.

In the classic *Mary Tyler Moore Show* episode "Chuckles Bites the Dust," Mary breaks up with laughter as the minister at Chuckles's funeral talks about some of the clown's funny bits. Her laughter is extremely embarrassing, but try as she might, she can't contain herself. Mary's predicament is excruciating, yet we laugh at her discomfort. The more she tries to stop, the more we laugh. Humor definitely has its aggressive side.

Superiority Theories

Superiority theories propose that when we laugh at someone, we triumph over them and increase our self-esteem at their expense. They are the ones doing the stupid things, falling prey to the embarrassing and ridiculous situations and looking foolish; we're above that. Laughing at the misfortunes of others makes us feel better about our own situation.

In *The Jerk*, we laugh at the Steve Martin character when he indignantly asks the waiter to remove the disgusting snails that are all over the plate. And how about a nice new bottle of wine instead of the old stuff you brought us?

Such *misunderstandings* are a useful comic device. We know the truth, while others misunderstand. In *The Court Jester*, the joke is based on who knows and doesn't know what. Those at the castle don't know that Hawkins is a member of the Fox's rebel band masquerading as the Jester. He doesn't know that the Jester really is a skilled assassin hired by the king's advisors to remove some rivals. For a while he thinks the villains are his confederates, even as they think he is their assassin.

At one point he is hypnotized so that a snap of the fingers transforms his normally fainthearted self into a dashing, confident swordsman, and back again; since he doesn't know what's going on, the results are hilarious. During one of his castle performances, he knows that the baby true king is in the basket, but the court doesn't. And so on and on for a splendid romp. And we are in on the whole thing.

We enjoy seeing a narrow escape, and our enjoyment is heightened if the character doesn't realize the danger until afterwards. If they never realize it, we laugh at their obliviousness.

Humor that belittles specific groups reinforces our own group identity and ego. Unfortunately this is also a staple of ethnic, racial, national, and gender jokes.

Tension Release Theories

Tension release theories suggest that we laugh as a release for excess nervous energy. *Psychoanalytic theory* says that humor serves as an acceptable outlet for repressed aggression and sexuality, which might explain why we so enjoy sexual innuendo and bodily functions humor.

However, recent research indicates that laughter at joke punch lines may actually increase (or at least maintain) arousal and that this arousal will be sustained for some time. So while there is no longer much support for the strict Freudian catharsis theory of humor, comedy and laughter do seem to involve some sort of relief of psychological and/or physical tensions.

Social Function Theories

Social function theories stress the role of laughter as a socially corrective process that restrains unwanted eccentric behavior. These primarily conservative theories depend on codes of civility and propriety.

Bizarre behavior is permitted in comedy, where it is the object of ridicule (thereby reminding us that it is inappropriate in society). A sneeze at the wrong moment, a funny walk, ridiculous clothes—these are seen as unseemly human behavior to be laughed at, not emulated. *Wayne's World* belongs on film, not in real life.

Incongruity–Resolution Theories

Incongruity–resolution theories are currently in favor. They assert that a joke contains two elements or "scenarios." The joke begins in one direction with the first scenario, then suddenly at the punch line/resolution switches direction to the other scenario. While we are following one line of meaning, we are surprised by a new one.

But the switch is not completely arbitrary. On one level, the two scenarios are incongruous, but at another level they are related and make sense together. Release of tension from the first expectation being reduced to nothing by the switch to the second scenario is what creates the humor.

Consider the classic Henny Youngman one-liner, "Take my wife—please." The first scenario sets up our expectation for the rhetorical "Take my wife, for example." The "please" reverses this to a scenario that asks us to take her off his hands. Both scenarios are incongruous, yet they fit.

"Please" doesn't fit with our first notion of "take my wife," but it does fit the second meaning—taking his wife away from him. The incongruity is established then resolved as we suddenly get the joke. The incongruity—and the joke—is even stronger since it implies an opposition—seeing your wife as a useful example versus wanting to get rid of her.

In *Sleeper*, the Woody Allen character says, "As a kid I was beaten up by Quakers." Our expectation is shocked; Quaker's don't beat people up, yet they are connected with violence by being the opposite—being non-violent.

In *Airplane!* as the plane readies for takeoff, a mechanic checks the hood and the oil, as if the plane were a car. Then the pilot pays for the gas with a credit card. The action is absurd—this doesn't happen at an airport. But planes do get gassed up and checked before takeoff. We relate getting gas with a service station. It's incongruous, but works on another level.

In a sense, *we* are the incongruity—capable of moments of transcendence, yet incapable of controlling ourselves.

SOME COMEDY ATTRIBUTES

A certain *detachment* operates in comedy—the *comic distance*. Knowing it is a comedy and "not for real" is reassuring. Rather than cringe at a slapstick character's physical pounding, our comic detachment allows us to laugh.

So Ben Turpin can get a foot caught in a rope attached to a car and have to hop down the road after it at fifty miles an hour. And Larry Semon can rush into a room to rescue an ingenue only to go out the window on the other side, dive down three stories and land on his head! In the next scene he is already into some other adventure. Cartoons, too, often follow this pattern.

Comic distance permits us to enjoy the comedy in a hopeless situation. James Agee describes the quintessential comic situation:

> Laurel and Hardy are trying to move a piano across a narrow suspension bridge. The bridge is slung over a sickening chasm, between a couple of Alps. Midway they meet a gorilla.[1]

Just as *suspense and surprise* are central to dramatic narrative, they are also important in comedy. In jokes, reverses, and switches, the *surprise* of the unexpected ambushes our expectations and we explode with laughter. The anticipated payoff of comedy *suspense* often occurs when we know something the character doesn't know and we anticipate the character's response when they find out.

In a classic *All in the Family* episode, ultra-conservative Archie believes he has saved a woman's life by giving her mouth-to-mouth resuscitation. However, we know that the recipient was not a woman but a transvestite. We wait expectantly for the moment when Archie finds out, and we enjoy his abashed reaction.

We enjoy *destructiveness* in comedy—car crashes, pie throwing that leaves the bakery in shambles. Total destruction can be enjoyable, such as when Laurel and Hardy demolish their adversary's house while he destroys their truck (in *Big Business*). In *Smokey and the Bandit*, it's funny when the Bandit's car jumps the broken bridge while the pursuing highway patrol cars fall on top of each other into the creek.

Comedy is often *iconoclastic*, destructive of aspects of our culture and society. Comedy is by nature impolite, even impious and sacrilegious, as is the great comedy of Chaplin, Tati, Sennett, Fields, Keaton, the Marx Brothers, Lenny Bruce, Monty Python, *Saturday Night Live*, *SCTV*, and Mr. Bean.

There is a broad range of *comic styles*. At one extreme is the farcical slapstick of the Keystone Kops and the absurdities of the Abrahams/Zucker movies that began with *Airplane!* Other comedies are easy, even tender (*Bagdad Cafe*, *A Christmas Story*). Still others are sophisticated and/or romantic (Neil Simon, screwball comedies, *Sleepless in Seattle*).

Television comedies similarly range from the zany *Monty Python*, to the eccentric *Fawlty Towers*, the angry social commentary of Norman Lear, and the milder *Mad About You* and *Friends*. "Black comedy" has a bitter, downbeat quality (*The King of Comedy*, *Dr. Strangelove*, *Pulp Fiction*).

Among *comedy genres* are slapstick, the buddy comedies of the 1930s, 1940s and 1950s (Laurel and Hardy, Abbott and Costello, Hope and Crosby, Martin and Lewis), and the screwball comedies that reigned from the 1930s through the early 1940s (*The Awful Truth*, *It Happened One Night*, *The Lady Eve*, *My Man Godfrey*, *Bringing Up Baby*).

Many effective comedies center around a prominent *comic character* (or pair) who carries the brunt of the comedy. A funny persona can lead to a series of films—Inspector Clouseau, the Hope and Crosby road pictures, Abbott and Costello, the Marx Brothers, Mr. Hulot, Ace Ventura, Mr. Bean.

Television sitcoms try to create endearing funny lead characters and "families" of characters—*Murphy Brown, Frasier, Seinfeld, Roseanne, Fawlty,* the *Friends* troupe.

Woody Allen has given us a number of funny films that feature a characteristic persona—neurotic, witty, urbane, cynical, self-centered, acerbic, worrying, and complaining (Alvy Singer of *Annie Hall* being one of the best).

Comic relief serves an important function in serious drama. A mixture of the very serious and comic can have a powerful impact; the serious seems all the more striking in contrast to the comic.

Beverly Hills Cop has a serious main story line (to catch the criminal) and a comic secondary story line (for Alex to outwit the pompous Beverly Hills cops). A number of action/adventure films combine humor with the adventure; their characters don't take themselves seriously and some of the action is played for laughs (*48 Hours, Lethal Weapon, Die Hard,* and the *Indiana Jones* movies).

Star Trek—the TV shows and the films—often mixes humor and drama. A classic moment occurs in *Star Trek IV* when Spock, the totally rational Vulcan, unsuccessfully tries to use late 20th century profanity.

Just as serious drama contains comic moments, so *comedy can include the serious* elements. *Arthur* contains the death of Hobson. In *Harold and Maude*, there is Maude's death.

In *SOB*, a man suffers a fatal heart attack on a lonely stretch of beach; his dog keeps a forlorn vigil over the body. The film periodically cuts back to the dog's faithful watch—a touch of pathos in a comic film.

WRITING COMEDY

When writing comedy, try to *establish the comic climate early.* Cue us that it's a comedy. This can be done through such devices as the film's title, the actors, the subject matter, music, dialogue, and initial action.

Comedy should flow naturally; it is most effective when neither the writer nor the characters are trying too hard to be funny. If we become too aware of the writer making a joke, it can detract. Let the comedy grow out of the characters—their conflicts, relationships, and the situations in which they find themselves.

Comedy is fast-paced. *Keep it moving.* If a funny bit is holding up the pace, consider dropping it. If you're writing a situation comedy, go for at least three laughs a page.

When pacing the humor, *allow for the laugh.* Pause for a brief moment after a comic bit to allow for audience response. You want to keep comedy moving, but if it moves too fast after something very funny, it steps on the laugh and loses part of what follows.

One theory (much oversimplified but still worth repeating) maintains that there are two common ways to develop a comedy:

Put a normal person in a crazy world.

Put a crazy person in a normal world.

In the first situation we identify with a normal protagonist coping with bizarre circumstances. In *King of Hearts,* a soldier in World War I goes into a town that's been deserted by everyone except the inhabitants of the insane asylum. *My Man Godfrey* plays the role of butler in a house of rich eccentrics.

The couple in *The Out-of-Towners* finds New York City a crazy place. The conservative dentist in *The In-Laws* is thrust into a bizarre world of international scheming and intrigue.

In a *Monty Python* sketch, a distinguished film director finds himself on a television interview show with a host who persists in calling him "Eddie baby" and other unacceptable names. In another Python sketch, a couple in a fancy restaurant mentions having a dirty fork—throwing the staff, chef, and owner into overreacting pandemonium.

In the reverse situation, consider *The Coneheads* or any Marx Brothers movie. We might also include *M*A*S*H, The King of Comedy*, and *Being There.*

Often in *Monty Python* (or *Saturday Night Live*) sketches, everything is played straight except for one element, such as combat training on how to resist attackers who are armed with fruit; people, including bikers, hassled by "Hell's Grannies"; the lumberjack sketch in which the manly song ends up divulging the singer's transvestism; and the killer joke (developed by the army as a devastating weapon).

The Comic Concept/Premise/Situation

> *Life is a tragedy when seen in close-up, but a comedy in long shot.*
>
> —Charlie Chaplin[2]

Selling a comedy is somewhat easier if it has a "high concept"—a premise that can be described in a few sentences. The premise of *Home Alone* is: a resourceful little kid is left home alone and has to outwit two bungling burglars. It suggests the comic possibilities.

So does the concept of *Tootsie*: an actor who is too temperamental to get work goes to an audition in drag and gets the part.

The Producers revolves around a down-on-his-luck Broadway producer who comes up with a scam that involves putting on a flop—*Springtime for Hitler*—but the scheme backfires when the show becomes a hit.

Comic Prop or Device

Film comedy has always had an affinity for the malfunctioning gadgetry of our modern world. Just about any machine can go berserk, and almost any object can serve as a comic prop.

Comedians have interacted with furniture, pianos, cars, escalators, paint cans, hammocks, and pets. A hand becomes stuck in a jar. An elevator door closes on a character. Machinery goes haywire (like the assembly line feeding machine in *Modern Times*). The Keystone Kops' Tin Lizzie automobiles go from one high-speed near-miss to another. W. C. Fields does wonders with a pool cue.

Charlie Chaplin was a master at using props. A bit of dough becomes bracelets, boxing gloves, quicksand, a slingshot, a discus, a mallet, even a chair. Empty pie tins and a pair of ham bones become a xylophone. Two beer bottles become binoculars. Chaplin shoots dice as though he were a pitcher delivering a hard-breaking curve ball. He passes out dinner plates as though he were dealing cards. Asked to inspect a clock, he applies a stethoscope to it, cuts open the lid with a can opener, examines it with a jeweler's eyepiece, a dentist's forceps and a hammer, takes an oil can to it, and finally returns it to the customer reduced to a collection of parts.

In *The Return of the Pink Panther*, Inspector Clouseau struggles with an enormously powerful vacuum cleaner that sucks in a painting, clothing, a slipper, and the bosom of a hefty masseuse. It even sucks a parrot into its canister. When Clouseau removes the top to release the bird, he, too, gets sucked in. The freed parrot rewards Clouseau by defecating on him (a topper). (The berserk vacuum cleaner was a common device in silent film comedies.)

A racing conveyer belt can drive workers crazy. Chaplin had one in *Modern Times*. In a now classic bit from *I Love Lucy*, Lucy and Ethyl are working at a candy factory wrapping chocolates that come down a conveyer belt. Needless to say, it speeds up and they end up throwing (and eating) candy as they try to control the onslaught.

Just think what contemporary comedies might do with computers and other cybernetic devices. Maybe.

Physical Comedy

Physical comedy works especially well in film. Entanglements with props and objects are effective because they fit the film's visual quality. Pies in the face, buckets of water on the head, and trips on banana peels are hallmarks of the silent comedies.

Comedy has always had a special affinity for the physical. If tragedy rarely shows a commode, comedy has a fondness for all the body functions and weaknesses to which our flesh is heir. Comedy enjoys outhouses, itches and scratches, toothaches, bellyaches, gout, ice packs, mummy-like bandages, sneezes, farts, toupees, smashed hats, long underwear, and fallen trousers.

One of the most-used gags in films is "walk this way," a *word-play misunderstanding* and visual gag in which one character says "walk this way," meaning to walk in this direction, whereas the other character perversely interprets it to mean to walk in the same manner as the speaker—especially if the speaker has a comic walk.

In *History of the World, Part I*, when an attractive woman says "walk this way" with a toss of the head and swish of the hips, the men proceed to imitate her. When Hope and Crosby are invited to "walk this way" by an attractive woman, they respond by saying they don't have the equipment.

Young Frankenstein reverses this well-worn joke by having Igor give the hero a small cane and indicate that he is to walk down the stairs in Igor's limping style.

COMEDY COMPONENTS

Here are some ways of classifying aspects of comedy that may make comedy easier for us to understand. The examples, like all the examples in this and other chapters, are designed to give you an idea of the range of options available to you.

Comic Sequence (Scene or Sketch)

Sometimes a *comic sequence* (scene or sketch) is there simply for its humor. In *The Pink Panther Strikes Again,* there's a sequence in which Inspector Clouseau tries to enter the castle although the drawbridge over the moat is raised. First he throws up a rope, but it's short and he falls into the moat. He tries again, but as he climbs up, the drawbridge lowers for a car to drive out and once again he ends up in the water. Clouseau then tries to grab onto the drawbridge as it lowers for a car, but when it rises he slips and lands back in the moat. In a canoe, Clouseau paddles under the drawbridge, but it lowers and drives him through the bottom of the boat. Finally, he tries pole vaulting, but the pole is too short and he's in the moat again. He never does get in. The sequence ends. The story resumes.

W.C. Fields has a wonderful scene in which he plays with a pool cue and table while telling a story. He endlessly lines up his shot, the cue ball bounces off the railing and flies back to hit him on the head, he breaks a cue stick, and pushes a cue stick through the table. A visual feast.

In *County Hospital,* Hardy is in the hospital with a broken leg. It's in a cast and elevated by a system of ropes and pulleys attached to weights that sit on the window sill. Laurel decides to use the weights to crack a nut he's trying to eat. When he lifts them, Hardy's leg drops. The doctor runs over to grab the weights, only to fall out the window, hanging on to the weights high above the street. Of course, this hoists Hardy to the ceiling. Laurel alternately tries to help one, then the other, only making things worse.

Comic Bit

A *comic bit* is a short comic segment, such as when a seducer has to deal with a pesky fly, or when the hero has to get his foot out of a wastebasket or gum off his shoe while trying to maintain composure.

The mirror bit is a classic. It usually begins with one character trying to escape detection by pretending to be the mirrored reflection of the person they are trying to avoid. Suspicious, the person tries various moves to make the "mirror image" mess up. This bit dates back to silent days and has been used by Harpo Marx, Lucille Ball, and Danny Kaye.

Visual Joke

A *visual joke* is the equivalent of its verbal counterpart—short and to the point. Harpo Marx is passing by a card game when someone says, "Cut the cards." Harpo instantly produces a meat cleaver and whacks the deck of cards in half (*Horse Feathers*).

In *Airplane!* someone makes a comment about the shit hitting the fan, and we literally see it happen. In another visual joke, we see a shot of an Air Israel plane with the long hair, locks, and beard of an orthodox rabbi.

Comic Reaction

The *comic reaction* deserves special mention because so often the laugh comes not so much from an action as from a character's reaction to it. Watch for this yourself. Comics Jack Benny, Oliver Hardy, and Lou Costello were famous for their reactions.

In *Young Frankenstein*, the creature and a young girl are throwing flowers into the well. Then she comments that they're all gone; what do they throw in now? The creature gives an ironic reaction (which is also an *allusion* since in the original Frankenstein story he threw the child in).

The Chase

The *chase* has been a comedy favorite since the silent movies had Model Ts tearing up the streets of Los Angeles. A chase that builds to a particularly fine payoff occurs in *What's Up, Doc?* Several cars are chasing a pedal wagon down San Francisco streets. At an intersection, workmen are crossing the street with a large plate glass window while overhead another workman on a very tall ladder is trying to hang a large banner. The workmen carrying the glass pane frantically dodge back and forth as the cars narrowly miss them on either side. Just when they believe they're safely on the sidewalk, a car turns around and knocks over the ladder—causing the workman hanging the banner to grab on to it for support. The banner breaks loose on one end. He swings on it and breaks the windowpane. (This is also an example of a comic *delay*. We are set up for a disaster that was narrowly averted, but just when it looks like all is okay, we get the payoff.)

COMEDY TECHNIQUES

> *In the end, everything is a gag.*
>
> —Charlie Chaplin[3]

If you can write effective comedy, you will be in demand; it isn't easy to make people laugh. Here are a variety of comedy techniques to help you along.

Exaggeration, Absurdity, the Incongruous, and the Outrageous

Exaggeration, absurdity, the incongruous, and the outrageous are basic to comedy.

Groucho says, "You can't burn the candle at both ends," only to have Harpo pull from his coat a candle burning at both ends. When a panhandler asks Harpo for money to get a cup of coffee, he pulls a steaming cup from his coat (*Horse Feathers*).

Buster Keaton throws an anchor in the water in *The Boat*—and it floats! While in *Steamboat Bill, Jr.*, he knocks a life preserver in—and it immediately sinks!

In *The Pink Panther Strikes Again*, a woman is tortured by a gloved hand with steel nails—which is drawn down a blackboard with a screech.

The character Bluto in *Animal House* is a premed major with a 0.0 grade point average who has been in college for seven years. Going through the cafeteria line, he shoves food in his pockets, eats it as he goes, takes a bite of something and puts it back, and piles his tray so high that food keeps falling off onto the floor.

The absurdity of Chuckles's death—he went to the circus parade dressed as Peter Peanut and a rogue elephant tried to shell him—is the hilarious premise of the "Chuckles Bites the Dust" episode on *The Mary Tyler Moore Show*.

In *Tootsie*, Jeff enters the apartment and finds Dorothy/Michael with John, Dorothy's ardent suitor. Believing that Jeff and Dorothy are lovers, John reassures Jeff that "nothing happened." Although he knows Dorothy is really Michael, Jeff turns to Dorothy/Michael and blurts: "You slut!"

Sometimes the obvious can be inane, as in: "Are you telling me I'm redundant? That I continually repeat myself? That I say things over and over?"

In *Dr. Strangelove*, a call to the President at the Pentagon to tell him of the unauthorized attack on Russia is refused because the caller hasn't the right change for the pay phone and the Pentagon won't accept the call.

When the film director in *SOB* is trying to kill himself by sitting in his car with the engine running, the gardener opens the garage door and removes the lawn mower, walking right by the running car without noticing a thing. Later the gardener returns and out of curiosity approaches the car. We think he will notice what is happening. Instead, he picks up a dead rat from the floor. Still later, when he notices the director in the car, he slips the car in gear, and, as a sort of *topper*, it goes through the wall and down the beach into the ocean.

Exaggeration can develop from taking a character trait to extremes. On *Seinfeld*, George has a streak of petty stubbornness. When he and another guy fight over the same parking spot—each with his car half into it—George determines to wait all night rather than lose the spot.

In another episode, George wants to break up with the woman he's dating, but when a friend taunts him about why he's still in the relationship, George stubbornly gets more deeply involved rather than admit he should break it off.

Understatement is sort of reverse exaggeration—serious subjects are treated lightly or trivially. In *Dr. Strangelove*, the President and the Soviet Premier talk childishly as war threatens.

Or exaggeration can come from *overplaying the trivial*. In a *Monty Python* sketch, the defendant makes a passionate plea before being sentenced. He begins humbly, but soon swells until he ends by giving an eloquent oration on the blessings of freedom and the need for mercy. Perplexed, the judge replies: "It's only a bloody parking offense."

Monty Python is filled with the exaggerated, the absurd, the incongruous, and the outrageous. One sketch features gangs of little old ladies (Hell's Grannies) going around tripping people, stealing, and beating up leather-jacketed motorcyclists. In another sketch, all the citizens are supermen (complete with costumes); when one has a bicycle accident we discover who their hero is—Bicycle Repairman!

A sketch featuring a man on television reading nursery stories to children starts rather typically, but then when the grown ups are asked to leave the room it quickly takes on a blatantly erotic twist.

In *Airplane!* an elderly woman haughtily turns down a drink of whiskey, only to sniff cocaine. There is a tough bar fight between two girl scouts. Driving to the airport, the steering wheel is held still while the view out the back window shows the car wildly rounding curves. The plastic Jesus on the "dashboard" of the plane covers his face with his hands over their predicament. Just as the plane is coming in for a landing, a character pulls out a plug that turns off all the landing field lights, then turns to the camera and says, "Just kidding." Whenever we see the establishing shot of the plane in the sky, although it's a jet, we hear the sound of propellers.

The Comic Build

Humor often builds to a payoff—the punch line. This can be a verbal punch line (a joke), or it can be visual—in *M*A*S*H*, the canvas of the shower tent is jerked away to reveal nurse Hot Lips in the altogether.

It can be the very quick build in *Duck Soup* when Trentino asks Harpo and Chico if they have Firefly's record (meaning his dossier). Harpo pulls out a phonograph record. Trentino grabs it and tosses it up behind him. Harpo draws a gun and shoots it (as you would in skeet shooting). Chico says, "Give the man a cigar." Harpo grabs one from the box on the desk, and slams Trentino's finger in the lid. All of this happens in a few seconds.

In his early Sennett films, Chaplin frequently takes someone's—anyone's—pulse as a sort of *running gag*. Then in *The Bank* he adds a punch line. He gratuitously takes the pulse of a waiting customer, then, showing great concern, asks the man to stick out his tongue. Chaplin promptly wets a postage stamp on the man's tongue and sticks it on a letter.

The famous stateroom scene in *A Night at the Opera* crams all sorts of people—travelers, engineers, maids, a manicurist, visitors, stewards—into the steamship stateroom. The payoff comes when someone opens the outside door and they all come falling out.

Jokes, One-Liners, Gags, Wisecracks, and Funny Stories

We're all familiar with jokes, but have we given them much thought? When writing a joke, structure it. Try to put the punch line close to the end of the joke, and put the key word at the end of the punch line.

Groucho Marx had great gag lines; his reply to being told that the garbage man is here was: "Tell him we don't want any." In response to "Mind if I join you?" he asked, "Why? Am I coming apart?"

In *Young Frankenstein*, Dr. Frankenstein's future wife arrives and is met by him and his young female assistant. He tells his other assistant, Igor, to "grab the bags." Igor's reply is pure Groucho *word play*: "You take the blonde and I'll take the one with the turban."

In *Back to School*, the protagonist tells us that "the football team at my high school was tough. After they sacked the quarterback they went after his family."

In the beginning of *Sullivan's Travels*, the idealistic director is talking with his producers about a film. The dialogue, in part, is:

> It died in Pittsburgh.
>
> Like a dog.
>
> What do they know in Pittsburgh?
>
> They know what they like.
>
> If they know what they like, they wouldn't live in Pittsburgh.

Mae West was the queen of the one-liners. "Men like women with a past because they hope history will repeat itself." "It's not the men in your life that counts, it's the life in your men." "When I'm good I'm very good, but when I'm bad I'm better." "Oh, Beulah, peel me a grape." In response to "Goodness, what beautiful diamonds," she replies, "Goodness had nothing to do with it, honey."

Word Play, Puns, and Malapropisms

Humor can come from how we use words: from misuse of words (a malapropism), from puns (words with similar sounds but different meanings, or one word with two different meanings), and from plays on meanings and word sounds.

The Marx Brothers were rich with puns and plays on words. Groucho: "One morning I shot an elephant in my pajamas. How he got in my pajamas, I don't know. But that's entirely irrelephant."

Being told he's shy for a lawyer, Groucho replies, "You're right, I'm shy. I'm a shyster lawyer." After asking a woman if she rhumbas, he tells her, "Then take a rhumba from one to ten."

"I used the past tense. But we're past tents now, we're living in bungalows." "You go Uruguay and I'll go mine." "That's three quotes—add another quote and make it a gallon." "You can leave in a huff—if that's too soon, you can leave in a minute and a huff."

Offering to marry two women and being told that's bigamy, he replies, "Yes, that's big of me, too." On houses being sold in a Florida development deal: "You can even get stucco—oh yes, you can get stuck-o."

Going over a contract, Groucho tries to explain to Chico about the contract being void if one party proves to be insane. It's a standard part of all contracts, "It's the sanity clause." To which Chico replies, "You can't fool me, there is no Santy Claus."

One of the most famous play on word sketches is the Abbott and Costello "Who's on First" routine. Abbott tries to explain to a confused Costello about a baseball team with players with such names as Who, What, and I Don't Know.

Mel Brooks's word plays in the skits that make up *History of the World, Part I* are often groaners, but still fun. As a narrator tells how primitive men treated death with a certain amount of awe, those standing around a dead body say, "Aw."

Caesar asks for a small lyre, so he is brought a small liar. Comicus says, "We got a god for everything except premature ejaculation. But I hear that that's coming quickly." The King reprimands his minister, "Don't be saucy with me, Bernaise."

In Brooks's *Young Frankenstein*, a wolf howls and Inga exclaims, "Werewolf!" Dr. Frankenstein asks: "Werewolf?" Igor points: "There." "What?" "There wolf, there castle."

Airplane! makes generous use of word plays. When the pilot gets calls from the Mayo Clinic and Mr. Hamm at the same time, he advises, "Give me Hamm on five, hold the Mayo." Asked in the control tower to check the radar range, someone checks out a microwave oven (Radar Range was a microwave brand name).

Two African American passengers talk a unique jive patois, some of which is translated by comic subtitles. When one of them says, "Shi-i-i-it" the title reads "Golly."

In reply to the order: "I want all the lights you can poured on that field," we see a dump truck dumping lamps on the field. When reporters are told to get some pictures, they start taking pictures off the wall.

Because Mork came from another planet, the television series *Mork and Mindy* often played with the meanings of words. Asked if he and Mindy are close, Mork replies, "Sometimes we stand right next to each other." When going to a picnic, Mork brings along a jar of ants—having heard that there are often ants at a picnic. Told "Those ants are revolting," Mork replies, "No, they're happy with their form of government." Entertaining someone who says "I'd like a little wine," Mork obliges by whining.

On *Home Improvement*, Tim tells his neighbor how he sold his treasured hot rod car. Surprised, the neighbor says, "I'm taken aback." To which Tim replies, "I can't take it back, I already gave it to him."

A marvelous play on words for their rhyming quality occurs in *The Court Jester* when the hero, to avoid facing death in a duel, has to remember which cup has poison and which doesn't. The message is in the rhyme "The pellet with the poison's in the vessel with the pestle, the chalice from the palace has the brew that is true."

Then they break the chalice from the palace, so now there's a flagon with a dragon. The hero keeps messing it up. His adversary's man overhears, but the adversary can't get it right either. Enjoyable whimsy.

Running Gag

The running gag is a visual, verbal, or sound bit repeated a number of times throughout the film, sometimes with variation, sometimes with some build to it.

In *Young Frankenstein*, Igor's humped back keeps shifting from left to right. And in a parody of a typical motif in horror pictures, each time the name "Frau Blucher" is mentioned, the horses neigh wildly.

The tourists are so concerned about his antics in *Mr. Hulot's Holiday* that each time he does something disruptive all the hotel windows suddenly light up.

When Hope and Crosby get in a tight spot in their road pictures, they often play pat-a-cake and end the refrain by punching their curious antagonists and escaping.

In *A Shot in the Dark*, Inspector Clouseau disguises himself as a balloon seller, but when challenged, he has no license so he is taken to jail. Then he disguises himself as a hunter. Because he has no license, he again goes to jail. Coming from a nudist colony, he drives a car naked and is again picked up and jailed. Each time he's arrested, the police wagon rushes through the streets with the siren blaring.

Airplane! has a number of running gags. We've already mentioned the sound of propellers for the jet plane. There's the hero telling his story to a number of different people, each of whom would rather kill themselves than hear any more. When the cockpit crew are too sick to function, they are carried to the back of the plane while intercom announcements distract the passengers.

There is a running gag in which the airport manager explains how he picked the wrong time to quit smoking . . . drinking . . . amphetamines . . . glue sniffing. Then there are conversations with the doctor that begin "Surely . . ." and his reply is " . . . and stop calling me Shirley."

In an example that also involves *word play and misunderstanding*, a character mentions a "message from headquarters." "What is it?" "A big building where generals work, but that's not important now." This recurs with the hospital (a big building with patients), and the cockpit (a little room in the front of the plane where the captain sits).

In *Duck Soup*, Groucho keeps trying to ride off on his motorcycle-plus-sidecar. First Harpo takes off on the bike, leaving Groucho and the sidecar behind. This happens again. Then Groucho hops on the bike and puts Harpo in the sidecar, which promptly zooms off leaving Groucho behind. (Also, *Rule of Three.*)

Misunderstanding/Mistake

A misunderstanding or mistake is a common catalyst for comedy. Romantic comedies frequently revolve around one partner mistakenly believing the other is involved with someone else.

In *The Gold Rush*, the little tramp mistakenly thinks a note from one woman to another was meant for him, so he fantasizes she loves him, leading to plot complications.

A *Seinfeld* episode has a reporter mistakenly believe that Jerry and George are gay lovers. Her story hits the papers with all sorts of complications. (As a *running gag* punctuating the episode, each time a character mentions the confusion over being gay, they always add ". . . not that there's anything wrong with it.")

A *Fawlty Towers* episode has Fawlty mistaking two different guests for the expected hotel inspectors; he is overly solicitous to them until he discovers his mistake, then he is vengeful and nasty, only to be caught acting this way when the real inspectors arrive.

Misunderstanding can also form the basis of a joke. In another *Fawlty Towers* episode, a hotel guest hears the Spanish waiter practicing his English, but thinks the voice is coming from a moose head sitting on the counter.

In *Caddyshack*, a candy bar gets dropped into the swimming pool. The prissy clubhouse lady thinks it is something else (!) and has the pool drained. When the pool cleaners discover it, one takes a bite out of it. The lady faints.

In the bar scene in *Airplane!* the heroine is disco dancing with a man who gets stabbed in the back. He tries to point to the knife, but she takes his movements as part of the dance and repeats them.

Seated in the plane for takeoff, the hero says he's nervous. His seat companion asks "First time?" He responds "No, I've been nervous lots of times." (Also an example of *word play*.)

When checking into a hotel, Inspector Clouseau sees a dog and asks the manager if his dog bites. "No." Clouseau leans over to pet the dog and gets snapped at. Why? "That's not my dog."

Reverse

We see an example of a reverse when the comic boastfully exclaims, "I'm not scared, I'm not scared," and then, when the hidden passage opens he admits: "I'm scared!" The following examples illustrate the wide range of the reverse as it appears in sequences, bits, visual jokes, an action/adventure show comic situation, and to structure an entire story.

In *Annie Hall*, Alvy urges Annie to take some adult education courses—the professors are so wonderful and interesting. But when she begins to get quite friendly with one, Alvy claims adult education is junk and the professors phony.

A reverse (or switch) occurs in *The Court Jester* when, having been bewitched, a snap of the fingers changes Hawkins from a nervous weakling into a debonair hero, then back again.

A character on *Hope and Gloria* is complaining to the boss about someone: "I hate her." The boss replies "She's my sister." So the character reverses to: "You both have such pretty eyes."

In *Road to Utopia*, Crosby and Hope are in a tough Klondike bar. Crosby orders "a couple of fingers of rot gut" (whiskey). Hope mildly requests "I'll take lemonade."

Crosby gives him a reprimanding look, so Hope adds with a stern face and snarl, "In a dirty glass!"

A typical Hope wisecrack occurs in one of his films when he and a woman friend are being shot at. The woman urges escape. He says bravely, "Do you think I'm yellow?" A shot hits nearby. "Shake hands with a lemon."

In *History of the World, Part I*, the King is out skeet shooting. He objects to rumors that he doesn't care enough for the people. He loves the peasants. "Pull," he commands, and a peasant for him to shoot goes flying through the air. The same film has a character cautioning friends about how to move through the city without being caught by the soldiers. "Whatever you do, don't panic. Whatever you do, don't panic." Suddenly soldiers see them and he yells, "Panic!"

In *When Harry Met Sally*, the two of them take their friends on a blind date. The evening over, each separately advises their friend that it's going well, but it would be best to go slow. Each friend agrees. Then one says he wants to get a cab and the other quickly adds, "I'll join you." They rush off together.

In *Ferris Bueller's Day Off*, they drop off Cameron's father's Ferrari at a parking garage and slip the attendant some extra money to watch it carefully. No sooner are they gone than the attendant and his partner hop into the Ferrari and roar out to joy ride the streets.

Visited by Sue Ann, Mary Richards (in *The Mary Tyler Moore Show*) offers her a cup of coffee. How does she take it? Sue Ann replies that experts advise that a good cup of coffee should be enjoyed hot and black. Then she tastes it and wryly adds, "I think I'll have a little cream and sugar." (Also a *putdown*.)

A visual reverse can occur on a cut. In *Manhattan*, the hero wants to take a walk since it's such a beautiful Sunday—cut to them rushing for shelter in the middle of a thunderstorm.

In *Lethal Weapon 2*, Murtaugh is trapped on a commode wired to a bomb that will go off if he gets up. His partner Riggs is trying to help. Feeling embarrassed by the situation, Murtaugh asks: "Riggs—let's try to keep this quiet, okay?" Riggs: "Trust me." Cut to: later and the street and house filled with all sorts of people.

The plot of "Chuckles Bites the Dust" is based on a reverse. Mary Richards has been putting down the station staff for making jokes about Chuckles's death. At the funeral, she starts laughing uncontrollably at the minister's remarks.

Switch

A switch is very much like a reverse. While a reverse usually means a 180 degree turn, a switch is more a change of expectation.

In a *Frasier* episode, Frasier, his brother Niles, and his father are in a cab with a woman cabby who starts to have a baby. At one point Frasier asks her, "Do you feel faint or short of breath?" His nervous brother Niles—speaking of himself—leaps in: "Yes, both of those."

A *Home Improvement* episode has Tim worried that a pimple on the back of his neck might be something more serious, needing medical attention. Since it's in a place hard for him to see, he asks his son to see what it is. "Sure, it's a pimple. The whole seventh grade is covered with them."

An Ernie Kovacs skit has a man shooting down wooden ducks at a shooting gallery. Suddenly a duck flips and a toy cannon behind the duck fires at the man.

In *Airplane!* the two girl scouts are fighting when one knocks the other into the juke box. Suddenly disco music begins, and the entire rough waterfront dive begins disco dancing.

An Abbott and Costello bit has them deciding who will open a door behind which danger lurks. Neither wants to do it. So Abbott says they'll decide: "Pick a number." Costello: "Four." Abbott: "Wrong, three." Costello starts to go in, but realizes he was conned. Let me do it, he says, you pick a number. Abbott: "Two." Costello reflects, chagrined. Shrugs. Starts through the door.

Topper

Often a punch line is itself "topped" with another punch line—the topper. Sometimes this occurs just as the laugh to the original punch line is beginning to diminish. Agee describes a comic situation in which an incredible number of tall men get out of a small, closed automobile. After a large number are out, one more—a midget—steps out. Then the auto collapses. (Agee sees the men getting out as the basic joke with the midget as the topper, and the collapse being the topper for the topper.)[4] Toppers can occur as part of a plot development, a comic bit, or a joke.

A noted scene in *When Harry Met Sally* involves Sally faking an orgasm in a restaurant. When she's finished, she smiles and resumes eating. (The joke.) Then we cut to a woman at a nearby table telling the waiter, "I'll have what she's having." (The topper.)

In a restaurant scene in *Frasier*, Frasier and a woman friend are seated. Looking around he determines he wants to buy the place. The waiter arrives to take their order. Frasier declares: "I'd like the whole place, from the wine cellar to the rafters!" The waiter reflects a moment, and then responds: "And for the lady?"

In one of his films, Chaplin is very polite and considerate to an elderly drunk in a flophouse. He makes up the man's bed. Then he hits the man on the head with a mallet to put him to sleep—and then he kisses him goodnight.

Buster Keaton and a woman friend are trying to move a tall, rickety house down the street (it's jacked up and on wheels), but it gets stalled on a railroad track. The train is coming; the house won't budge. The train comes and goes on a parallel track, missing the house. Suddenly another train comes from the other direction and demolishes the house. They put a "for sale" sign by the wreckage—the topper.

In a *Cheers* episode, Diane tells Sam that he better watch himself and not try to get physical or "you'll be walking funny (beat) or should I say, funnier."

In *The Pink Panther Strikes Again*, two assassins enter stalls opposite Clouseau's in a public toilet. Clouseau drops the toilet paper and reaches to pick it up just as they shoot, killing each other. He steps out to pick up the paper and someone sneaks in the stall behind him. He shrugs and returns the toilet paper—under the stall door—to the new occupant.

A *Seinfeld* episode has Jerry and George pretending to be two other people in order to get a free limousine ride from the airport (they know that the person expected missed the plane). But it turns out that the person George is pretending to be is being driven to give a major speech at Madison Square Garden. When he is handed the written speech, it turns out to be an anti-Semitic, anti-African American diatribe.

Rule of Three

This is not a rule, of course, but a guiding principle. When setting up a joke based on a verbal or visual series it is more effective to use two sets (or builds) and then the punch line—a total of three. Two seems too few, four too many. The Rule of Three occurs in many verbal and physical comic bits.

In *Mad About You*, Paul and Selby arrive late at a restaurant. Paul: "Sorry we're ten minutes late." His wife: "Twenty." Paul: "Fifteen."

In a *Family Ties* episode, Mallory's parents are upset that she is dating a biker type. Her father approaches the discussion with dismay—he doesn't want to appear authoritarian. He tells Mallory they would like to talk to her "about Nick. About you and Nick. About you and not Nick."

Here's a visual joke from *Annie Hall*. Duane has told Alvy about his urge to crash into oncoming cars. As they drive in the rain to the airport, the camera first shows us Duane's face as he drives, then pans over to Annie, then to the terrified Alvy.

In *Ferris Bueller's Day Off*, they debate taking Cameron's father's Ferrari. Cameron: "It is his love. It is his passion." Ferris: "It is his fault he didn't lock the garage."

A *Frasier* episode has Frasier trying to explain to the unreserved Roz how Daphne is so different from her. He tells her that Daphne is ". . . a bit shy and inexperienced. You're more . . . well, a lot more . . . actually, you'd be hard pressed to find anyone more. . . ."

The Rule of Three appears with a *reverse* in an interchange at a yard sale. The daughter is being urged to sell a quilt that her mother has said she should not sell. Buyer: "Your mother would be happy if you got $200 for it." Daughter: "I really shouldn't." Buyer: "$250." Daughter: "I don't know." Buyer "$300." Daughter: "Do you want it gift wrapped?" (*Family Matters*)

As the plane is facing a possible crash in *Airplane!*, those in the control tower read the newspapers: "Plane about to crash." Another says: "Passengers to die." Johnny grabs a paper and reads: "A sale at Penneys!" When we see shots of newspaper headlines, two of them are about the plane, the third is a tabloid that reads, "Boy eats own foot."

Deflating the Pompous, the Pretentious, and the Self-Righteous

A stuffy title for a common comedy technique. We enjoy seeing the pompous deflated, the haughty brought low, rigid officiousness punctured. They are asking for it, and we want to see them get it. Comedy is always a threat to dignity, especially if that dignity is pretentious. So if you're going to have someone get what they deserve, first show us how much they deserve it.

We enjoy seeing the self-righteous Inspector Clouseau continually getting himself in trouble while acting superior.

The early comics—Chaplin, Laurel and Hardy, the Marx Brothers—loved to deflate the pompous. Harpo is leaning against a building when a sarcastic policeman comes by asking him if he's holding it up. Harpo nods affirming he is. The outraged policeman yanks him away—and the building collapses.

In the "Chuckles" episode, pompous Ted Baxter, who was to have been Grand Marshal of the parade, goes to see if Mary can get Lou to change his mind and permit Ted the honor. But Mary says it's too late, they've already got a replacement. Haughtily, Ted asks who they got to replace him—the mayor? the governor? Mary replies, "Chuckles the clown." (Also the *Rule of Three*.)

Indiana Jones deflates the pompous when he's confronted with a haughty, show-off swordsman who threateningly demonstrates his skill—only to have Indiana pull his gun and shoot (*Raiders of the Lost Ark*).

Recall or Repeat

A comic bit that is used and then used again later in a different context or with variation is all the funnier when we recall its original use.

A *Monty Python* sketch features a secretary who tells a boss a very poor joke, then bursts into tears and says, "But it's my only line." Later there's another sketch about a newly married couple shopping for a mattress (featuring the same actress as the wife). They are advised not to say the word "mattress" because when the salesperson hears it he puts a paper bag over his head and the others in the store must go through an elaborate (and ridiculous) ritual to get him to remove it.

When the husband slips up and says the word, they go through the ritual. Then he mistakenly says it again. Everyone is aghast that someone said it twice. The ritual takes longer this time, but it works and he removes the bag. Then the wife says, "We'd like a mattress." (*Rule of Three*.) How could she?! She plaintively replies, "But it's my only line!" This is funnier as we flash back to the earlier sketch and the line used there.

In "Chuckles Bites the Dust," Lou explains to Ted that they're making jokes over Chuckles's unexpected demise as a release—we laugh at death knowing death will have the last laugh on us. He quotes the classic line, "Ask not for whom the bell tolls, it tolls for thee." Later, when the minister recites the same line during the funeral oration, Ted leans over and whispers, "Hey, Lou, he stole your poem."

In *Tootsie*, Julie tells Dorothy that she would respond to a guy who's honest enough to say he finds her interesting and would like to make love to her. Later when Michael meets her at a party and tries this very tactic, he gets a drink in the face. (Also a *reverse.*)

In a *Mad About You* episode, a friend, Selby, comes in with a bag of fast food and says he'd like to hang out for awhile. He's in the 10K (ten kilometer marathon race). But he only starts the race, then waits it out, and joins it again at the end—when there are lots of attractive women waiting with towels to wipe you down. He settles on the couch. At the end of the episode, the couple gets a call from Selby on their answering machine, "Guess what, I won the 10K!" His action was funny earlier, this tops it.

Delay

A delay occurs when we are set up for a joke or punch line, but then it is delayed a beat (pause) or longer. In Richard Lester's *The Three Musketeers*, a man is seen carrying a very large basket of eggs while a fight is occurring nearby. The fight knocks over some barrels, which roll toward the man. He watches them coming, but the barrels stop just as they reach him. The expected fall doesn't occur. The man walks a few steps—then trips and falls into the basket of eggs.

There's a series in *Airplane!* in which, as the hero burdens various passengers with his story, they kill themselves in one way or another (hanging, seppuku). The last occurrence is with an Indian who pours gasoline over himself, ready to immolate himself. He strikes the match, but then the flight attendant interrupts in order to invite the hero to fly the plane. The Indian holds the burning match expectantly as they talk. The hero agrees to fly and leaves. Relieved, the Indian blows out the match. *Then* there is an explosion.

Often we see a delay in a *delayed reaction* or a *double take*; there's a brief reaction, then a stronger one as the point sinks in.

The Suggestive: Sexual Innuendo and Double Entendre

Sexual innuendos and double entendres, for better or worse, are here to stay. Done well, they can be fun. Done poorly, they seem sophomoric and cheap.

In *Young Frankenstein*, the doctor asks his attractive associate to "elevate me." There is a beat as she reacts with hesitation, so he clarifies. "Raise the platform."

In *History of the World, Part I*, the steward is pouring wine for the Empress Nympho. "Say when," he requests. "8:30," she replies. When an attendant says, "If they're captured, they're hung," Nympho replies, "Not necessarily." (Also *switch* and *word play*.)

With the crew ill, the stewardess in *Airplane!* blows up the inflatable auto pilot (a life-size plastic doll) by blowing through a valve in its lap. The doctor looks in and—seeing her bent over the smiling doll—gets the wrong idea and leaves. (As a *topper*, we later see her sitting next to the smiling auto pilot and smoking a cigarette—typical after-sex behavior.)

A cute scene from *High Anxiety* combines a *reverse, misunderstanding*, and *sexual innuendo*. Richard is calling Victoria from a phone booth, but before he can identify himself, an assassin breaks through the glass and starts to strangle him. From his panting and choking, Victoria imagines this is an obscene phone call. At first indignant, she soon gets interested and starts to ask leading questions: Where did he get her number? What's he wearing? Jeans? Bet they're tight. Richard finally manages to best the assailant, and identifies himself on the phone. Victoria pretends she knew it was him all the time and went along with it for a laugh (of course, he doesn't know what she's talking about).

Here are two comic relief sexual innuendoes from the James Bond film *Octopussy* (the title itself is suggestive). Getting a tour of Q's technical department, James observes a technician trying to perfect the Indian rope trick in which a rope is thrown in the air and stands straight up. But the attempt doesn't work, the rope bends over. Bond coyly asks: "Having problems keeping it up, Q?"

Later, Bond meets an Indian confederate who is disguised as a snake charmer, blowing a flute to charm a cobra in a basket. They take a taxi, and as the confederate leaves, Bond hands him the dildo-like flute he left in the cab: "Oh, here, you may need this to play with your asp."

Mae West used many delicious sexual innuendoes.

Allusion/Reference

With allusion, a joke or comic bit becomes funny (or funnier) because of its reference to something else. We enjoy the connection humor, and get some satisfaction from realizing the reference.

If we saw the earlier film, we understand why Indiana feels confident in *Indiana Jones and the Temple of Doom* when facing a pretentious swordsman. This time, however, when Indiana cavalierly reaches for his gun, he's not wearing it!

In *The Pink Panther Strikes Again*, Inspector Clouseau disguises himself as a hunchback. The phone rings. He rocks his head and groans, "The bells, the bells." This is funnier if we recall *The Hunchback of Notre Dame*. In addition, the name of Clouseau's assistant, Cato, alludes to the assistant in the old radio show, *The Green Hornet*.

A line in *Beetlejuice*—"She's still upset because somebody dropped a house on her sister!"—refers to *The Wizard of Oz*, with the implied *put-down* that the woman is a witch.

In *True Lies*, the wife learns that her husband is really a spy, and blurts out, "I married Rambo!"

As Dr. Frankenstein rides into a train station in *Young Frankenstein*, he asks a shoeshine boy on the platform, "Pardon me, boy, is this the Transylvania station?" The boy replies, "Yah, yah. Track twenty-nine. Oh, can I give you a shine?" The allusion is to a line from a 1940s song, "The Chattanooga Choo Choo."

The Simpsons uses numerous allusions. One half-hour show includes references to *The Devil and Daniel Webster*, *The Twilight Zone* episode about a gremlin attacking an airliner (only here it is a school bus), and *Dracula*. In another episode, Lisa is acting up at school. The principal asks her what she's rebelling against. She replies, "What have you got?" (Referring to the classic Brando line in *The Wild One*.)

Seinfeld did a wonderful homage to the famous scene described earlier from *Marathon Man* about a former Nazi walking down a street in New York's diamond district. This time Kramer is the one trying to be stopped by the woman who calls out, "Stop him. Stop him. I will stop him." If you know the allusion, you especially admire the cleverness of the scene.

In the *Northern Exposure* episode analyzed in the television chapter, while Holling and Barbara are boxing, Maggie and Marilyn sit at ringside knitting—an allusion to Madame LaFarge, who sat knitting by the guillotine during the French revolution.

As the doctor lies to the passengers his nose grows longer and longer—just like Pinocchio's; other *Airplane!* allusions will be dealt with in the next section.

Allusions and parodies shade into each other. An allusion does not always make fun of another work—it need only refer to it. Parody, of course, makes fun of what it parodies.

Satire, Irony, Parody, and Burlesque

Parody and burlesque make broad comic use of other films, television programs, or literary works. They spoof their target by exaggerating it. Satire, often used for social comment, is usually not so broad. Irony can refer to an entire style, or simply a meaning that is the opposite of what is actually being said or done. Such devices can be used as contrast, understatement, imitation, or mockery—often masked in politeness.

At one point in *Dr. Strangelove*, the Air Force general and the Russian ambassador are scuffling. The President ironically admonishes them, "You can't fight in here, this is a war room."

Mel Brooks has practically made a career of parody: *Blazing Saddles*, *Young Frankenstein*, *Spaceballs*, *Robin Hood, Men in Tights*, and *Dracula, Dead and Loving It*. *High Anxiety* spoofs Hitchcock films with references to *Psycho*, *Vertigo*, *North by Northwest*, *Spellbound*, and *The Birds*. Many of his films feature a dance number that lampoons the grand Busby Berkeley musicals.

Dr. Strangelove is a classic satire of cold war politics. *Beat the Devil* satirizes detective dramas like *The Maltese Falcon*. *The Court Jester* parodies swashbuckling movies.

The ending of *The King of Comedy* implies that Rupert could become successful because of—not in spite of—his audacious kidnapping of a talk show host.

Airplane! has its many parodies and *allusions*. The film itself is a spoof of the *Airport*-type movies, particularly *Zero Hour*, on which it was loosely based. The opening refers to the opening of *Jaws*, using that music, and with a plane's tail stabilizer cutting through the clouds like a shark's fin.

As the plane takes off, a young woman runs along the runway (knocking over some pylons) saying goodbye to her boyfriend who stands in the door of the plane in a spoof of the scene from the World War II drama, *Since You Went Away*. The kissing on the beach scene mimics a famous one in *From Here to Eternity*.

The disco dance sequence toys with *Saturday Night Fever*. We hear that a fellow pilot, George Zip, asked if they would "win just one for the Zipper," a take-off of the Gipper line in *Knute Rockne*.

Love at First Bite is a spoof of vampire films: "Do you know what it's like to go through eternity dressed like a head waiter?"

Zorro, the Gay Blade—need I say more?

Anticipation

When we're ahead of the characters and anticipate some coming bit of humor, we especially savor the superior position of being in on the joke (this is not unlike suspense expectation). Once the Hope and Crosby Road pictures established the pat-a-cake routine, audiences looked forward to it in each of their subsequent films.

Often the anticipation comes when we see the comic do or say something that we know will result in some catastrophe. In a *Young Frankenstein* bit, Frankenstein tells his assistant that he'll put his body between the closing bookcase panel and the wall. We know this will be a disaster and we anticipate it—which may in part explain why we don't see him actually getting squished. We don't need to; our imagination does it wonderfully. We hear only an "oof," and then see the results.

Laurel and Hardy used anticipation well. We know Hardy will get himself in trouble (or Laurel will do it for him). In one of their bits, Hardy criticizes Laurel for not being able to light the gas oven, and goes to the kitchen saying he'll do it himself. Needless to say, the resulting explosion sends him flying.

In *The Pink Panther Strikes Again*, when Clouseau says he will slip into his new hunchback disguise, we know it will result in some delicious predicament. And later when we see the disguised Clouseau inhaling laughing gas, we know it will lead to a major mess up.

Anticipation is a useful device that exploits our imagination and comic suspense for its effect.

The Insult, Cut, and Put-Down

Verbal comedy can be as cruel as visual comedy. Jokes at the expense of others or of oneself are common. Put-downs were standard fare on *The Honeymooners*—with Ralph taking swipes at his wife and vice versa. On *The Mary Tyler Moore Show* barbs were constantly flung at Ted Baxter. Archie Bunker and others in the "angry" sitcoms of Norman Lear continue this tradition, which we now see in more contemporary comedies (*Married With Children*, *The Simpsons*).

On sitcoms we often find gentle put-downs, said in fun between friends. These are obviously played for laughs and are not meant to be taken too seriously.

Airplane! features a dandy put-down when a young boy on the plane checks out a girl and decides to make a move on her. He comes up and offers her coffee. She accepts, but when he asks her how she takes it, she replies that she likes it black—like her men!

Groucho Marx could do his share: "You're the most beautiful woman I've ever seen, which doesn't say much for you."

Naivete, Foolishness, and Stupidity

We laugh at the foolishness and stupidity of others. Costello frequently appeared foolish and a bit stupid. Recall the sketch in which he and Abbott are deciding who will enter a room and confront the danger inside. Even when Costello thinks of a number, he isn't able to pull off the con.

A Jackie Gleason skit has Norton playing a blindfolded mind reader identifying various chosen objects. Gleason, his assistant, gets a ring, and cues him by saying, "I hope you *ring* the bell on this one." Norton replies assuredly, "It is a bell."

Homer Simpson is generally portrayed as stupid. In an emergency, he grabs the phone, dials the operator, and says: "Quick, operator, give me the number for 911."

Inspector Clouseau's inane antics are all the funnier because of his attempts to act as if he did nothing wrong.

Dumb and Dumber—need I say more?

Cleverness and Ingenuity

We find enjoyment in an ingenious bit or ploy. We admire imagination and inventiveness. So much of Chaplin's comedy has these qualities. In one film, Chaplin is being chased by the police and hides amongst some mechanized figures on a store front, pretending to be one of them. The added touch is that as he turns in the required automated manner he hits one of his adversaries over the head and then laughs mechanically, all the time staying in character.

Buster Keaton has his own ingenious qualities. Once he has a house front fall on top of him, but the door frame falls over him so he isn't hurt. (He really did the stunt—a few inches either way and he would have been severely injured if not killed.)

Another Keaton sketch features a house in which everything is rigged for efficiency. Dining condiments are suspended by strings from the ceiling so they can be easily passed (swung) back and forth. The bread basket is on wheels so it can be rolled from one side of the table to another. Leftovers are dumped through a slot in the wall to awaiting pigs. A sink is hidden in a roll-top desk. The table top is swung to the wall above it. The dishes, which are stuck to the table top, are rinsed off by a hose. A bathtub is tipped up to become a couch, and the water flows outside where some ducks swim in it. The bed tips up and the underside is revealed to be a piano. The table top on the wall is then flipped over to reveal a framed placard that reads, "What Is a Home without a Mother." It all happens very quickly, and we enjoy the inventiveness.

In *Adventures in Babysitting*, the baby-sitter and her charges, running from the pursuing criminals, find themselves in a blues club and are told they can't leave until they sing the blues. They resourcefully improvise "Babysitting Blues."

Offscreen Sound and Dialogue

Imagination plays a big part in our comic response, which is why much can be done with offscreen sound and dialogue. In *Young Frankenstein*, Frankenstein is playing darts and doing badly. One hits the wall, another he throws backwards and we hear a cat yowl. With the next throw we hear the crash of a window breaking. Inspector Clouseau falls down stairs and we hear a prolonged crash; we imagine the rest.

In a *Taxi* episode, Louie plans to expose an old lady con artist who faked a car injury. He doesn't realize that this time she really did get hurt. To demonstrate what he thinks is a fraud, he sends her wheelchair flying out the courtroom doors—and we hear it bump down nineteen flights of stairs.

The offscreen sound of a toilet flushing is frequently used in *All in the Family*—one classic moment being when we hear the flush as everyone is waiting for Archie to come down for Mike and Gloria's wedding.

Background Comedy

Sometimes while the main action is going on in the foreground, there's something comic happening in the background. A scene in the control tower in *Airplane!* has someone in the background loading their wash into the washer-like "door" of a radar scope. The scene in which they walk through the VA hospital grounds in *Harold and Maude* has patients collapsing on the grass behind them as Harold's uncle extols the virtues of military life.

A COMEDY EXAMPLE

We'll conclude this chapter with a breakdown of highlights from one of the best of the Pink Panther films, *The Pink Panther Strikes Again*. I chose this film for a number of reasons. It contains many excellently structured comic sequences. They are fast-paced, build masterfully, and usually have great payoffs. The film is well written and acted—Peter Sellers makes Inspector Clouseau one of the classic comic film characters. The comedy is broad and easily accessible. And there is a clear, if rather absurd, plot.

Inspector Clouseau is the bumbling French detective who, although totally inept, thinks he is masterful, and is always trying to cover up his missteps. In the end, he always manages to bungle through.

This fifth film of the series opens with Clouseau as Chief Inspector (he drove his nemesis—Dreyfus, the former Chief Inspector—to a mental institution).

The story line, once it begins, is straightforward. Clouseau wants to capture the mad Dreyfus who in turn wants the world to turn Clouseau over to him so he can have his revenge—or else he will destroy our cities with his new death ray. (This part gets rather preposterous, although by this time we are so amused we don't much care.)

There are five major comic sequences:

The opening in which Clouseau unhinges Dreyfus.

The fight with Cato, which develops along with Dreyfus's attempt to blow up Clouseau.

Clouseau investigating the kidnapping in the English mansion.

Octoberfest, and the assassins failing to kill Clouseau.

Clouseau disguised as a dentist attempting to pull Dreyfus's tooth.

The opening is a marvelous example of how to reduce someone to a babbling idiot in a few minutes. Former Chief Inspector Dreyfus proves he is cured and is about to be released following a routine hearing. Clouseau arrives, offering to—groan—testify in support of Dreyfus.

While Dreyfus is seated by a pond on the sanitarium grounds, Clouseau casually hits a croquet ball that ricochets off a tree and hits Dreyfus on the head, knocking him into the water. Clouseau tries to pull him out with the croquet mallet, but the head comes off and Dreyfus falls back in. Once Dreyfus is out, Clouseau gives him mouth-to-mouth resuscitation, which two passing ladies mistake for sexual activity—one whacks Clouseau with her bag.

Sitting on a bench, the two talk for a bit. Then Clouseau gets up, making the bench tip down and sending Dreyfus back into the water. Climbing out, Dreyfus steps on a rake that Clouseau has left there, and it swings up and hits him in the head (again knocking him into the water).

By this time he has gone completely berserk and chases Clouseau to the car threatening to kill him. This is a nine-minute introduction; opening credits follow.

Clouseau is about to enter his apartment when he spills some of the sugar he is carrying. Since the woman who lives across the way is watching him, he tries to cover his foolishness by pretending to do a soft shoe dance on the spilled sugar. He puts his key—attached to his pants—into the lock, then reaches over to pick up the woman's dropped wallet, and rips his pants down the leg.

Inside his apartment, Clouseau moves around suspiciously. (A running bit in the series is that he and his manservant Cato keep each other alert by surprise attacks.)

Meanwhile, in the apartment below, Dreyfus prepares to blow Clouseau to bits. He begins by drilling holes in the floor into which he inserts a small periscope so he can locate Clouseau. But when Clouseau opens the door of the refrigerator looking for Cato—absurd in itself—food falls out and catsup spills down the drilled hole and onto Dreyfus. Clouseau looks in the washing machine, and the soapy water that pours out falls down onto Dreyfus.

Cato appears, and he and Clouseau fight throughout the apartment, using nun chuks, wooden swords, and staves. They demolish much of the apartment. In the course of the chase, Clouseau bumps into the periscope and sends Dreyfus falling off his perch. Then the phone rings, and Clouseau calls a halt, but then after taking Cato's weapon, gives the trusting friend a final hard whack.

During the call, a new hole is drilled right next to Clouseau. To clear it for a better look, Dreyfus puts his finger through it, only to have Clouseau step on the finger. In pain, Dreyfus knocks over his support, dangles by his finger, and then falls. The call alerts Clouseau that Dreyfus has escaped and is after him, but he dismisses it.

Clouseau shows Cato his new disguise—the humpback outfit. He ignores the warning not to overinflate the hump. Dreyfus calls him on the phone to keep him in place while planting the explosive. Slowly the hump fills with helium until an unaware Clouseau begins floating out the balcony doors.

There is some suspense because Dreyfus is hurriedly setting the explosives. Suddenly aware of being high in the air, Clouseau drops the phone, which swings back and hits Dreyfus who blows himself up. Clouseau instantly deflates the hump; the escaping gas sends him zooming over Paris and into a pond. A wild and very funny twelve-minute sequence.

Now it's time for some plot. A criminal being transported by train is rescued by a helicopter. Dreyfus, his rescuer, asks him to build a super crime gang. They rob a bank to finance Dreyfus's plans, and they kidnap a noted scientist in England.

Clouseau goes to England to investigate the kidnapping and another comic sequence begins. At first he messes up only on obvious things. He misses the light switch but instead turns on an exercise conveyer belt, which he walks on until the error is revealed.

Claiming to have been an expert, he takes a leap on the parallel bars in the house gym and goes over, falling down the stairs to where people are awaiting him. "That felt good," he says to cover his clumsiness.

He questions those waiting, messing up their names. He gets his hand caught in a suit of armor's glove and mace and can't remove it. He accidentally whacks the beekeeper with the mace. Trying to swat a bothersome bee, he swings the mace and destroys a priceless piano. Standing by the fireplace, the ball and glove dangle over the flames and get hot. He manages to get the glove off his burned hand, but trying to cool the hand, plunges it into a flower vase and gets it stuck there. Falling back into the gun case, he sets off a shotgun that shoots a newly arrived police superintendent in the derriere.

Clouseau next tails a suspicious motorcycle to a club where the singer turns out to be the scientist's butler in drag. Clouseau is picked up in a raid on the club.

At the castle hideout of the deranged Dreyfus, the scientist is forced to construct a doomsday machine or else his daughter will be tortured (by having to listen to fingers on a metal glove dragged screechingly across a blackboard).

Dreyfus then appears on television warning the nations of the world to give him Clouseau or he will create a holocaust. As a sample, he vaporizes the United Nations building. The nations send their top assassins after Clouseau.

Meanwhile Clouseau has followed Dreyfus to Germany. At an Octoberfest celebration, there is another comic sequence as the assassins try and fail to kill an unwary Clouseau.

The first one tries to stab Clouseau but stabs through his attache case instead and is himself killed when Clouseau unwittingly presses the case onto him. At Octoberfest, the assassins kill each other instead of Clouseau. Just as one assassin is about to shoot Clouseau, he is accidentally stabbed by one of the others. A second man is then shot by someone aiming at Clouseau. A third assassin in drag with large daggers protruding from his/her bosom stumbles and is stuck to a table.

A dwarf assassin is accidently killed by a musician assassin blowing a poisoned dart through his horn. In the toilet scene described earlier, two assassins shoot each other when Clouseau bends down. Soon only the Russian and Egyptian assassins are left.

The Egyptian disguises himself as Clouseau and finding the beautiful Russian assassin in Clouseau's apartment, masterfully makes love to her. Later he ends up dead in the bathtub, a victim of Dreyfus's man. (Dreyfus now thinks Clouseau is dead.)

The Russian agent is so enthralled with his amours, that she mistakenly thinks she is in love with Clouseau and tells him the whereabouts of Dreyfus's castle headquarters. Clouseau leaves to pursue him.

Next follows the music-driven sequence of Clouseau trying to break into the castle through the drawbridge, described earlier. The series of attempts all end in failure.

At the castle, Dreyfus is suffering from a painful toothache. Back at the hotel, Clouseau learns that the castle needs a dentist. He disguises himself as one and goes. We're now ready for the last major comic sequence.

Clouseau's disguise includes thick glasses through which he can't see very well. The glasses make him fall down a flight of stairs when he tries to clobber Dreyfus.

Clouseau offers Dreyfus nitrous oxide—laughing gas—as an anaesthetic and indulges in some himself. Both men start to laugh. In the heat inside the castle, Clouseau's disguise starts to melt. Dreyfus receives the message that Clouseau is not dead. They continue to laugh wildly, but when Clouseau pulls the wrong tooth Dreyfus realizes the dentist is Clouseau. We go to a chase in which Clouseau manages to escape.

Just as Dreyfus is about to destroy England with his death ray, Clouseau enters disguised in a suit of armor. First he swings on a rope and, missing, falls through a window into a pig pen outside.

Then he sits on a catapult and when a goat chews on the rope Clouseau is flung up and lands on the doomsday ray, which swings around and starts to dissolve Dreyfus and the castle. All escape to safety, except Dreyfus who insanely plays "Tiptoe Through the Tulips" on an organ as the castle vanishes. The world is saved.

Back in his Paris apartment, Clouseau is about to join the beautiful Russian spy in bed (after being unable to remove his tie or pants) when Cato stages a surprise attack. The folding bed flies up and smashes the wall, and all three are flung through the wall into a pool.

The end of a very funny movie. The plot is silly, but moves quickly and holds our interest. The comic sequences are hilarious.

Comedy is fun! Film and television comedy has given pleasure to millions. If you can write top-notch comedy, you have a promising career in this business. And the privilege of a great gift—being able to make us laugh.

SUMMARY

The chapter began with comedy theories: disparagement or aggression, superiority, tension release, social function, and incongruity–resolution. Comedy characteristics described aspects of comedy, including comic distance, suspense and surprise, destructiveness, comic styles, comedy genres, comic characters, comic relief, and the serious in the comic.

Writing comedy considered the comic concept; the use comedy makes of props and devices; physical comedy; and such comedy components as the comic sequence, the comic bit, visual jokes, comic reactions, and the chase.

Comedy techniques presented a number of techniques for creating laughter, each with various examples from the media. Topics covered were exaggeration, absurdity, incongruity, the outrageous, the comic build, jokes, one-liners, gags, wisecracks and funny stories, word play, puns and malapropisms, running gags, misunderstanding, reverse, switch, topper, the "Rule of Three," deflating the pompous, the recall, delay, the suggestive, allusion/reference, satire, irony, parody and burlesque, anticipation, the insult, cut and put-down, naivete, foolishness and stupidity, cleverness and ingenuity, offscreen sound and dialogue, and background comedy.

The chapter concluded with a description of *The Pink Panther Strikes Again*.

ENDNOTES

1. Agee, J. (1958, 1964). "Comedy's greatest era." In *Agee on Film*. Boston: Beacon Press, p. 8.

2. Quoted in Wilson, S. (1990). *Eat dessert first*. Pickerington, OH: Advocate Publishing Group, p. 50.

3. Wilson, p. 65.

4. J. Agee, p. 11.

CHAPTER *12*

Adaptations

*Look, you can't be faithful to the book. Or, if you're faithful to the book, it's
only where it's coincidental. You've got to be faithful to the audience.*

—Nunnally Johnson[1]

Why should you do an adaptation? If it's of something you don't own the rights
to, don't bother; you will probably be wasting your time and effort. If it's for a
writing sample, you would be better off writing an original script that demonstrates
your own imaginative ideas.

However, if you become a successful screenwriter, you will undoubtedly be
asked to do adaptations. Some of the best films and television MOWs have been
adapted from novels, short stories, and theatrical plays—or based on true-life stories. By far, the most Academy Awards for Best Picture have gone to adaptations.
Most mini-series and nearly half of all MOWs are based on other material, and the
vast majority of those that have won Emmys are adaptations. Adaptations are often
moneymakers.

Here are some films that were adapted from other material. From novels: *The
African Queen, Blade Runner, Casablanca, The Color Purple, Dances with Wolves,
Deliverance, Field of Dreams, Frankenstein, The Godfather, Gone with the Wind, The
Graduate, The Hunt for Red October, Howard's End, Jaws, Jurassic Park, The Maltese
Falcon, My Left Foot, One Flew Over the Cuckoo's Nest, The Secret Garden, Sense and*

Sensibility, Schindler's List, Slaughterhouse Five, The Third Man, Tom Jones, The Warriors, and *The Wizard of Oz.*

From comic books: *Batman, Superman.* From short stories: *All About Eve, High Noon, It Happened One Night, It's a Wonderful Life, Stagecoach, The Wild One, 2001.* From theatrical plays: *Front Page, Glengarry Glen Ross, Harvey, Sabrina, Six Degrees of Separation, Streamers, Who's Afraid of Virginia Woolf?* From true-life stories: *Chariots of Fire, Dances with Wolves, Malcolm X, My Left Foot, Patton, Romero, Stand and Deliver.*

The popularity of adaptations is understandable; they represent material that has usually demonstrated audience appeal and critical response. Adaptations are, in effect, presold. Interestingly, some of the best films have been made from mediocre novels, perhaps because they can be more freely adapted.

One issue in making an adaptation is how closely to follow the original work. There is no prescribed answer. Some adaptations stay very close to the original (*The Maltese Falcon, Who's Afraid of Virginia Woolf?*). Others are less similar to the original, and may be described as "freely adapted" or "based on" the original (*Blow-Up, 2001*). With famous or best-selling novels, you might hesitate before eliminating major characters or events.

A successful film adaptation will be more of a paraphrase than a translation since every medium has characteristics that preclude a direct translation. It is important to retain the key elements from the original—the qualities that made it popular. This means catching its flavor—the "personality" or feeling-tone of the original. A quick read-through should give you this sense. Identify the vital elements, and try to retain them when translating to film or television.

The basic approach to writing an adaptation is straightforward. First you want to review the material for an overall sense of its unique elements. In subsequent readings, analyze the work's structure, characters, and themes.

Do an outline of the work as is. Understand how it is constructed. Then—using the principles we've discussed—restructure the story and characters into film form.

This will involve many changes. Characters will be eliminated, merged, and perhaps even added. Themes in the original will need to be dramatized and visualized. Dialogue will be shortened and made conversational. Some scenes will be condensed, some will be eliminated, others will be added.

With a loose adaptation there is little need to remain faithful to the original, so you may merely want to identify elements in the work that excite you and build on them. Or you may pick out a single essential element from the work—an unusual premise, intriguing situation, or character—and write the story from this.

If the adaptation is to be close to the original work, analyze its deep structure and build from it, trying to retain the flavor of the original.

In keeping with the visual impact of film, try to show actions and events that are described in the original rather than having the characters talk about them.

A narrator might help in overcoming problems, as might flashbacks showing past events (to clarify the backstory). However, these are rather awkward devices and risk messing the story.

NOVEL AND SHORT STORY

A novel will need to be condensed. Subplots, events, and perhaps even characters will have to be eliminated. Where a novel is introspective, the script will have to find ways to externalize the events with behavioral detail or filmic metaphor.

If there is no clear conflict/objective or climax, you will need to rework the story to build these into an effective story line. If the novel doesn't have a clear major protagonist, you will have to pick one. The same is true of the antagonist. Be sure the story line is clear and clean. Add or drop other story lines, as needed. You may need to add a powerful hook to the opening.

A short story needs to be expanded. You will probably add characters and secondary story lines.

THEATRICAL PLAY

A theatrical play may also need to be expanded. Certainly you must expect to open it up by including locations and actions only alluded to in the play or by adding new ones. Break loose from the stagy feeling the setting of a play imposes. Try to present as much as you can visually. Cut down the dialogue of the play. If the play is not that realistic—and many aren't—you will probably have to make it so.

TRUE-TO-LIFE STORY

In adapting a true-to-life story, be sure to structure it into a strong film story line with a clear objective/problem and climax. Make sure it develops and builds through a series of crises. Try to restrict the time period of the story so that it doesn't span an entire lifetime. Have a likable main character and (most likely) an antagonist.

It is often easier to adapt an incident rather than an entire life story. An incident leaves the writer freer to dramatize the story. Take some care before too drastically changing facts, events, or characters. Try not to change history. Avoid making changes that may damage the real people involved.

FROM FILM OR TELEVISION

You might even adapt a work from film or television. Early films, television, or foreign films are sometimes remade (*The Addams Family, The Birdcage, Breathless, The Coneheads, Cousins, Fatal Attraction, The Fugitive, The Magnificent Seven*). If you are adapting an older film, you will need to update it for today's audience. Modify cultural references and locations. If the adaptation is of a foreign film, be sure to rework cultural differences.

RIGHTS AND OPTIONS

Rights and options are important considerations when working with someone else's material. If the work is in the public domain—which at this writing is fifty years after the death of the author—you may use it freely. Also in the public domain are public records and newspaper stories.

It is always safer to get an option, even if you believe the material is in the public domain. This means tracing down the rights to the work—often through the publisher or the writer's agent—and buying an option, which gives you the exclusive right to buy the rights to the work by paying a larger amount (to be agreed on at the time of the option) within a certain time period (typically six months or a year).

Whenever you deal with someone else's work, be sure you have the rights. Don't write a script with the hope that if it's good, the producer will negotiate rights. This will most likely be a waste of time and energy.

The best advice is to consult a knowledgeable attorney whenever you negotiate for rights or options. For a fuller discussion of this as well as a sample contract, see Linda Seger's *The Art of Adaptations: Turning Fact and Fiction into Film.*[2]

SUMMARY

This chapter reviewed some considerations for adapting from another work. With a close adaptation, you will try to keep the key elements and feeling-tone of the original. With a loose adaptation, you can range more widely. In any event, you will need to analyze the original work, then recast it in the structure we have discussed.

ENDNOTES

1. Johnson, N. Quoted in Froug, W. (1972). *The screenwriter looks at the screenwriter.* New York: Dell, p. 246.

2. Seger, L. (1992). *The art of adaptation: Turning fact and fiction into film.* New York: Henry Holt. This is a useful book to consult if you're doing an adaptation. Another possibility is Portnoy, K. (1991). *Screen adaptation.* Boston: Focal Press. (If you only look at one, I'd give the nod to Seger.)

CHAPTER 13

Marketing Your Script

Let me tell you about writing for films. You finish your book. You drive up to the California state line, take your manuscript and pitch it across. No, on second thought don't pitch it across. First let them toss the money over. Then you throw it over, pick up the money, and get the hell out of there.

—Ernest Hemingway

Marketing a script isn't easy. It may turn out to be harder than the writing. Hollywood is a small community that has developed its own ways of operating. If you want to sell to this mainstream market, you'll need to fit into those ways. People work around the system every day, but don't count on being one of these exceptions.

Here is some advice to ponder as you go about trying to sell your script.

If you are a novice writer, the odds are that you will not sell your first script; you are probably better off not trying to.

Write two or three screenplays before you try to get an agent.

Understand the way the industry works and how it handles new material.

Be able to handle rejection; don't take it personally.

If this is your first screenplay, you're justifiably proud of it. Your impulse is to try to get it right to a producer's desk. Unfortunately the odds are that your first script is not that good. You will improve with each subsequent script, so work on a second screenplay and then a third. (If your first script turns out to be that very rare gem that is marketable, it will still be so after you've written other scripts.)

If you have a contact in the business that you can get your script to, use it. People in the industry are bombarded with scripts. If you send them a poor one, they'll be less inclined to look at your second script. So only use contacts when you've got something worthwhile. Few first screenplays are.

The most common path to becoming a professional screenwriter is through an agent. It may take some doing, but you will eventually find an agent to read your scripts.

Agents are interested in developing writers' careers. They have a long-term commitment in mind; if you have only one script, there's always the suspicion that you might be a "one-script wonder." Or the agent may think it shows promise and ask what else you have; if you have nothing else to show, things can cool rapidly. Have two or three scripts ready when you approach an agent. That way, they can get an idea of what your writing is like and what they can sell.

Know how the business works. Read the references at the end of the chapter. Know the process of getting material read and sold.

Screenwriting can be rewarding; it can also mean long, lean periods without work. It means having your work turned down and rewritten—sometimes with poor results. Don't let it get to you. This is part of the business. You will get rewritten—bank on it. You will get rejected—don't take it personally.

Remember William Goldman's dictum about the industry: Nobody knows anything. *Airplane!*, *All in the Family*, *E.T.*, *Platoon*, and *Star Wars* are just some of the many films that were first rejected—often repeatedly. Don't take it personally.

THE STATE OF THE BUSINESS

The state of the business is always in flux. There are rich and lean periods. Right now, things look pretty good for the movie industry. Revenues are setting new records. More films are being produced than ever. Video sales and rentals are growing, as is the foreign market.

In television, the picture is not so clear. The networks have been in trouble, but this could change. As cable channels expand, there will be more demand for writers. Markets other than feature films and television networks look promising.

Top writers and good scripts are always in demand. As any reader or producer will tell you, over ninety-five percent of the material they receive—most all of it from agents—is junk. Of the few good scripts, only a small percentage will be made into films. And of the films produced, perhaps one-quarter will never get theatrical release (most of these are made by independents rather than by the major studios). If you have talent, the entertainment media need you.

Not only will you have to be good, you'll be competing against thousands of other aspiring writers to get your material read. The Writers Guild registers some

20,000 scripts a year. There are a lot of people writing, but most are not making a living at it. Of some 8000 Guild members, perhaps 3000 are actively writing, and of these, some 500 writers turn out most of what we see on film and television.

Outside the traditional movie industry, there are growing opportunities in alternative markets including cable, films produced directly for home video, television programs made directly for syndication rather than for the networks, animation, children's programming, radio, public broadcasting, and non-fiction industrial, training, and educational production. Also promising are interactive video, CD-ROMS, and video games.

FEATURE FILMS

The Hollywood market for feature films works like this. Studios, producers, and many stars receive script submissions, nearly all of these from agents. Scripts are sent to story analysts/readers for coverage (a summary of the script and recommendations). The small percentage that get recommended are read by studio executives and producers. If they think the script is worth considering, it will be put into development where it will be rewritten to make it more effective. (Expect that your script will be rewritten. It's virtually a given in this business; you will be rewritten.)

At this stage, your script will either have been optioned or bought outright. If you are a beginning writer, the studio may turn your script over to one or more established writers for rewriting (six to a dozen writers is not unusual on a film). If your script is bought, the contract typically specifies that you will do one complete rewrite, perhaps some additional revisions, and a polish.

A script may spend months or years in development during which time the studios will be trying to adapt it to their needs—or they may be looking for the right actors. It is estimated that only one out of forty scripts in development is ever produced. The others are shelved or put in turnaround and made available to other studios and producers. Many writers make a decent living from having their work optioned and bought—even though none of their work has ever been produced.

TELEVISION

Prime-time television series are made by production companies who in turn make deals with the networks. Each production company has a team of producers, story editors, and staff writers. A series may sometimes accept scripts from freelance writers. The goal of most television writers is to get on staff. From there they can move up to become series producers. New series and movies-of-the-week are almost exclusively developed in-house by established professionals.

Breaking into television is often a matter of getting scripts read by someone on a show. Your agent can probably do this better than you, but feel free to try it yourself—contacts always help.

Surprisingly, advice for a novice writer is to send a series a writing sample script for another series rather than theirs since they are so familiar with their show that they will see all the faults in your script while a script for another series could show them that you have writing ability.

GETTING AN AGENT

The best way to break into the business as a screenwriter is to get an agent. It can be done without one, but it is much more difficult. You can get a list of agents from the WGA (Writers Guild of America). Send an agent a well-written query letter asking if he or she will look at your work. Advice on how to make these contacts will be found in the books listed at the end of the chapter.

PITCHING

The books at the end of this chapter will also offer advice on how to pitch a story idea. A good pitch is invaluable. The producer or story editor has only limited time available. You need to be able to give an exciting overview of the script in a few minutes.

A good pitch must catch the audience's attention. It needs a strong opening, a clean spine, one or two dynamite scenes, a definite sense of the growth of the main character or of character relationships, and a strong climax ending. (Not unlike a good basic story.) Pitching is an invaluable skill for a freelance writer. There are even workshops that help writers develop pitching skills.

LOOK PROFESSIONAL

Be sure that your script has a professional look. Use the correct format; be sure to have clear copies with a clear typeface. Give the script the standard stiff paper cover—don't try to be fancy. Make a good professional impression.

SCRIPT PROTECTION

Be sure to protect the script before you send it out. There are two ways to do this. One is to send an unbound copy of the script to the WGA Registration Service. They register it for five years, with an additional five-year renewal possible. As of this writing, the fee for registration is $10 for members, $20 for non-members.

The other protection is to copyright your script through the U.S. Copyright Office (information on copyright is available in most libraries or can be obtained from the Copyright Office, Library of Congress, Washington, DC 20559). Copyright gives some additional protection that registration doesn't. It is advisable to do both.

WRITERS GUILD OF AMERICA

The Writers Guild of Amerca (WGA) represents screenwriters. Like similar professional organizations, it offers benefits (such as health insurance) to its members. It negotiates general contracts with producers, studios, and production companies. Most major producers are signatories to the Guild and pay at least WGA contract minimums. After making some script sales you will be eligible to join the Guild.

Writers Guild of America, West
7000 W. Third Street
Los Angeles, CA 90048-4329
(213) 951-4000

OTHER AVENUES

There are other possibilities for getting your scripts considered. There are screenwriting competitions to which you can submit material, but beware of those with high entrance fees—they may be ripoffs. Similarly, avoid script consultants who say they will read your script and critique it for a fee.

Colleges and universities have screenwriting courses; the instructors often have professional contacts and can get an outstanding script from one of their students to someone who should see it. Some studios have new talent development programs, especially for women and minority writers.

There are numerous regional screenwriting groups that publish newsletters announcing opportunities and competitions. Many have meetings where writers can share their work. These are to be found all over the country. (For example, The Freelance Screenwriter's Forum, Baldwin, Maryland.)

A promising recent innovation is marketing your script on the Internet. GreatScripts.com creates a personalized Web Site for you on which you can post loglines and synopses of your screenplays. From here they can be searched—by author, genre, and location—by registered filmmakers worldwide (and only by those who have registered, thereby providing some ownership protection). An interested filmmaker can then contact the writer (or agent, if you have one) for a copy of the script. The cost is surprisingly low (as of this writing, $45 per year to writers, no cost to filmmakers). The service maintains a useful digital trail of all filmmakers who have accessed your site and when they did so. Contact GreatScripts.com, 9399 Wilshire Boulevard, #105, Beverly Hills, CA 90210, 310-278-9292; e-mail: writer@greatscripts.com.

Marketing your work isn't easy, but if you are talented and you've honed that talent over a number of scripts, you have a good chance to become a professional screenwriter.

Plan to go to Los Angeles. It's difficult—but not impossible—to get into the business from anywhere else. Give it your best shot. Good luck.

MARKETING REFERENCES

Here are some books that deal with marketing your script and related issues.

Field, S. (1989). *Selling a screenplay: The screenwriter's guide to Hollywood.* New York: Dell.

Katahn, T. L. (1990). *Reading for a living: How to be a professional story analyst for film and television.* Los Angeles: Blue Arrow Books.

Kosberg, R. (1991). *How to sell your idea to Hollywood.* New York: HarperCollins.

Sautter, C. (1992). *How to sell your screenplay.* New York: New Chapter Press.

Seger, L., and Whetmore, E. J. (1994). *From script to screen: The collaborative art of filmmaking.* New York: Henry Holt.

Silver, D. (1991). *How to pitch & sell your TV script.* Cincinnati: Writer's Digest Books.

Stuart, L. (1993). *Getting your script through the Hollywood maze.* Los Angeles: Acrobat Books.

Whitcomb, C. (1988). *Selling your screenplay.* New York: Crown.

Zaza, T. (1993). *Script planning.* Boston: Focal Press.

CHAPTER *14*

Script Formats

"Begin at the beginning," the King said, very gravely, "and go on till you come to the end: then stop."

—Lewis Carroll

Your script should look professional. You want to make a good initial impression. Avoid giving readers any reason to be turned off to your work. Here is how to make a script look like a script.

GENERAL SUGGESTIONS

Be sure the script is clean, easy to read, and neat—neatness counts. There should be no misspelled words. Submit a clean photocopy of the original.

Be sure the script is the right length—many readers check this out first. A feature script will be from 105 to 125 pages (comedy usually runs somewhat less: 95–115 pages). A one-hour television show will be around 60 pages (but check with the show, some like longer scripts so they can be cut). Half-hour, live-on-tape scripts are 40 to 50 or more pages.

Feature scripts and filmed television follow the same format (except for indicating the television acts); half-hour, live-on-tape sitcoms use a different format.

Filmed scripts time at a minute a page; a 120-page script will run two hours. Live-on-tape scripts time at about half a minute or slightly longer a page.

Try to make the script as easy a read as possible. This can mean a great deal of "white space" on the page, which is another way of saying, don't cover the page with words, long dialogue speeches, or lengthy descriptive segments. Break up the latter so that no description section runs more than a half-dozen lines. One rule of thumb is to make the page half white and half black. This can be taken with a grain of salt, but the principle stands—don't overfill your page.

Write the script in master scenes, that is, each scene as it might be shot as a whole, without breaking it up into smaller shot segments such as medium or close shots.

Except for rare instances where the material demands that you indicate a shot, don't call shots. Let the director do that.

Don't right justify your description or dialogue. Leave the right edge of description and dialogue jagged, not aligned.

Don't center each line of dialogue on the page. Dialogue lines should each begin at the indented dialogue left margin.

In description, avoid contractions (use them in dialogue, not in description).

Try to write description with active-voice verbs and generally try to avoid "to be" verbs.

Keep character descriptions to a minimum.

Don't use the "we" form of address ("we see," "we hear"), it's out-of-date.

Be sparing with parentheticals.

Avoid boldface.

Avoid abbreviations with obvious exceptions such as Mr., Mrs., Sgt., and Capt. (even these last two could be written out). Write out: Doctor, five dollars, department, okay. Write out numbers smaller than three digits (for example, "thirty-seven"); it may even be better to write out all numbers. If you are in doubt, write it out.

Don't include a synopsis. Don't include a list of characters or sets. Don't suggest actors for the roles.

Don't use a fancy cover, just a heavy card stock in any color but white. Fasten the script with two brass brad fasteners (even though you punch it with three holes). Be sure the brads are the right size—not too long to be awkward, not too short to come out. Acco #5 is recommended.

Use Courier typeface (typewriter style), ten characters to the inch (Courier 12 for computer printers), with equal spacing for all letters (*not* proportional spacing).

There should be a plain title page with the script's title and your name. Near the bottom, include a line stating it is copyrighted and/or registered with the WGA (don't include the registration number). Your agent's name and address could also be included near the bottom on one side, but some present usage discourages it. Don't include the date—this could date your material.

Begin your script with "FADE IN" and end it with "FADE OUT" followed by "THE END."

MOTION PICTURE/FILMED TELEVISION FORMAT (SINGLE CAMERA)

Margins for the script are one-and-a-half to two inches on the left (to make room for the brads) and an inch on the right. Leave an inch to an inch and a half at the top and bottom of the page (not including the page number). Don't crowd the bottom of the page.

Pages are numbered in the upper right-hand corner or the upper middle of the paper, three or four lines down.

Horizontal Spacing.   The spacing is generally as follows (with the paper edge as zero and counting ten spaces to the inch. These suggestions allow for a two-inch left margin; if using a one-and-a-half inch left margin deduct five spaces, et cetera:

20	Scene headings (slug lines) and description. FADE IN.
30–60	Dialogue
35	Parenthetical (Business)
40	Character name (CAPITALIZED)
60	Transitions such as DISSOLVE TO, FADE OUT, CUT TO (as CUT TO is implied, it isn't necessary; contemporary usage advises against it)
75	Page number if in upper right-hand corner

(This spacing is general. Sometimes these spacings are adjusted two or three spaces to the left. It is a minor distinction.)

Limit transitions. Fades within a script are rather old hat. Unless you have a good reason to do otherwise, let the director decide on fades, dissolves, and wipes. "CUT TO" is always implied so it needn't be put in; preferred usage is not to use CUT TOs.

Scene Heading or Slug Line.   It is all in caps. It begins with the location of the scene as interior (INT) or exterior (EXT), followed by a period and a space. Then comes the location of the scene, followed by a space, a single dash, and a space. Then DAY or NIGHT.

EXT. ALLEY - NIGHT

INT. TEA HOUSE - DAY

Description.   Always follow a slug line with some description, never go directly to a line of dialogue.

Restrict the number of lines of your description; if longer than five or six lines, break it up by skipping a space and continuing with another few lines of description. This makes for an easier read.

Capitalize.   Within description, capitalize technical cues—sound, music, camera directions (for example, CAMERA PANS across the demolished room, phone RINGS). In description, capitalize the name of a character, even a minor character, the first time they appear in the script, but not thereafter.

Characters' names above a dialogue speech are also capitalized.

Scene Numbers and CONTINUEDs.   If you read a copy of a produced script, you will notice that it has scene numbers written in. It also has "CONTINUED" at the bottom right and the top left of pages to indicate that a scene is continuing. These are put in by typists when a script is being prepared for production. It is best to leave them out. (Certainly leave out scene numbers; CONTINUEDs are optional but probably best omitted.)

Vertical Spacing.   *Single-space*: scene description, dialogue, between the character's name and dialogue. (That is, there are no blank lines between these elements.)

Double-space: between FADE IN and a slug line, between a slug line and description, between description and a character's name (above dialogue), and after a dialogue speech. (That is, there is a one-line space between these elements.)

Triple-space: between scenes (before the slug line of a new scene). (That is, there are two one-line spaces between these elements.)

Parentheticals (Business).   These give advice on how a speech should be delivered. Use sparingly. If used, keep them short.

A longer interrupting comment—"He walks over and gingerly lifts up the lid"—should be written out as description rather than squeezed into a parenthetical.

Parentheticals begin with a lower case letter, not a capital letter: (sarcastically).

Don't embed a parenthetical comment within a dialogue line; put it on its own line and continue the dialogue on the next line.

Miscellany.   For a pause in dialogue or action, use "(pause)"; for a short pause use "(beat)." These are either used in description or as parentheticals (on their own separate lines within a dialogue speech, not embedded in a dialogue line).

Use three dots (. . .) for a pause within a speech when the speaker pauses; four dots if a speech trails off and concludes without formally ending the sentence.

A dash (—) can also signify a speech that trails off, but it is more likely to mean a break in thought or an interruption by another speaker. It can be used at the end and beginning of a dialogue speech, especially if the dialogue is in rapid-fire phrases.

When a dialogue speech is broken by description, begin again with the character's name, followed by (CONT'D). For example:

```
                         WEAVER
              We'd better check this out.
              Stand back.

Weaver walks over and gingerly lifts up the lid.


                     WEAVER (CONT'D)
              Stand back!
```

Although some use small letters for cont'd, the preferred usage is to put anything that appears in the character name line in caps. Some scripts use "(continuing)" as a parenthetical rather than writing "(CONT'D)" after the name:

```
                         WEAVER
                      (continuing)
```

If you happen to have a longer dialogue speech that falls at the bottom of the page and you have to break it and continue it on the next page, write "(MORE)" centered right under the speech, without skipping a line, then on the next page put the character's name, centered as usual, followed by "(CONT'D)."

Avoid leaving a lone slug line or character's name at the bottom of a page. Try to avoid breaking a sentence from one page to another. It's also wise to avoid cutting a joke in half with part of it on one page and the rest on another.

If we hear a character's voice over the phone, indicate this by writing "(FILTER)" or "(FILTERED)" after the character's name: MINDY (FILTERED). This is also seen as "(filtered)," appearing as a parenthetical. When you want to indicate that a character is speaking into a phone (or mic), you can add "(INTO PHONE)": BOYD (INTO PHONE).

Two abbreviations that are often confused are O.S. for offscreen and V.O. for voice-over. Both appear in parentheses after the character's name above the dialogue speech.

O.S. is used when the character is around—as in the next room—but not on camera. (Live-on-tape scripts use O.C., Off Camera, rather than O.S.)

V.O. refers to a character's voice when the character is not in the scene, as in narration. Also for a voice on a radio or television set in the room. It may also refer to a character's thoughts. Sometimes V.O. is used for telephone calls: HANNAH (V.O. FILTERED) although HANNAH'S VOICE (FILTERED) is also used. V.O. sometimes appears without abbreviation periods: VO. If you use these within description, use lower case letters: o.s. and v.o.

Sometimes characters talk simultaneously. In such cases, their speeches are placed side by side on the page.

At the end of the script, type "FADE OUT." Then, just below, centered and underlined, type, "<u>THE END</u>."

FILMED TELEVISION SCRIPTS (SINGLE CAMERA)

Filmed television scripts are broken into television acts. On the first page (after the cover page) list the series title in all-caps and underlined, centered about six lines down: <u>NORTHERN EXPOSURE</u>.

Double-spaced under this, list the episode title—centered, in quotation marks, not in caps. Sometimes underlined, sometimes not: "<u>Spring Break</u>."

The act numbers are written, capitalized, centered, and underlined double-spaced below this: <u>ACT ONE</u>.

When you finish an act, write END OF ACT ONE centered and double-spaced after FADE OUT. At the end of the script, write, centered and double-spaced below, FADE OUT: END OF EPISODE.

Begin each new act of a television script on a new page.

Since television is filmed so quickly, directors have limited time to prepare productions. Teleplays will have some shot references that wouldn't be in a feature film script. These are not so much LS, MS, CU as they are broader indications of a change of shot such as: ANGLE–PAM, ANOTHER ANGLE, CLOSE TWO SHOT–PAM AND HEIDI, CLOSE ANGLE–LAWRENCE, NEW ANGLE.

HALF-HOUR, MULTI-CAMERA SCRIPTS (LIVE-ON-TAPE OR LIVE-ON-FILM)

Half-hour, multi-camera live scripts are similar to single-camera filmed scripts, beginning with series name, episode title, and act number as above. Centered and double-spaced under the act number is the scene designation. Different series have different preferences. Some write out Scene 1, but more common is to label the scenes with letters A, B, C, and so on—written, centered, and in parentheses: (A). Then skip down eight lines before writing the first slug line. At the top of the page, just under each page number, place the scene letter in parentheses.

DISSOLVE TO.   Use these between scenes in the same act. Start each new scene on a new page. For a new scene within the same act, go down a dozen lines and write the new scene designation: (B). Begin the scene another dozen lines below this.

FADE OUT and FADE IN.   Use this between acts, and indicate the end of the act, as above: END OF ACT ONE.

Begin a new act on a new page. Go down ten spaces and mark the act: ACT TWO. Centered under it, double-space and put the new scene: (C). After FADE OUT at the end of the program, double-space, center and write: END OF SHOW.

Format for the half-hour multi-camera live script is very different from a single-camera filmed script. However, the exact format is likely to vary somewhat for different shows.

Many shows want a wider margin on the right side: two-and-a-half to three inches. This is for the actors, director, and crew members to write in notes. Other shows are less concerned about this. Best advice is to put in a somewhat wider right margin.

Don't indicate shots.

Dialogue is double-spaced and written in lower case type. All other material appears in all capital letters. (The only words written in lower case type are what is spoken.)

Description is single-spaced.

New scene locations and visual instructions such as <u>FADE IN,</u> <u>DISSOLVE TO:</u>, <u>INT. HALLWAY - MORNING</u> are all capitalized and underlined. Character entrances and exits are usually underlined as well: <u>GEORGE ENTERS</u>.

Parentheticals are placed within dialogue lines and capitalized (they aren't spoken).

The following examples should help.

Example of Single-Camera Film Style Format

```
INT. RESTAURANT - DAY

Peter and Curry continue their conversation. SHADE,
a young woman in her mid 20s, enters. Curry sees
her, Peter does not.

                    CURRY
          Are you sure?
          You look like you make dirty
          movies.

                    PETER
          I don't make dirty movies!

                    SHADE
          —But you'd love to, wouldn't
          you?!

                    PETER
                 (abashed)
          Uh, hello, Shade.
          I bet you didn't expect to
          see me.

                    SHADE
          I bet you don't expect me to
          talk to you!
                 (to Curry)
          This is him! The X-rated
          producer I told you about.

                    CURRY
                 (mock shock)
          No! Well, well . . . .

They all glare at each other.

                                    DISSOLVE TO:

INT. RESTAURANT - LATER THAT NIGHT

Curry, Shade, Walt, and Brad are relaxing at this
late hour. Curry is stretched out on the bar. Shade
and Brad are playing gin rummy. Liz comes sailing in
full of her usual vigor.
```

Example of Multi-Camera Live Script Format

```
                        ACT TWO

                          (C)




FADE IN:

INT. RESTAURANT - LATER THAT NIGHT

THE LAST FEW PATRONS LEAVE AND CURRY CLEARS
AWAY THE LAST GLASSES. PETER ENTERS.

                        PETER

          May I come in?

CURRY SHRUGS, POURS HIMSELF COFFEE

                        PETER (CONT'D)

          I came to see Ms. Altman-Shade.

          I tried her apartment, but there's

          no answer. Do you know—

SFX: CLOCK STRIKING TWO AM

                        PETER (CONT'D)

          (INSTANTLY RESUMING) I must

          see her.
```

Glossary of Common Script Format Terms and Abbreviations

SHOTS

AERIAL SHOT   Camera shot as taken from a plane.

ANGLE   Used to indicate a new angle in the scene without trying to specify exactly what the shot should be. Also seen as: ANGLE ON HAROLD, ANGLE—IN-CLUDING GEORGE, ANGLE—JAN, ANOTHER ANGLE, ANGLE WIDENS, NEW ANGLE, REVERSE ANGLE.

BACK TO SCENE, SCENE   Often used after an INSERT to indicate a return to the scene as it was previously shown.

CLOSE, CLOSER   A general direction to move the camera closer, as: CLOSE ON MONITOR, CLOSER ON HILDA, CLOSER ANGLE.

CLOSE SHOT Head and shoulders of character.

CRANE SHOT   Camera is high in the air on a crane.

CU, CLOSE-UP   Closer than a CLOSE SHOT.

ECU, EXTREME CLOSE-UP   As of the eyes.

ELS, EXTREME LONG SHOT   An extremely long shot as of a village, or of charac-ters appearing very small in the distance.

ESTABLISHING, TO ESTABLISH   A shot to establish a location or setting, often seen in the beginning of a script. This can be included as part of the slug line, just after the location, and before DAY or NIGHT, as:
EXT. BEACH - ESTABLISHING - DAY
Or it can go on the next line under the slug line, as:
EXT. BEACH - DAY
ESTABLISHING

FAVOR, FAVORING   To compose the shot so that it favors one person over others, as: FAVOR MEREDITH.

FULL SHOT   A long shot. Sometimes used to refer to showing the full-length person.

INCLUDE   To include in the shot someone who was previously not there, as: INCLUDE MARION, INCLUDE GUESTS.

INSERT   A very close shot of some object in the scene, usually inserted into shots of characters, as: INSERT— BOTTLE.

INTERCUT   To intercut back and forth between elements, as: INTERCUT: GEORGE—GLORIA.

LS, LONG SHOT   A shot of two or three persons, showing the complete person.

MCU, MEDIUM CLOSE-UP   Tighter than MEDIUM SHOT, looser than CU.

MLS, MEDIUM LONG SHOT   Tighter LS.

MS, MEDIUM SHOT   From waist up.

OS, OVER-SHOULDER   A shot of someone over the shoulder of someone else, as: OS—JEAN.

POV   Point of View. A shot taken the way a character would see something, as: JOHN'S POV.

RESUME   A return to a shot after cutting away for an insert or point of view, as: RESUME—JEAN.

TCU, TIGHT CLOSE-UP   As of a face.

TWO-SHOT   Two persons, usually in medium shot.

VLS, VERY LONG SHOT   As of a crowd.

TRANSITIONS

CUT, CUT TO: An abrupt shot transition. Usually not typed in script, but assumed to be there if no other transition is given. May be used to indicate an abrupt change within a scene.

DISSOLVE, DISSOLVE TO: A transition from one shot or scene to another, involving an overlap during the transition.

FADE IN:, FADE OUT: To come up on a picture from a blank screen, and to go out to a blank screen. Used to begin and end a film. Also sometimes for internal transitions that involve a large change of time and space, but used sparingly today.

MATCH CUT   Matching the subject, objects or visual look of one scene with the next.

SEGUE   A smooth transition from one element to another, usually used for the transition from one music segment to another.

Other less common transitions included the WIPE, SPIRAL, DEFOCUS–FOCUS, SWISH PAN OR WHIP, BLUR, PAN TO, SHOCK CUT.

CAMERA MOVEMENTS

ARC   A combined dolly and truck, almost always with the camera moving in as it moves right or left. Can be used to maintain constant subject distance as camera moves sideways. Often used in live television.

CRANE SHOT   The camera moves up and away. Sometimes used to end films.

DOLLY IN, DOLLY OUT, DOLLY BACK   Camera moves toward or away from the subject. Sometimes seen as PULL BACK or MOVE IN.

MOVING, MOVING SHOT   Camera moves with character or object.

PAN   Left or right movement from a stationary camera.

TILT   Up or down movement from a stationary camera.

TRAVELING   A general term meaning the camera moves. Useful when following action. Also FOLLOW.

TRUCK   Right or left movement of the camera.

WIDER, WIDEN   To pull back and take in a wider view with the shot.

ZI, ZO, ZOOM IN, ZOOM OUT   In or out movement of the zoom lens of the camera.

OTHER SCRIPT ABBREVIATIONS AND TERMS

AD LIB   Extemporaneous dialogue lines made up by the actors. To be used only in cases where this will be very easy, such as when greeting arriving guests.

b.g.   Background

EXT.   Exterior location.

f.g.   Foreground

FILTER, FILTERED   Using a filter to reproduce the sound of a voice on the telephone and so indicated in the script.

FREEZE FRAME   A frame of the film is frozen as a still picture.

INT.   Interior location.

MONTAGE   A series of (usually short) shots combined for their total effect.

MOS "Mit Out Sound" (without sound) as when the scene is shot without any recorded sound, or is played without sound originating in the scene.

O.C. Off camera, used in live television production instead of O.S.

O.S. Offscreen; describing an action or sound happening outside the view of the camera. Put in caps when after a character's name, in lower case (o.s.) when in description.

RP Rear projection, such as a city skyline outside an apartment window on a soundstage set.

SFX Sound effects (a technical cue).

SPFX Special effects, such as an explosion (a technical cue).

SPLIT SCREEN Dividing the screen—usually into halves— with different action in each half, such as when showing two characters talking to each other on the phone.

STOCK A shot from a stock footage library.

SUPER, SUPERIMPOSITION The superimposition of one image on top of another for a double-image effect.

V.O., VO Voice-over—a narrator's voice laid over the visual image.

SCRIPTWRITING TERMS

Act breaks The plot points that end Acts I and II in the three-act model; high points that spin the story around and send us into the next act.

Action Activity within a scene. What happens within a scene as opposed to the story point (beat) being realized.

Arc, Transformational Arc The growth and changes in a character (character arc) throughout the script.

Backstory Events that happen before a script begins that are important to the story, often a character's previous history.

Beat A plot point, the units of a story line. (Also a short pause in the action or dialogue.)

Bits Short pieces of comedy—visual or verbal (jokes).

Business Activity to keep an actor busy while on screen. Also parentheticals (q.v.).

Button The ending of a scene so that it comes to a definite close rather than seeming to terminate abruptly. Often with a strong bit of action, dialogue, or humor.

Climax The emotional and often physical high point of the film. The climax resolves the suspense of the story line.

Crisis   A challenge, threat, problem for the protagonist. The middle section of the story develops through a series of crises. The largest crisis usually comes just before the climax.

Denouement   The short wind-up of the story that occurs after the climax.

Deus ex machina   Literally, "god out of the machine" from Greek drama where sometimes at the end of the play a god would be lowered in a basket ("machine") to solve the complex twists of the story. Refers to any unconvincing, too convenient way for the writer to wind up the story and the hero's difficulties.

Empathy   Feeling for the character; sharing the character's emotions and tensions.

Exposition   Information given the audience about something that happens off-screen or before the story begins (backstory).

Fillers   Excess words added to dialogue to give it flavor. Best avoided. These include: "Uh," "Well," "Yeah," "Like," "Hey," "You know."

Foreshadowing   Setting up events to come. Used both in suspense and preparation.

Genre   A designation of films or television programs that relate to each other because of stylistic or other elements—for example, western, sitcom, film noir, screwball comedy.

Hook   A plot twist or development that grabs the audience's attention and compels them to keep watching (or reading).

Identification   The psychological process of putting ourselves in the character's place.

Jeopardy   A character in physical or emotional danger. A typical way to end a television act—with a jeopardy beat.

Master scene   The complete scene shot as a whole rather than the way it could be broken up with shots. Screenplays are written in master scenes.

Mise-en-scene   The physical setting and look of a scene.

MOW   Television movie-of-the-week.

On-the-nose   Dialogue that is too obvious and heavy-handed.

Option   A fee paid to the writer for the right to try to sell the script to a studio or to otherwise get it into production. Made for a specific length of time, after which rights revert to the writer. Often renewable.

Parenthetical   Comments to the actors on how to deliver a line or direct a comment. Use sparingly.

Payoff   The realization of an earlier preparation; the punch line of a joke or humorous-bit build.

Plant   A preparation technique in which an object or person is presented so that it may be used later.

Points   A percentage of a picture's income granted in addition to the up-front money paid (for a script). Don't expect any income from points.

Preparation   A technique to set up the audience for something that will be important later.

Reverse   A twist in the plot. Specifically, a story or story moment in which there is a reverse of character (as from bad to good) or character fortune.

Runner   Recurring bit, not necessarily comic. Used a few times.

Running gag   A recurring comic bit that crops up throughout the film.

Slug line   Familiar name for a scene heading.

Story line   A complete story with beginning, middle, and end. Often one of a number of story lines in the story.

Subplot   A story line contained within the larger story, often involving characters other than the principals.

Subtext   Meaning that lies beneath the words, that is different from the literal meaning of the words. The true meaning that is being conveyed in the character interaction.

Tag   The short segment at the end of a television program.

Teaser   The short segment at the beginning of a television program.

Theme   The larger cultural meaning, message, or significance of a story.

Treatment   A narrative version of the script describing action but containing little or no dialogue. For many writers, a step in the writing process before they begin the script proper.

WGA   Writers Guild of America.

Resources for
the Screenwriter

The past few years have seen a proliferation of books on screenwriting. I've already indicated some suggested reading on marketing your script. Here are some screenwriting texts, many of which I have already mentioned.

Armer, A. (1993). *Writing the screenplay* (2nd ed.). Belmont, CA: Wadsworth.

Dancyger, K., and Rush, J. (1991). *Alternative scriptwriting*. Boston: Focal Press.

DiMaggio, M. (1990). *How to write for television*. New York: Prentice-Hall.

Egri, L. (1972). *The art of dramatic writing*. New York: Simon & Schuster.

Field, S. (1982). *Screenplay: The foundations of screenwriting*. New York: Delta.

———. (1984). *The screenwriter's workbook*. New York: Dell.

Goldman, W. (1983). *Adventures in the screen trade*. New York: Warner Books.

Hauge, M. (1988). *Writing screenplays that sell*. New York: McGraw-Hill.

Hunter, L. (1993). *Lew Hunter's screenwriting 434*. New York: Perigee Books (Putnam).

Kaminsky, S. M. (with M. Walker). (1988). *Writing for television*. New York: Dell.

King, V. (1988). *How to write a movie in 21 days*. New York: Harper & Row.

Lucey, P. (1996). *Story sense*. New York: McGraw-Hill.

Miller, W. (1980). *Screenwriting for narrative film and television*. New York: Hastings House.

Rockwell, F. A. (1975). *How to write plots that sell.* Chicago: Contemporary Books.

Root, W. (1979). *Writing the script.* New York: Holt.

Seger, L. (1987). *Making a good script great.* New York: Dodd, Mead.

————. (1990). *Creating unforgettable characters.* New York: Henry Holt.

Vale, E. (1982). *The technique of screen and television writing.* (2nd ed.). Englewood Cliffs, NJ: Prentice-Hall.

Wolff, J. (1988). *Successful sitcom writing.* New York: St. Martin's Press.

Wolff, J., and Cox, K. (1988). *Successful scriptwriting.* Cincinnati: Writers Digest.

For special books on formatting screenplays, there is: Haag, J., and Cole, H. (1980, 1984). *The complete guide to standard script formats.* Hollywood: CMC Publishing. It comes in two parts. The first is for screenplays, the second for teleplays. There is also: Reichman, R. (1992). *Formatting your screenplay.* New York: Paragon House.

Screenplays can be found in many libraries, or ordered at reasonable prices, through Samuel French, 7623 Sunset Blvd., Hollywood, CA 90046; write for their *Film Book Catalogue.* Or from Script City, 1765 N. Highland Ave., #760, Hollywood, CA 90028.

Writing books and screenwriting software programs are available from The Write Stuff Catalog, 21115 Devonshire St., #182-153, Chatsworth, CA 91311.

Index